The fourth estate

THE FOURTH ESTATE

An informal appraisal of the news and opinion media

by **JOHN L. HULTENG** and **ROY PAUL NELSON**
University of Oregon

HARPER & ROW, PUBLISHERS
New York, Evanston, San Francisco, London

THE FOURTH ESTATE: *An informal appraisal of the news and opinion media*

Copyright © 1971 by **John L. Hulteng and Roy Paul Nelson**

STANDARD BOOK NUMBER: 06-042988-7
LIBRARY OF CONGRESS CATALOG CARD NUMBER: 70-137808

Contents

33421

13 NEWS UNDER LICENSE   231

14 WHERE MADISON AVENUE CROSSES MAIN   256

The communication of ideas and information can be a simple process or an exceedingly complex one. A casual conversation with a friend is one kind of communication; reading a newspaper or watching a television news broadcast is another.

In the first instance the one-to-one relationship allows each party to evaluate the information exchanged. Chances are, you know the friend well enough to have reached a judgment about his trust-worthiness as a bearer of news; you also have some idea of his motives and are aware of the personal biases that may affect the way in which he passes on a bit of information or an opinion about something or somebody.

But you very likely are not in as good a position to assess the information or ideas that come to you from one or another of the media of mass communication. You probably do not know much about the way these media work or why they function as they do.

Yet from the time we leave the formal educational system, all of us are very heavily dependent on these channels of information. Once we are out of school or college, teachers and textbooks are no longer primary sources of information or ideas for us. The average adult learns new concepts or new bits of information largely from the media of mass communication. Even the ideas and news items he picks up in conversation with friends very likely came to those friends in the first place from one of the mass media.

These channels show us the shape of events, of persons, of ideas. They provide us with the basis for judgments we reach and opinions we form. The men and women who operate the media of mass communication are intellectual gatekeepers who let through some facts and ideas and hold back others. Sometimes the picture of the world around us that is presented by the channels of information is a true and complete one. Sometimes it is as misleading and distorted as the image in a fun-house mirror.

This makes it important that all of us find out how these media function, what pressures affect them, what motives activate the men and women who staff them.

We need to know their limitations and their possibilities. Most particularly, we need to be aware of their possibilities. For as consumers of the product that the mass media produce, we are important to those media. If we as customers insist on good service, we can get it. But we can't ask for good service if we don't know enough about the media of mass communication to tell whether they are serving us well or poorly.

That is why this book has been written. Its purpose is to help readers become more understanding and more discriminating consumers of the products that the mass media thrust at us every day, and nearly every hour, of our lives.

J.L.H.
R.P.N.

CHAPTER ONE

The press and society

If a man is deprived of a continuing flow of fresh air, death swiftly follows. In very much the same way, the liberties and freedoms of a people weaken and die when access is cut off to a continuing flow of honest and uncensored news about what is happening in the state, the nation, and the world.

Dictators have always been quick to sense this fundamental truth, and to act on it. Rigid control of the media of information became one of the first and most urgent objectives of Adolf Hitler in Germany, Juan Perón in Argentina, Francisco Franco in Spain, Joseph Stalin in Russia, and Fidel Castro in Cuba. When the Russians sent tanks and generals into Czechoslovakia in 1968 in an effort to crush the "democratization" process underway in Czech communism, one of the first actions taken was the imposition of strict press censorship.

Once the press is under control, the people no longer are exposed to anything other than the doctored propaganda the state permits them to read or hear. Behind the intellectual curtain thus set up, totalitarian forces can complete their grasp on a nation. The media of information thus constitute the jugular vein of a democracy; strike there decisively and the wound is mortal.

The importance of the information media to the survival of democratic freedoms stems from the basic concept of a representative system of government: if the people are fully and accurately informed, they will be able to choose their governors wisely.

If the press provides the people with a continuing and complete picture of what is happening in the world, and particularly with a complete account of the way in which their elected representatives are conducting the public business, then the people will know how to register their judgment at the polls when election day comes around.

If the people do not have a true picture, they have no sound basis for their election-day decisions, and may be swayed by emotion, fear, or propaganda.

An eighteenth-century legal philosopher, Jeremy Bentham, saw the value of press publicity for the public business:

Without publicity on the entire governmental process, no good is permanent; under the auspices of publicity, no evil can continue. Publicity, therefore, is the best means of securing public confidence.

How the constitution-makers viewed it

A similar awareness led Thomas Jefferson to make his often quoted comment on the role of the press in a democracy:

. . . Were it left to me to decide whether we should have a government without newspapers, or newspapers without a government, I should not hesitate a moment to prefer the latter.

He and others of the Founding Fathers saw to it that the First Amendment to the Constitution contained a guarantee against government interference with the freedom of the press, putting that freedom on a par with freedom of speech and of religion.

That parity is worth noting, because it underlines the original concept of press freedom in our society. It was to be a freedom belonging to the people, as were freedom of speech and freedom to worship. It was not intended to be the right of only a privileged few.

As has been the case with other ideas embodied in the Constitution, this concept has never been fully realized. At no time in our history has freedom of the press been available equally to all citizens. Perhaps this was more nearly the case in the post-Revolutionary period, when an occasional pamphlet or a weekly newssheet could be launched with very little capital, and when population centers were small. But even then, as a practical matter, the channels of communication were utilized by a relatively small number of persons; then, as now, economic and other factors tended to limit the access of most citizens to the means by which information was disseminated to the public.

In today's world, newspapers, magazines, and television stations are enormously costly enterprises (the Philadelphia *Inquirer* and *Daily News* were recently sold to Knight Newspapers for $55,000,000).[1] And they are also few in number, considering the size to which our national population has grown (there are now around 1,750 daily newspapers, 9,300 weeklies, 6,500 radio stations, and 840 television stations serving 200,000,000 Americans). Most citizens, despite The First Amendment guarantee, have few opportunities to exercise freedom of the press.

This makes it important to note the remainder of that celebrated quotation from Jefferson about preferring newspapers without government, a part that is not so often cited:

But I should mean that *every* man should receive those papers, and be capable of reading them.[2]

Part of Jefferson's concern has been met in today's society. Literacy is at the highest level ever in our country; and the new electronic media of information communicate even with the illiterate.

But the access of the people to the channels of communication is far more limited than was contemplated by the architects of the Constitution who sought to protect this key aspect of a representa-

---

[1] Weekly newspapers have sold in recent years for prices ranging from $25,000 to $1,000,000. Their value depends on the size of circulation, quality of equipment and facilities, and the presence or absence of competition.

[2] It should be noted that Jefferson did not consistently argue the importance of a free and accessible press. On another occasion he wrote: "The man who never looks into a newspaper is better informed than he who reads them, inasmuch as he who knows nothing is nearer to the truth than he whose mind is filled with falsehoods and errors."

tive democratic system. Because the channels of information are now few in number, and because they are under the control of a relatively small number of persons, all citizens need to monitor their performance knowledgeably and critically.

Who sets the standards?

Various methods of ensuring quality performance by the media of information have been tried or proposed over the years. Some of them will be taken up in detail in a later chapter. At this point, it is enough to note that, as a practical matter, there are only two quality controls operating on the media today: the conscience of those who own and run the media, and the expressed demand of the consumers. And only one of these is effective.

Most consumers of mass media products make their needs known only rarely and inexactly. And in a competitive market situation, the working of consumer preference more often favors the shoddy product than the quality one where the media of information are concerned. This leaves the burden of maintaining responsible standards of performance very much on the shoulders of those who make the operating policy for the media of information—the owners and their hired representatives.[3]

Whether a given community is well served or not by its local newspaper or broadcasting station is often dependent on the accident of inheritance or purchase. For if the owner, however he came into ownership, wants to publish a good, balanced newspaper, he can do it. If he wants to milk the property for profits and ignore his responsibility to inform the public, he can do that, too.

If the lack of quality in his product becomes too obvious, the consumers theoretically might rebel and encourage a competitor to enter the market. But this does not often happen. In many cases, the readers or viewers simply aren't aware that they are the vic-

---

[3] In its obituary editorial on the death of Arthur Hays Sulzberger, publisher of the New York *Times*, *The Wall Street Journal* observed (December 16, 1968) : "Around newspaper city rooms and press rooms it is traditional to underrate the role of publishers in the making of a newspaper. But the truth is that no newspaper can be greater than the vision and integrity of the man who makes the ultimate decisions."

tims of bad journalism; they aren't familiar enough with the media to recognize the signs. Even if they should sense that they are poorly served and attempt to encourage corrective competition, the odds are steep. In very few instances in recent years has a competitor, even with widespread community support, been able to move in successfully on an established daily newspaper.[4]

In the last analysis, it is usually up to the newspaper owner and his staff to determine whether a community will enjoy responsible journalism or suffer mediocrity.

So far, we've been pretty lucky

Fortunately for all of us, most newspaper publishers, editors, and staff members through the generations have responded in at least some degree to the central ethic of journalism: that the people be informed. Many journalists have shown extraordinary dedication to this mission.

Joseph Pulitzer, one of the makers of American journalism, saw his responsibility clearly as he guided his New York *World* and St. Louis *Post-Dispatch* through the final decades of the nineteenth century and into the twentieth:

We are a democracy, and there is only one way to get a democracy on its feet in the matter of its individual, its social, its municipal, its national conduct, and that is by keeping the public informed of what is going on. There is not a crime, there is not a dodge, there is not a trick, there is not a swindle, there is not a vice which does not live be secrecy. Get these things out in the open, describe them, ridicule them in the press, and sooner or later public opinion will sweep them away.

There have been many other editors and publishers who sensed their obligations as clearly as did Pulitzer. And they have not all been big-city journalists by any means.

---

[4] A group of conservatives made the attempt in Atlanta, Ga., hoping to capitalize on local dissatisfaction with the liberal policies of the Atlanta *Constitution*. Although the newcomer's backers were well-heeled, the venture failed. So did another on a smaller scale in Lima, Ohio, where an attempt was made to oppose the ultraconservative local daily owned by the Hoiles group.

A recent example is Hazel Brannon Smith, publisher of the small weekly Lexington, Miss., *Advertiser,* who persisted in informing her readers accurately about the integration movement of the 1960s, despite the bitter opposition of the White Citizens' Councils and most of the important business interests of her community. She followed in the tradition of publisher J. N. Heiskell and editor Harry Ashmore of the Little Rock, Ark., *Gazette,* who put that paper behind the move to bring Negro children into the schools in the 1950s even though most of their readers took exception to the policy. And in another sector of the country, 85-year-old Thomas Storke won the Pulitzer Prize for his Santa Barbara, Calif., *News-Press* by having the courage to publish a documented exposé of the John Birch Society in one of the strongholds of that right-wing organization.

But there have also been editors and publishers who were indifferent to the role of the press in society, or who deliberately abused their control of the channels of communication in order to wield political power or fatten their fortunes.

The national chain of newspapers owned by William Randolph Hearst, Sr., reflected his personal biases not only in the editorial page columns of opinion but also in the news columns where readers assumed they were getting an undistorted report. Col. Robert R. McCormick's Chicago *Tribune* was guilty in his lifetime of similar tampering with the news in order to reinforce the owner's bitterly anti-British views and political conservatism. And the Wilmington, Del., newspapers served for years as examples of journals that were operated largely as house organs for the Du Pont Corporation, which owned them and most of the other newspapers in the state.[5]

In a number of small towns today the local editors deliberately follow a comfortable, "don't rock the boat" policy in covering hometown news. They thus avoid antagonizing advertisers or officials and keep the profit margins sound. But they also neglect their chief reason for being: informing the people fully and honestly.

In short, the picture now, as it has always been, is a spotty one. The controls are uncertain, and it is usually the owner's sense of integrity and responsibility that determines how good or how bad

---

[5] Ben H. Bagdikian, "Case History: Wilmington's 'Independent' Newspapers," *Columbia Journalism Review,* Summer, 1964, p. 13.

the service will be. It is this haphazard quality which makes observers and critics of the press agree that there is an increasing need for the readers and viewers, the consumers of the media, to become a more knowledgeable and more effective influence on the level of performance of the channels of mass communication.[6]

[6] Additional background on the development of the press and on its role in American society can be found in the excellent journalistic history, Edwin Emery, *The Press and America*, 2nd ed., Prentice-Hall, Englewood Cliffs, N. J., 1962. A more condensed discussion can be found in John Tebbel, *The Compact History of the American Newspaper*, Hawthorn Books, New York, 1963.

CHAPTER TWO

The representative medium

The various media of mass communication deliver to their readers, listeners, and viewers a mixture made up—in varying proportions— of news, opinion, entertainment, and propaganda. The concern of this book is chiefly with the news content in this mixture, and to a somewhat lesser degree with opinion and propaganda. There will be little consideration of the entertainment aspect of the media, except incidentally.

In the ways in which they package and deliver news to their customers, the various media differ considerably from one another. But many of the problems involved in gathering, writing, editing, and evaluating the news are common to all: newspapers, radio, television, books, magazines, and films.

An examination of the ways in which news reaches us through the channels of mass communication should logically begin with the newspaper. This second-oldest of the information media (books came first) has the most elaborate news-gathering and news-processing apparatus of all—and the one from which the approaches taken by the other media have been adapted.

So this chapter and several that follow will take a detailed look at the functioning of the newspaper as a *representative* medium of mass communication; later chapters will consider in turn the distinctive characteristics of the other media.

Some terminology

Like any profession or trade, newspaper journalism has developed a language of its own. While some of it is jargon and therefore of interest only to newspapermen, some of it is useful to readers.

The newspaper industry has been called the *Fourth Estate*. This goes back to the early days of the British Parliament, with its three estates of man: Lords Spiritual, Lords Temporal, and "Commons." "The gallery in which the reporters sit has become a fourth estate of the realm," wrote Thomas Babington, Lord Macaulay.

One of the most versatile terms in newspaper journalism is *editorial*. As a noun, it means an essay or article on the editorial page, usually without a byline, that expresses the opinion of the editor or editorial writer on an issue or event that is often controversial. A regular column, supplied by a syndicate, even though it deals with controversy and appears on the same page, is not considered an editorial. Papers usually run their editorials—or *edits*, as they are sometimes called—on the left-hand side of the editorial page, often in wider columns than other material on the page.

As an adjective, *editorial* is used to distinguish the nonbusiness from the business side of the paper. A newspaperman is an editorial worker if he doesn't work in advertising, circulation, or printing departments. In other words, reporters as well as editorial writers work on the editorial side. Sometimes newspapers use the term *news-editorial* for *editorial* to show that both news and opinion are involved.

On the news side, a reporter writes a *story*, and yet it is not a story in the classic sense. Technically, it is a *news report*. But newspapermen seldom call it that.[1]

Any item of entertainment in the newspaper is called a *feature*.

[1] Magazines use "story" for a short piece of fiction, reserving "article" for their news and opinion pieces.

Feature is also a verb, meaning *to give prominence to;* a newspaper may feature, let's say, a picture series on its front page.

Some readers have trouble with the significance of the words *publish* and *print. Publish* is the broad term covering all aspects of putting out a publication, including its printing. To *print* something is simply to make multiple impressions from type or plate. A newspaper *publishes* a story, it doesn't merely *print* it.

Another term commonly misused is *masthead.* A masthead is a box or table, usually on the editorial page, listing top editors and offering other information about the paper: frequency of publication, place of publication, and the like. The name of the paper, running across the top of page 1, is the *nameplate* or *flag.*

ORGANIZATION

Who does what

No organization chart can trace precisely a daily newspaper's chain of command. Some departments and some executives defy categorization. Duties overlap. Short cuts develop. And no newspaper organization exactly resembles the operation of another. Even the titles of top executives vary.

The chief executive officer usually is the *publisher.* He manages the entire operation. On some newspapers, the owner is publisher; on others—especially the big dailies—the publisher is a hired hand, although a very special one. Ideally, he has a background on both the news-editorial and business sides of journalism.

Two top-level executives answer directly to the publisher: the *executive editor* or the *editor-in-chief* (or simply, the *editor*) in charge of the news and editorial side; and the *business manager,* in charge of accepting and soliciting advertising and of printing and circulating the publication. Other executives may work directly with the publisher on public relations, personnel, and other administrative matters.

The editorial side

An *editorial page editor*—or *chief editorial writer,* as he is called on many newspapers—and a *managing editor* work with the editor-in-chief.

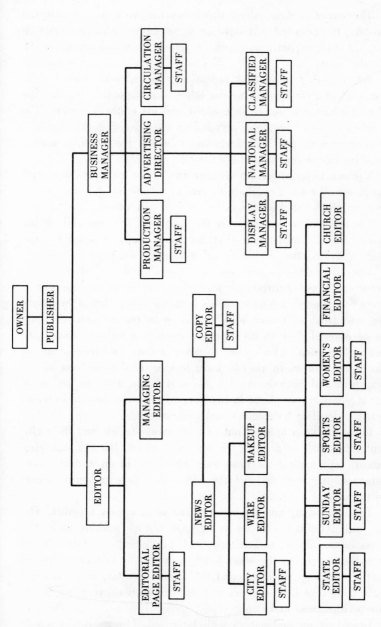

The chain of command in a daily newspaper

The editorial page editor supervises the work of the editorial writers, the editorial cartoonist, and the staffers who edit the syndicated columns, select and edit the letters to the editor, and make up the page.

When during a political campaign a newspaper comes out in favor of one candidate over the other, that support represents the thinking of the editorial page editor and his editorial writers. The publisher—the owner, too—may influence the decision. But reporters and other staff members, including those on the ad side, usually play no role in decisions on editorial policy.

The managing editor, who is concerned more with news than with opinion in the paper, works with various subeditors, the most important of which are the *news editor* and the *city editor*.

The news editor watches over the process of selecting and editing national and international (but not local) news, copy-editing the stories, writing the headlines, and making up the pages.

The city editor assigns regular "beats" and special stories to reporters. He also directs photographers. He gets ideas for stories from tips phoned and written him, from watching what other papers do, and from a "future book" he keeps to remind him of events to be covered. Not all his reporters qualify as writers; some may act as "leg men" who go out to cover a story and then phone in their information to rewrite men, less aggressive perhaps as researchers and interviewers but more at home with the language. Or a reporter may phone in his story to a rewrite man in order to make a deadline he couldn't make otherwise.

Reporters keep opinion out of their news stories, and their city editor has little to do with the editorial writers. But the managing editor, representing the news side, often sits in on editorial conferences, primarily to brief the editorial writers on developments in the news.

The city editor and the news editor work closely together. The city editor sends his stories to the copy editor (working under the news editor) to have them copyread, headlined, and finally fitted into the pages. On the other hand, some of the editors of special sections (the sports editor and the women's editor, to name two) have their own little empires and do their own copyreading, headline writing, and make-up.

Important on newspapers with large out-of-town circulations is the *state editor* or *county editor*. He works with both full-time reporters and "stringers." The stringers—or correspondents—turn in stories on a piecework basis, whenever something newsworthy happens in their communities; they often work under an arrangement that pays them by the story or by the published inch. Their "string" is a paste-up, one following the other, of stories written for a particular month.

The *Sunday editor* puts out the locally edited magazine section and, unusual among newspaper editors, buys some of his material from free-lancers. Some newspapers in their Sunday issues offer readers a syndicated magazine section—like *Parade*—in place of, or in addition to, a locally edited magazine. The newspaper's own staff, of course, plays no role in the production of the syndicated magazine.

Other editors on the organization chart hold less vital though still important jobs, supervising smaller staffs than that of the city editor. In some cases they represent one-man departments where they work more as writers than as editors.

A large newspaper would also have a number of minor editors not included on this chart: for instance, an entertainment editor, an automobile editor (a holdover from the time automobiles were a novelty), a science editor, an aviation editor.

The business side

The *business manager* shares equal billing with the editor-in-chief. Working directly under him is a *production manager*, in charge of typesetting, photoengraving, and printing; an *advertising director*; and a *circulation manager*.

Some organization charts show the production manager directly under the publisher, because he does, after all, serve both news-editorial and business departments. His typesetters, for instance, set news stories and editorials as well as advertising copy.

The advertising director supervises the work of three managers: one in charge of display advertising (ads placed mostly by local retailers), one in charge of national advertising (ads prepared by advertising agencies for manufacturers of brand-name merchandise), and one in charge of classified advertising (the want ads).

The circulation manager uses three different methods for distributing the paper: mail, newsstands, and home delivery. The copies that go into the mail may differ from those sold on newsstands. And the copies delivered by paper boys may differ from the other two. All the copies published for a certain day make up the *issue* for that day. A single issue may consist of several *editions,* published at different times during the day; editions change slightly as the news day wears on and emphasis shifts. For example, an afternoon paper may put out a "suburban" edition at 1 P.M., for distribution to the outlying areas of its circulation district, then a "city final" at 2 P.M. for carrier distribution within the city proper, and still later a "market final" carrying the closing stock market quotations and designed to be sold on midtown newsstands.

The chart does not show the subtleties of relationships between departments and executives. Nor does it show how isolated some departments are from others. For instance, most newspapers discourage communication between the advertising and news departments. The advertising department lets the news department know what parts of inside pages are reserved for advertisers; the news department fills in the remaining areas with stories. The contact ends there. The news department may not even know what the ads will say or who the advertisers will be.

An organization chart for a weekly newspaper, of course, would be much simpler. It would still show an editor-in-chief and a business manager, but the supporting cast would be much smaller or, in some cases, nonexistent. For instance, there is no need for an editor or a staff to process national and international news. As far as weeklies are concerned, all news is local.

A few weekly newspapers are so small that a single person serves in both an editorial and a business capacity. On such a paper it would not be unusual for that one person to sell some advertising space while he was out to cover a story. And maybe to sweep out the place when he gets back.

An organization chart for a magazine would show no news editor, wire editor, city editor, state editor, or Sunday editor on the editorial side and no local advertising manager on the business side. It might add a fiction editor. It would feature prominently one staff member overlooked by newspapers: an art director. Not yet convinced of the value of integration of the visual aspects of communication, or not finding such integration practical, newspapers employ photo editors and staff artists to draw charts and cartoons, but they leave make-up of the pages to their word-oriented editors. We may see a change in this attitude in the next few years as newspapers compete for readers in an increasingly visually oriented society.[2]

The wire services

Much of what goes into a newspaper comes from the outside. Serving the editorial side are two different kinds of organizations: *feature syndicates* and *wire services*.

Feature syndicates supply comic strips, editorial cartoons, columns, and other items of opinion and entertainment. (See Chapter Nine.) The material arrives in the newspaper office either in mat form, ready for casting into plates, or in mimeographed form, ready to be set in type.

Because they are concerned with news, wire services—sometimes called "press associations"—use leased wires to get their stories and pictures (wirephotos) into the hands of editors minutes after they are written or snapped. Newspapers have the option of getting wire service stories on punched tape, which can be fed directly into the Linotype machines.

The two major wire services are Associated Press, a cooperative, and United Press International, a profit-making organization that resulted from a merger in 1958 of United Press Associations and International News Service. UP and INS had been formed independently by newspaper owners who quarreled with AP service or who could not get it. The United Press, unencumbered by members' votes, had pioneered in the development of full service to broadcasters. Today both AP and UPI serve broadcasters as well as the print media.

Technically, AP has *members;* UPI has *clients.* AP members are obliged to share stories developed by their own reporters when the stories have regional or national significance. But both wire services have their own reporters, called *correspondents.*

AP and UPI argue about which is the larger, but AP, if it doesn't have the most member/clients, probably handles a bigger volume

[2] For more detailed treatment of the role of various staff members see Eric Rhodin, *Newspapermen,* The Odyssey Press, New York, 1967.

of business. For a long time AP was thought to be the most accurate of the American wire services. UP was livelier, but sloppier. Such a distinction would be hard to document today.

As the number-two wire service for so many years, United Press had to try harder. Its reporters scrambled to cover their beats and make their deadlines. They were never happier than when they scooped the AP.[3]

Newspapers have access to a number of other wire services, including the world's third largest, Reuters, a British organization. Several large newspapers, including the New York *Times,* the Chicago *Daily News,* the Chicago *Tribune,* and, in concert, the Los Angeles *Times* and Washington *Post,* syndicate some of their stories to other newspapers. Some newspapers have gone into the feature syndicate business, too.

Newspapers subscribing to any of these services or features pay for them on the basis of circulation. The smaller the paper, the less it pays. This puts syndicated materials within the reach of every newspaper.

Syndication is essentially a pooling of resources. It brings the biggest names and best talents in the business to the most remote publication. But it also tends to standardize content.

What goes where

The person who moves from one city to another and there subscribes to a newspaper new to him may complain at first that he "can't find anything." The crossword puzzle isn't in the usual place. The TV schedule is in an unfamiliar part of the paper. The differences, though, are superficial. Chances are, the basic organization

---

[3] Some reporters couldn't take the strain. Joe Alex Morris in his *Deadline Every Minute,* the story of the United Press, tells about a staffer in an undermanned bureau in Raleigh. The poor fellow was trying to run two teleprinters at once. He'd punch on one for a while, then run over to punch on the other. When the one going to Atlanta stopped, the man in Atlanta punched this message to Raleigh: WHAT'S THE MATTER? CAN'T YOU PUNCH? The Raleigh man punched back: ONLY HAVE 2 HANDS. The Atlanta man then sent this message to the boss of the man in Raleigh: SUGGEST YOU FIRE THE CRIPPLED BASTARD. Another story has a man quitting UP with this terse letter of resignation: "Pay too low. Hours too long. Life too short." Morris's book was published in 1957 by Doubleday and Company, New York. For a history of the AP, see Oliver Gramling, *AP: The Story of the News,* Holt, Rinehart and Winston, New York, 1940.

of the paper is about what it was for the paper in his old home-town.

For over the years editors have developed an order of presentation of the newspaper fare that almost never varies: first, the important local, national, and international news on a page uninterrupted by advertising. Then more of the the same on the inside pages, where large ads start to intrude. On the third from the last page of the first section, a left-hand page, the editorials. On the first page of the second section, more local news (national and international news in the paper is now largely forgotten), followed by regular departments, women's news, and—on Wednesday and Thursdays to accompany all these grocery ads—food and homemaking features. A third section offers sports news and financial news, followed by the comics and, finally, classified ads. Another page or so of news, most of it relatively unimportant, and the issue for that day is complete.

A table of contents usually appears on the front page to spell out exact page numbers, but only for the regular features. The paper may use its *ears*—little display areas on either side of the name at the top—to promote special stories inside.

The name of the paper on the front page appears usually in Old English letters. If readers were not used to it, it might strike them as inappropriate, because Old English does not say "new" or "news." Far from it. Newspapers originally adopted Old English for their nameplates simply because it was the blackest of types then available. They use it now because, somehow, it conveys dignity. And what newspaper is not concerned about its image?

The look of the page

In spite of the fact they use more pictures, run them larger, cut down on the size of headlines, and allow a little more white space on their pages, newspapers today look much like newspapers of a hundred years ago. A few have modernized their formats dramatically, employing wider—and fewer—columns, doing away with typographic clutter, substituting graceful and readable typefaces for the clumsy ones they had been using.[4] But the constant pres-

---

[4] See, for instance, the redesigned "The Week in Review" section of the Sunday New York *Times*.

sures of the newsroom and poor production facilities preclude the kind of graphic beauty one finds in some magazines and books.

Newspapers continue to regard the upper right-hand corner of the front page as their prime position for news, even though logic dictates the upper left. Emphasis on the upper right is an outgrowth of the days when newspapers frequently ran banner headlines; where the headline stopped, that's where the story began.

And newspapers continue to regard the entire upper half of the page as more important than the lower half, a carryover from the days when newsstand sales were more important than they are now.

The front pages of each section give the editor his only chance for full display. Inside pages are cluttered by ads arranged in stair-shapes in order to give them maximum exposure. Because advertisers buy space for specified days, their ads must fit into the page first. The "news hole" is what's left over; its size and shape does not lend itself to good design.

The count is king

Newspapers' resistance to change is nowhere more evident than in their headlines. Slowly, painfully, newspapers have made adjustments in the shape and typography of headlines, but they have made virtually no change in what headlines say and how they say it.

Headlines today, with fewer lines, take up less space. No longer do they have to form a shape that is a perfect rectangle or inverted pyramid; their lines can be uneven at the right. Nor need they shout any more. In the 1920s newspapers began setting headlines in capital *and* small (lower case) letters rather than in capital letters only. In the 1960s many newspapers went to all lower case letters except for the first letter of the first word and the first letters of any proper nouns, making headlines easier to read.

But the affectations of style remain. The headline—*head*, as it is called—must be summary in nature: it must deal with material from the first few paragraphs of the story.

It is always written in present tense, even though the story itself is in past tense. People aren't already dead in the world of head-lines writers: they *die*, now, right before our eyes. Sometimes, in order to fill out the space, the headline writer adds a "when": Tuesday, say. Then the headlines read as if somebody has put the finger on somebody else: JOE BLANK DIES TUESDAY, when the fact is that poor Joe Blank has already gone on to his reward.

The mannerisms of headlines puzzle some readers. The headline writer uses single rather than double quote marks. He drops all nonvital words like "a," "the," and "and." In the place of "and" he uses a comma. He doesn't use a period at the end of his headline, but when his headline consists of two sentences, he uses a semicolon to end the first sentence. Most of these practices grew from the headline writer's need to save space.

The biggest deterrent to effective communication in headlines is the newspapers' insistence that the lines fit a given space. Even in the more relaxed "flush left" headlines (with the several lines of type even at the left margin, but uneven on the right) headline writers can fit only so many letters and spaces into a line (the limit is called the "maximum count").[5] Headlines are written as much to fit a space as to communicate with readers. Magazines—the general circulation magazines anyway—write their headlines or titles first, and then find the room for them.

Lack of space results in a lack of precision. Consider this headline from a newspaper of the 1950s: TV RAPPED BY KNOWLAND. A general criticism of TV as a medium? The reader might think so. Only when he gets into the story does he find that the Republican Party is being criticized by one of its leaders for thinking it can win a presidential campaign using television alone. Senator William Knowland was saying the party had to get the candidate out to meet the people.

Here's a more recent example—from *Publishers' Weekly*, a magazine that runs newspaper-like headlines: MAX RAFFERTY BANS BLACK AUTHORS. The story mentions only *two* books—*Soul on Ice* by Eldridge Cleaver and *Dutchman* by LeRoi Jones—banned for black studies courses in San Francisco high schools. They were banned because they contained, in Rafferty's opinion, "unbridled obscenity and pornography," not because they were written by blacks. Seventeen other books by blacks remained on the reading list. Rafferty made an easy enough target for criticism without misstating the case against him.

Examples of misleading headlines are all too easy to find.

[5] One of the advantages of the wider column now being used by many newspapers is an increased maximum count for headlines.

MOTHER OF 16 SEEKS/DIVORCE TO GET RELIEF describes, it turns out, not a woman pestered by her husband but a woman who has discovered that she can get her family on the welfare rolls only if there is no employed man in the home. AGING REPRESENTATIVE/IS LUNCHEON SPEAKER refers to an area representative for the Administration on Aging, not a man who is himself in his last years. CHAMPION DAIRY ANIMALS/SHOWN BY BORING FARMERS and VIRGIN WOMAN/ GIVES BIRTH/TO TWINS make more sense when you get into the stories and discover that Boring is a town in Oregon, Virgin a town in Utah.

"Writing to fit" results not only in a lack of precision in headlines but also in an irreverence not in keeping with the stories themselves. But who could blame a headline writer for using "Ike" rather than "Eisenhower" when he has room for only a dozen or so letters per line? Or "JFK" for "Kennedy" and "LBJ" for "Johnson"? Interestingly, Nixon never became RMN because his set of initials count out to five units—the same number of units as his full name;[6] and headline writers would prefer to use the full name. Anyway, when he became President, Nixon dropped his middle initial.

A newspaper's bias enters into its irreverence too. In the 1968 presidential campaign, the New York *Daily News,* which was for Nixon, referred to Hubert H. Humphrey in headlines as "Hubie." "Hubie" counts out as five units. "Humphrey" was too long. But the paper could have used "HHH," certainly more dignified than "Hubie," and saved itself half a unit.

Whatever a headline's defects, the reader must not blame the reporter. Reporters don't write headlines. The reporter, when he turns his story in, does not know where the story will run or how important it will be in relation to other stories that day; he doesn't know the size of the headline or what its "count" will be. So the job is left to the copyreader. That headlines are written by someone twice removed from the source of the news explains some of their inaccuracies.

[6] Most newspapers use this unit system for "counting" headlines: each lower case letter counts as one unit; each capital letter counts as one and one-half units. Exceptions include unusually narrow or wide letters; for instance, the capital "M" counts as two units. In "Nixon," the "N" is one and one-half, the "i" is one-half, the other letters each one—for a total of five. In "RMN" the "R" and "N" are each one and one-half; the "M" is two— for a total of five.

THE FLOW OF THE NEWS

News: what it is

Textbooks for students of journalism typically contain numerous definitions of news. Two of them are particularly useful in the context of this book:

1. News is anything that interests you and that you didn't already know.

2. News is whatever the editor decides is news.

These two suggest most of the essential dimensions of news. It is possible to be a good deal more detailed and much more technical about the components of news; some writers catalogue the 10, or 15, or 20 components of newsworthiness (consequence, conflict, suspense, proximity, progress, and the like). But no reporter sits down to write a story with such a catalogue before him, checking off the items as he packs them into the paragraph. Nor does an editor gauge a wire service story against a checklist to decide whether he should put it in the paper. Most of the decisions about news—whether the reader's decision to look at a certain story, or the editor's decision to play up a specific feature—are made by intuition.

What's new and interesting

Consider that first definition above: News is anything that interests you and that you didn't already know.

Both elements are typically present in an item of news a reader selects from the smorgasbord put before him in each day's paper. But they may not be present in equal degree. If a story deals with something that deeply interests a reader, he may spend time on it although it tells him only a few more things than he already knows about the subject. But even if everything in the story is new to him, he may skip it if the topic is one that holds no interest for him.

His interest may be generated in a number of ways. The story may deal with a subject that has directly to do with the reader's trade or profession; it may appear to offer him some help in a role-playing situation he faces (e.g., a father might be drawn to a story about a community approach to teen-age drug experimentation) ; or it may contain the ingredients of vicarious experience (an account of a suspenseful rescue, or a sports story).

The most newsworthy story of all, from the reader's point of view, is one about himself. No matter how flatly written it may be, no matter how prosaically dull it may be to others, a story that deals with the reader himself earns his close and repeated attention. Look to the family scrapbooks, or to the bureau drawers where fading newspaper clippings are carefully folded away; you won't find the story reporting the first heart transplant, or the account of the initial landing on the moon. Instead there will be the wedding story, the obituary, and the account of the son of the family being promoted to first assistant cashier.

From the other side of the desk

Before the reader has an option to choose or ignore a given story, others have had a hand in the matter. This is where the second definition above comes into focus: News is whatever the editor decides is news.

Events by the billions take place every day. A microscopically tiny fraction of these become news—because someone decided they were newsworthy.

A city editor drawing up his assignment sheet makes some of these decisions even before the events take place. He sends a reporter to cover the school board meeting, but decides that there will not be coverage of the Fortnightly Club's panel discussion on the draft. He may make the decision simply because he doesn't have enough reporters to cover both events and he has to pick one as more important than the other. Or he may make the decision on the ground that the club meeting wouldn't interest enough readers.

The reporter who goes to cover the school board meeting also plays a decision-making role. During the meeting a dozen items come up for discussion. He picks out three or four as being important and of interest, and includes them in his story. Some others may be summed up in a final paragraph beginning "In other business . . ." while still others may be ignored altogether. Thus some events of the evening become the stuff of news; others subside into the official records of the school board to gather dust.

In some cases the decisions made by the news gatekeepers—the editors and reporters—may not be ones that individual readers might have made in the same circumstances. Most of us have had the experience of having some part in a news event about which we later read in a newspaper account; and in all probability we snort: "That wasn't the way it really happened!"

Walter Lippmann, in his book *Public Opinion* published in the 1920s, wrote that ". . . each of us tends to judge a newspaper, if we judge it at all, by its treatment of that part of the news in which we feel ourselves involved."

In some of the cases where the reader's recollection of an event differs from the report he finds in the paper, there has been a failure somewhere in the flow of the news. The reporter may have missed a significant point, or he may have jotted down a wrong figure or misspelled a name.

In a good many other cases, however, the problem may be one of differing priorities. The reader who was also a participant in the news event quite naturally remembers best the part in which he was involved; for him, it looms in the foreground. The reporter, in his role as a disinterested party, has a different perspective. His account, balanced and complete in his judgment as observer, may stint the facet of the event in which the indignant reader had taken part, or in which he had a particularly strong interest. In this, and in other ways, the mechanics of news reporting, writing, and editing have an effect on the shape of the news as it is presented through the media of information.

Distilling the essence

A news report, whether transmitted by newspaper, magazine, or television, is necessarily an abstraction or condensation of the original event. A presidential candidate may make a 5,000-word speech before a national television audience. If the event is important enough it may perhaps be broadcast in its entirety; some persons may have time to watch through the whole of it. Most of us, however, will get our impressions of the speech at second or third hand.

A television newscast later that evening may show excerpts totalling two and a half minutes of the original half-hour speech; the commentator may sum up in another 60 seconds what in his judgment were the salient points covered by the speaker.

The newspaper may offer a somewhat fuller report, perhaps as many as 700 words in a summary story studded with pertinent quotations from the speech. The headline written for the story will represent an attempt to boil it all down to a half dozen or so expressive words.

A newsmagazine published three days later may deal much more succinctly with the event than did the newspaper and infuse into its report some analysis and evaluation as well.

However an individual gains his various impressions of the candidate's speech, they will necessarily be different from the impressions he might have obtained had he been present for the original delivery (though it should be noted that he very likely will have a clearer picture from the reports than he might have gained on the spot, with his attention distracted by the surroundings, by the incipient indigestion induced by the bad luncheon served, or by the conversation of his table partners).

Distilling the central significance out of a sprawling, complex news event is part of the job of the reporter. If he is skilled at the task and impartial in his approach, he can accomplish this without doing any violence to the meaning of an event or the theme of a speech. If he is inexpert, or if he has an axe to grind, he may misrepresent the nature of the news in the condensing process.

Such misrepresentation—whether unintentional or deliberate— can often be detected more readily in headline treatment than in the body of a news story. Consider the following case.

An assistant philosophy professor at UCLA was dropped from her position by action of the board of regents of the University of California system. She was a Negro, and also an avowed Communist. The news account of the dismissal appeared in two different daily papers under these two headlines:

| **Marxist Professor** | and | **UC Regents Fire** |
| **Ordered Dismissed** | | **Black Professor** |

The difference in emphasis is of obvious importance. In each case, the headline establishes a mental set for the reader as he approaches the story to follow. Why two different editors, viewing the same story, chose to focus on different aspects of the incident cannot be determined just on the face of the matter. Whether an honest difference in news judgment was involved, or whether a deliberate attempt to put a special spin on the story dictated the choice of words is impossible to tell from a distance. But the difference certainly is there to be seen, and it undoubtedly had at least some effect on the readers of the two stories.

That top-heavy pyramid

Conventions govern the way in which news is packaged for presentation to the consumer, whether in the newspaper or over the air waves.

There is not enough space in the paper, or time on the air, to tell about a news event in complete detail; so the report is condensed as has been noted above. But there are also other differences between the original event and the news report.

An event takes place according to a certain chronology; there is a beginning, and an end. A reporter writing a news story typically rearranges the elements in an order different from the one in which they occurred.

A news story might begin:

An eight-year-old South Chicago youngster was killed today when a driverless car rolled down a hill and into a crowded school playground.

Rarely would a reporter approach such a story on a chronological basis, telling first how a driver had parked his car on a hillside in order to go into a neighborhood store, then how the worn-out handbrake had given way, how the car had gathered momentum down the hill, how passers-by had shouted warnings in vain, how the eight-year-old had started to run from one end of the playground toward the other, and how the car broke through the chain-link fence and struck him down.

A few stories have such strong elements of pathos or humor in them that the reporter decides he can bring out their significance best if he uses a chronological sequence and a climactic ending. But in most cases involving "spot" news (recent, fast-breaking events) the kind of beginning sentence quoted above (it is called a summary lead) would be preferred. And that lead sentence would be followed by additional details to fill out the story—all arranged in order of descending importance. Thus the end of the story, far from carrying the climax, might contain the home addresses of participants or other wrap-up details. This story form with the major element of news first and less important material following, is the "inverted pyramid" style of news story construction. It is preferred in most spot news for two reasons.

First, it helps the reader sort out the news quickly. If every story begins with a summary lead that provides a quick capsule version of the account to follow, the reader can quickly skim through a dozen such leads before zeroing in on one that indicates to him that here is something of particular interest.

The editor is realistic about his readers. He knows that they are likely to spend only a relatively brief time (half an hour to an hour for most readers) going through his entire paper. So he tries to make it as easy as possible for them to locate quickly the items of news on which they would most like to spend that time.

The inverted pyramid story also has a secondary value. A newspaper is put together rapidly, over a brief period of time. Changes are made up to the last minute. When a story needs to be cut down in size to make room for a new bulletin a few seconds before deadline, it is useful to the make-up man to know that he can simply pull out the last couple of paragraphs; they contain the least important elements of the story. The essential points will still be intact in the earlier paragraphs.[7]

The inverted pyramid form, for all its usefulness, is something of a literary corset. It is artificial rather than natural in sequence. If it is utilized unvaryingly in every column of every page in the paper, the effect on the reader is wearying.

Readership studies have demonstrated that most readers will take more interest in a news account presented in chronological, narrative form than in one written in the inverted pyramid form. Heeding these findings, editors have turned more and more to a

---

[7] A third reason for continued use of the inverted pyramid construction is internal and mechanical. If the story is thus arranged, the headline writer can quickly develop a theme for the headline. However, a good desk editor ought to read through the entire story in any case before attempting to write a head for it.

narrative approach, particularly for feature stories that do not deal with spot news and can be held until a day on which there is room to run them. But the inverted pyramid is still with us in most newspapers, for most of the top stories of the day. And since the two reasons for its use are still valid, it is likely to be around a while longer.

The blue-pencil boys

When a news story leaves the hands of the reporter, whether in chronological or inverted pyramid form, it still may undergo some more changes before the reader's eye falls on it.

On a newspaper, the city editor, the copy-desk editor, and an assistant managing editor may wield their pencils on the story, cutting out a superfluous phrase here, clarifying an obscure point there, perhaps even rewriting an entire paragraph to bring out some meaning that the reporter had left half-buried.

In a radio or television newsroom a news editor or news director may perform similar functions, and on a magazine the departmental editors and senior editors go over writers' copy exhaustively, sometimes rebuilding it almost beyond recognition.

The editors' role is to backstop the reporter. If in his haste to get a story written the reporter has been guilty of errors in fact, or lapses from clear style, it is the responsibility of the various editors to clean up the copy before it gets to the reader or listener. The editor on a newspaper also decides whether or not a given story is of sufficient importance to go in the paper at all, and if so, on what page it should be placed and under what size headline it should be displayed.

In all of these various functions, the editor has opportunities to alter the impact of a news story. He is another of the gate-keepers through whom the reader's picture of the world is filtered.

Getting through—just barely

The communication process can be diagrammed in an all-purpose model that serves to represent any of the several media of information.

NEWS EVENTS — X — REPORTER — X$_1$ — EDITORS — X$_2$ — READER or VIEWER — X$_3$; X$_n$

The communication process

In this model, X represents a news event of some kind. The first screen through which the event is viewed is the reporter (or someone else who bears tidings, such as the neighborhood gossip) and X$_1$ represents the reporter's *version* of the original news event, X. The reporter's version is not the same as the original—at the least it is condensed, paraphrased, summarized. It is an abstraction of the original, thus X$_1$.

Next there are various editors who may in a number of ways work changes in the reporter's version. The version that emerges from this second screen at the editors' desks is different from the reporter's and is represented as X$_2$, a second level of abstraction. Finally, the news report reaches the reader or viewer. He may note only part of the story and react to it in terms of his own frame of reference (a third screen); in other words, he perceives it in still another version, X$_3$, a further abstraction of the original. And his perception of the event may be still further conditioned by versions that have come to him from other of the media of information, or from friends who pass on word-of-mouth impressions—all of these other versions being represented in the model as X$_n$.

When the communication process is thus viewed, and all the possibilities for alteration or error are analyzed, the wonder is that the news reaches us at all.

At each stage along the way the mechanics of the communication process require some changes to be made in the account. At each stage along the way, the news account is processed by men and women with individual backgrounds, attitudes, biases, and reactions. As professionals, the news gatherers and editors try to keep their own attitudes and prejudices out of the picture. But inevitably these factors color their judgments.

And at the end of the line, the reader himself colors the final version of the news account according to *his* biases and background, selectively perceiving those elements in the news that accord with his view of the world, and tuning out those elements that conflict with his beliefs and hopes.

To appreciate the implications involved, assume that the news event in question is an announcement by a college president that fraternities and sororities will be abolished on the campus.

Assume that the reporter who covers the story is a student who is a part-time campus correspondent for the newspaper. As he writes the story he must try to keep his own reactions under control, even though he is a fraternity member and deplores the move.

Assume that the desk editor on the newspaper downtown who scans the reporter's story has a dozen others to weigh against it that day and decides to trim it down, thus cutting out some of the explanation with which the college president accompanied his announcement.

And then consider the infinitude of readers who find this story before them that evening—the outraged alumnus whose happiest memories were of the old Sigma Zeta house, the teen-ager who had been planning to enter the college next fall, the gas station attendant who has built up a grudge against the hot-rod college boys who roar in and out of his station, the restaurant owner who wonders what this might do to the profitable homecoming weekend business he counts on each year, and so on and on.

The communication of news and ideas to a mass audience is an intricately complex process. At every step of the way there are possibilities for alterations that affect the way in which the account will be perceived by the final receiver—the reader, listener, or viewer—in his home, surrounded by his own special framework of learned attitudes and unconscious biases.

CHAPTER THREE

The disappearing daily and other illusions

Except perhaps for marriage, no institution in our society is more frequently a subject of criticism than is the press. But—so far as the press is concerned, at least—the critics frequently aim wide of the mark. They attack imagined faults and overlook genuine weaknesses. They complain about minor or nonexistent abuses and fail to perceive some real and urgent problems.

Many of these uninformed criticisms are repeated often enough so that they achieve widespread currency and acceptance. Thus a smoggy mixture of myth and fact has accumulated around the press, and it is difficult for the average reader to distinguish the reality from the illusion.

The advertiser as dictator

For example, many newspaper readers are firmly convinced that important advertisers call the tune for editors. If you buy enough advertising space, the theme runs, you can tell the editor what to keep out of the paper, and what position to take on a controversial issue. After all, the newspaper's chief source of revenue is advertising, and money talks (income from subscriptions typically represents only about a quarter to a third of newspaper revenue; the rest comes from sale of space to advertisers).

In earlier eras of American journalism, when competition among papers for the advertiser's dollar was fierce, this claim had some substance. And even today, in some cities, there is truth in it. But to most daily newspapers in our time, it simply doesn't apply.

Most daily newspapers in this last third of the twentieth century do not have local newspaper competition. The advertiser needs the newspaper more than the newspaper needs the advertiser, since the paper usually represents the most effective way for the advertiser to get his sales message to the potential purchasers in the community. This semimonopoly (not a complete monopoly, since the local electronic media provide a kind of competition) allows the newspaper to be independent of advertiser pressure, even when it is applied.

This independence was illustrated dramatically in the 1950s in Portland, Oregon. The management of the largest department store in Portland, and the heaviest advertiser in the city's two newspapers, became angry with the Portland *Oregonian* because the paper insisted on printing news of a strike at the store. To bring pressure on the paper, the store's managers pulled all their advertising from the *Oregonian,* many full pages a week. But the editors stuck to their guns. In time the store's advertising manager came around, hat in hand, to put his advertising back in the paper. He had found he couldn't get along without this access to the community, even though there was a competing newspaper in Portland as well as several radio and television channels.

But if most dailies can afford to be indifferent to advertiser pressure, and to other outside forces, that is not necessarily the case with weekly newspapers or with radio stations. It is far less costly to introduce competition into the weekly newspaper field, or into a radio market. A group of disgruntled advertisers in a small town could very possibly withdraw enough advertising revenue from the local weekly publisher to put him in serious trouble. If they combined to set a competitor up in business, they might well be able to drive the original publisher out. It has happened in more than one rural community or small town.[1]

Because they are aware of this possibility, many small town publishers tend to walk warily with respect to local issues and local advertisers. Generalizations are usually misleading when the press is under discussion, since it is by no means a monolithic institution; but it is fair to say that there is less editorial crusading on local issues among weekly newspapers than among dailies. Many weeklies do not carry any editorial comment at all. One important reason for the muted editorial voices in the small towns is the recognition by the editors that they are indeed vulnerable to some kinds of pressures.

But it would be wrong to leave the impression here that the small community editor or publisher is invariably a milquetoast when it comes to local controversy or advertiser pressure. Many are, but some are as boldly independent as their metropolitan brethren, as witness this editorial response in a small Northwest weekly (the Sandy, Oreg., *Post*) that had been subjected to pressure by a telephone utility:

Our Editorial Page Is Not for Sale

In legal circles, it might be called attempted bribery. Others might refer to it as financial pressure or an advertising subsidy. We prefer to look upon it as downright stupidity. . . .

We were told bluntly that if we wish to continue receiving advertising from the West Coast Telephone Company, it is advisable that we lend our support to the company in its demand for higher rates, whether we approve the sought increase or not.

This is to advise the West Coast Telephone Company, together with its advertising and public relations agents, that so far as this newspaper is concerned they have rung the wrong number.

It so happens that we do not presently know whether or not the telephone company is justly entitled to an increase in its telephone rates. Offhand, we would suggest that there might be considerable doubt as to the justice of their cause. The mere fact that they are attempting to pressure the weekly newspapers which carry

[1] Some radio stations in small communities are equally vulnerable, although the necessity of obtaining a Federal Communications Commission frequency allocation may limit the opportunity for the introduction of competition in the electronic field.

their advertising to support their plea causes us to look with grave concern on the merits of the case. . . .

The elevator syndrome

There is at least one substantial qualification to be entered to the general assertion that daily newspapers are well armored against advertiser influence.

A wry comment on the newspapers of England once ran:

> You cannot hope to bribe or twist
> Thank God! the British journalist.
> But, seeing what the man will do
> Unbribed, there's no occasion to.[2]

It has been suggested by some critics of the American press that even though the advertiser may not be able to put any pressure on modern daily newspapers, he really doesn't have to—the publishers share his philosophy anyway and reflect it in their papers.

It is true enough that most newspaper publishers tend to be conservative on economic and political issues, as do most businessmen. In both groups there are notable exceptions, of course.

It is also true that the attitudes of a newspaper owner seep out into the staff generally, sometimes by directive, sometimes by a kind of osmosis or as a result of the "elevator syndrome" (employees overhear the publisher's comments as they ride with him up and down in the office elevator, and either consciously or unconsciously reflect his prejudices in their own approach to their jobs).

An anonymous employee of the Louisville *Courier-Journal* put into the newsroom suggestion box a list of the persons and institutions that he felt were regarded as "sacred cows" by the news staff simply because the publisher or someone else in management had indicated an interest in them. His note said:

News sources or topics don't really have to be considered by the publisher to merit special treatment. . . . However, if someone in the editorial chain of command *between* the publisher and the news gatherer believes the publisher has a special interest, the effect is the

[2] By the English poet, Humbert Wolfe. Quoted in "Queries and Answers," *The New York Times Book Review*, May 7, 1961.

same on the reporter. Or, if one of the executives in this chain has himself a special interest, that interest is transferred down the line, too. It is rare—although it happens here—for an editor to say "be careful, you know how the publisher feels about this one," but the way stories are edited, the questions asked reporters by editors about them, and sometimes just a tone of voice can quite effectively get across the message that this is "of special concern."[3]

As a counterbalance to this effect, there is the fact that many working journalists—reporters, editors, broadcast newsmen—tend to be liberal rather than conservative in their personal outlook. Though they may strive to keep their own views out of their handling of the news, these views inevitably exert some influence, perhaps enough to nullify the ripple effect of the publisher's attitudes.

In any case, both publisher and staff member tend to resist, and resist strongly, any overt attempt by an advertiser or other outside pressure source to influence the handling of the news. They may sometimes arrive at the same policy decision that the advertiser might have enforced if he had had the power; but they usually arrive at the decision for reasons of their own, not because they have knuckled under.

"Anything to sell a few more papers"

Another widely held belief about the newspaper press is that it is a business conducted only to sell papers, and that to this end the columns are crammed with sex, crime, and sensation.

If you're on the lookout for them, you can find individual papers that serve as prime exhibits to illustrate the truth of this claim. (It is also true that you can find a Biblical quotation to support almost any thesis, and statistics to back up almost any theory.)

Critics point to the fact that the largest circulation newspaper in this country is the New York *Daily News* (2,000,000 copies a day), which does indeed base a substantial amount of its appeal to readers on cheesecake pictures and overplayed crime stories. In New York City the *News* outsells the New York *Times,* the country's finest quality newspaper, about six to one.

The critics also call attention to the lurid look of some tabloid

[3] Quoted by Robert U. Brown in "Shop Talk at Thirty," *Editor & Publisher,* September 13, 1969, p. 72.

and metropolitan papers in other cities where lively competition still flourishes. When a tight battle for readers is on, even a normally staid newspaper tends to put more emphasis on sensational and human interest news, heralded by outsize, multi-colored headlines, in order to win the war of the newsstands.

But the observer who looks over the whole spectrum of American journalism, and not just at the gamiest sectors, is likely to come away with quite a different impression from that of the critics.

Nearly all newspapers carry news of crime (the *Christian Science Monitor,* as a matter of policy, carries hardly any) and stories that center on human interest elements, including sex. But in most newspapers—big city, small town, and community weekly—these stories are only a part of the daily mix. They are not sensationalized or overplayed in order to sell a few more papers. They are included in the paper because they are legitimately a part of the news of the day.

As citizens we need to be informed about news of crime. We need to know what crimes are being committed, what the law enforcement officers are doing about them, and how the courts are dealing with persons accused of crimes. If we are not well informed about these matters, we can't be alert to abuses that may readily develop in the working of the machinery of law enforcement, we can't be aware of the festering corners of our society in which crime is bred, we can't be discerning voters when the time comes to pass judgment on those who have been elected or appointed to balance the scales of justice on our behalf.[4]

So news of crime, criminals, and the machinery of the law properly belongs in the paper. But it should not be given undue emphasis, or presented in the kind of morbid detail that feeds the fantasies of sick minds. That is sensationalism. In some papers, crime news is indeed given sensationalist treatment, but in most American newspapers, there is not as much sensationalism as the casual critics would have us believe.

If you were to take a ruler and measure out the inches given to crime news in the average newspaper, you would discover that it constitutes a very small percentage of the total news hole. If you were to make a simple content analysis of most crime stories, you

---

[4] *Life* magazine's 1969 revelations about Supreme Court Justice Abe Fortas's extracurricular activities led to his resignation, the first such departure under fire in the history of the nation's highest court.

would discover that the language is largely legalistic rather than sensational.

Why, then, does the typical reader nod in agreement when he hears the charge that the newspapers are full of crime? Why does it seem to him that there is so much of this kind of news?

There are, of course, the horrible examples, the individual papers of which the charges are all too true. But a large part of the answer lies with the readers themselves.

Communication is, after all, a two-party process. The newspaper presents news stories; the reader selects and reads those that interest him. Crime stories interest the average reader greatly. He will seek them out, even in the back pages, and pore over every line. He remembers them when he has quickly bypassed or forgotten the story on tax reform or water pollution. Even though they may not take up much of the over-all news hole, and even though they may be presented in strait-laced fashion, crime stories leap up from the page and into the reader's mind. And because he selects them out, and gives them loving attention, he is left with a distorted impression of the place they occupy in the over-all news budget.

Editors are well aware, of course, of the reader's built-in interest in crime and similar news. An editor who had no other purpose than to make a successful newspaper from a cash register viewpoint would find this a simple matter. Some have done precisely that.

But the fact is that most editors do not take this easy road to success. They include in their papers the crime and human interest news they feel readers need and want to know about. But this is typically only a small part of the whole; the editors fill out the rest of their papers with the news of consequence and importance that we must know about if we are to function as citizens—even if that news is of far less interest to us than the crime stories or the human interest features.

If the motto in the editorial room really were "anything to sell a few more papers," we would have 1,750 sensational sheets rather than a handful.

And everyone knows monopoly is bad

If you're looking for a scare statistic, try this one: in about 96 percent of all the American cities with daily newspapers there is only one newspaper, or else a single newspaper owner with a morning-evening combination. In other words, in only 4 percent of our cities is there any genuine newspaper competition.

Whether or not those percentages are familiar, the tags "monopoly journalism" and "one-newspaper town" are known to most of us. And the connotations they call to mind are always bad. The assumptions are usually made that the absence of competition is a disaster, and that any one-ownership situation must inevitably be injurious to the community.

Fortunately, the picture is not as bleak as it seems.

In the first place, the one-newspaper town is usually not even close to a true monopoly. In addition to the one daily, the citizens are typically served by one or more weekly newspapers or shoppers (free-circulation throwaways consisting mostly of advertising with a sprinkling of local news). Readers also have access to local radio and television channels, regional newspapers, and national news magazines.

There are, to be sure, some few communities in which one owner controls newspaper, radio, and television. That comes close to being an absolute monopoly, at least of the channels through which local news is available to the community.[5]

But in the vast majority of towns and cities embraced by that fearsome 96 percent statistic, the newspaper constitutes only a semi-monopoly, considerably tempered by the competition of the electronic and other media that reach the citizens of the community.

It should not be assumed from this, however, that the talk about monopoly journalism is a false alarm. Even the semimonopoly situation is an inherently unhealthy one in that it represents a narrowing of the channels through which the citizen can obtain various reports and interpretations of an event in the news. But matters are by no means as serious as they would be if the 96 percent figure reflected absolute monopoly conditions.

There is an additional element of comfort, too, in the fact that the consequences of a one-newspaper situation are sometimes anything but inimical to the public interest. In fact, it can be argued

---

[5] According to the Federal Communications Commission, in 1969 there were 72 cities, all with populations under 100,000, where the only daily newspaper controlled the only local radio station and where there were no television stations.

that a monopoly or semimonopoly publisher can *afford* to publish a good paper just *because* he does not have competition. He is freer of advertiser pressure than he would be in a competitive situation, as was noted earlier. Also, his paper very likely has a good profit margin, which should enable him to plow money back into a quality staff and modern facilities.

Some one-ownership towns such as Louisville (*Courier-Journal* and *Times* one-ownership combination) clearly illustrate the fact that monopoly journalism can be of superior quality.

A striking instance of the advantages of a monopoly situation over competition is to be found in New England. In Boston there is still lively competition among several papers, most of them mediocre; 35 miles away in Providence, R. I., a monopoly morning-evening combination (the *Journal* and the *Evening Bulletin*) provides that community with vastly better journalism than most readers in Boston have available to them.[6]

Again, however, the hasty generalization must be avoided. These are a couple of examples; quite a few more could be listed. But an equally lengthy list could be compiled of communities in which a monopoly publisher has taken advantage of his comfortable situation to lapse into a shoddy, slovenly, nickel-nursing mockery of journalism in which the public interest is coldly ignored.

The point is that once a one-newspaper situation has been established, it can go either way. The potentiality for improved service is there; so is the opportunity for neglect of responsibility.

The chain gangs

Another cause for concern (and one about which much less is heard) is the growth of newspaper chains, or "groups" as they are now euphemistically termed.

[6] A *Newsweek* essay ("What's Wrong with the Press?" November 29, 1965) observed that "Where bitter competition still exists, as in New York or Boston, papers still appear that are hardly worth the dime they cost, while monopoly cities boast such responsible papers as the Kansas City *Star*, the Minneapolis *Tribune*, the Providence *Journal*, and the Louisville *Courier-Journal*." It is true that Boston is also the city of publication for the *Christian Science Monitor*, a fine journalistic product. But the *Monitor* is more a national, daily news magazine than a local newspaper. One of the criticized Boston local dailies, the *Globe*, has been making an effort to improve in quality in recent years, with some success.

In 1940 a few more than 300 of the country's daily newspapers belonged to chains (a chain is made up of a number of newspapers controlled by a single owner or ownership syndicate). By the late 1960s there were close to 900 chain newspapers, half of all the dailies in the country. In the field of broadcasting there is a similar concentration of ownership. Chains own 31 percent of all AM and FM radio stations. Networks control about 95 percent of local prime time on television.

As was noted in the case of monopoly, the fact that a newspaper or a broadcasting station is owned by a chain system does not necessarily mean that it is a poorer paper or station than it would be if it were independently owned. But the potentiality is there for a decline in the quality of service. And in many cases the decline is realized.

There can be an absolute slide in quality, as when a chain owner insists on a step-up in profits at the expense of the news content of his papers. Or the effect can be subtler.

At the least, there is likely to be a homogenization of the product produced by the chain publishers. In one national chain, editorials on national issues are written at the chain's central headquarters, and then run word-for-word in all of the member papers (the local publishers have autonomy with respect to editorial comment on local or regional matters, however).

In some chains an honest effort appears to be made to resist this homogenized effect. The individual publishers of the 21 Newhouse papers insist that they are free to set editorial and news policy without reference to the central ownership. The editors of the Gannett group, a New York and New England chain, meet regularly to discuss editorial policy, but then go back to their offices to make the final decisions on their own.

Yet on balance, the spread of chain or group ownership of the channels of communication must be viewed as an ominous trend; in the eyes of some observers of the journalistic scene it is more ominous than the growth of the one-newspaper-town statistic. They are particularly chilled by the specter of foreign control, as represented by the Thomson group. Lord Thomson of Fleet, a British newspaper publisher, has built up an international chain which during the 1960s expanded rapidly on the American scene. Most of his American acquisitions have been small-city dailies.

"The newspaper is dead"

Finally, what of another widely circulated belief about American journalism—that the day of the newspaper is drawing to a close?

What reality is there in such books as *The Disappearing Daily*, by the former editor of *The Nation*, Oswald Garrison Villard, or *The Fading American Newspaper*, by a long-time Gannett editor, Carl Lindstrom? Their theme is suggested by their titles, and it finds reinforcement in the pronouncements of prophet Marshall McLuhan, who celebrates the death of print and the dawn of the era of electronic tribalism.

The doom-sayers have some persuasive statistics to offer (*everyone* has statistics, including the authors of this book). They point out that there were once more than 2600 daily newspapers in the United States, and that now there are only 1750. They point out that the development of radio and television, and the proliferation of magazines, have drained away much of the advertising revenue on which the newspaper's survival depends. They point to surveys that show that people are turning more and more to television for news. And they cite findings of pollsters that people tend to believe what they hear and see on television more than what they read in the paper.

For the defense, spokesmen for the newspapers point to the steady and continuing increase in newspaper circulation. They emphasize that while some national advertising revenue has been lost by newspapers, revenue from local advertising has more than doubled in the last two decades ($1.5 billion a year to $3.6 billion) and neither radio nor television has been able to cut seriously into this field. And they point to polls of their own that demonstrate that readers still get *most* of their news and information from newspapers, although they may get the first flashes from the electronic media. Even the fans who sit through a TV ball game grab for the paper the next morning to "read all about it."

When the prophecies, claims, and counterclaims are all sifted down, it seems reasonable to predict the survival of print media in some form for the foreseeable future. The advantages of a permanent report that can be consulted at the reader's convenience, and consulted again later if need be, are compelling. And the kind of depth reporting that the print media can provide is increasingly needed as the flow of news becomes more complicated and more difficult to understand. A half-hour newscast's skimming of the top of the news is not enough for a still substantial number of consumers. They will continue to want a fuller report.

The format of the newspaper undoubtedly will undergo alterations, perhaps even radical ones. Distribution of the newspaper of the future may be by electronic means rather than carrier boys. But the survival of some form of print medium to disseminate news, opinion, entertainment, and advertising messages seems worth betting on.[7]

---

[7] For additional insights on newspapers and newspapermen consult Jonathan Daniels, *They Will Be Heard: America's Crusading Newspaper Editors*, McGraw-Hill, New York, 1965, and Louis M. Lyons, ed., *Reporting the News*, Belknap Press of Harvard University Press, Cambridge, Mass., 1965.

CHAPTER FOUR

Some shots on target

As was noted in the last chapter, some of the most widely circulated criticisms of newspapers are not altogether valid. But there are some other complaints about the newspaper press that land on target, some in the bull's-eye.

Certain of the genuine shortcomings of the press are evident even to that mythical creature, the average reader. Others can be spotted only by the practiced eye of an informed critic (there have been a few professional critics of the press in every era; for a sampling, try Upton Sinclair, *The Brass Check*; George Seldes, *Lords of the Press*; A. J. Liebling, *The Wayward Pressman* and *The Press*; and some of the articles by a current critic, Ben H. Bagdikian, in *Esquire* and *Columbia Journalism Review*).

Something (but not much) for everyone

One weakness of newspaper journalism, its tendency to superficiality in coverage of any given area of news, is sensed sooner or later by nearly all readers.

The daily newspaper is put together so that it will appeal to a very wide range of potential readers; it is, quite literally, a mass medium. It is, in addition, catholic (small c) in its approach; the world, the nation, the state, the community, the serious and the comic, the portentous and the trivial—all are a part of the sprawling, constantly changing picture of reality that the newspaper attempts to provide for its readers.

Newspaper writers and editors are skilled at encapsulating large events in small packages of type; they are practiced at distilling the meaning from lengthy documents or speeches.

But despite their skills, the end product is inevitably a less-than-complete account of most of the news. Some major news events (a national tragedy, like the assassination of President Kennedy, or a national spectacle, like a British coronation) may be given such saturation coverage by all the media that even the most intensely interested and most deeply informed readers find out all they want to know. But most news stories, most of the time, are sketched out only in essential outline.

This outline is as much as most readers may want. But to some who have a special stake in the event, and to others who may have considerable expertise in the field of news involved, the newspaper's coverage seems shallow and inadequate.

The reader who has himself been a participant in a news event (as a speaker at a conference, or as a witness in a trial) rarely feels that the subsequent news coverage provided a full and satisfactory report. The reader who is an economist by profession is invariably impatient with the brevity of the news story on a rediscount rate increase or a proposed tax reform. The lodge member who has just been elected Grand Redeemer is outraged when the one-paragraph newspaper account or the 30-second radio report fails to convey the solemnity and significance of his elevation.

In each case, the newspaper provided *most* of its readers all they wanted to know about the various news developments; in each case, the informed insider with a special interest found the coverage wanting.

Novelist Mark Harris, who is himself a former newspaper man, observed that

Newspapers are ceasing to be useful to me. In areas where I know a little something—say, news of colleges and universities, books or the theater—I've discovered the paper is just a clue to what's going on. And if I assume papers are wrong in my field, I begin to assume they're wrong in all fields.[1]

This is a shortcoming inherent in any mass medium. Radio and television offend even more than newspapers, since they have comparatively much less space or time to give to the over-all news report.

All the media have been trying during the last two decades to respond to the criticism of superficiality. Newspapers have been scheduling more and more background or interpretive articles that seek to present a news development in several dimensions. The electronic media have developed some effective hour-long documentary treatments of complex and controversial issues.

But all such efforts are extremely costly, both in dollars and in terms of space and time. It seems inevitable that the mass media, by their nature, will continue to be vulnerable to the criticism of superficiality in the coverage of many areas of news.[2]

How about the rest of the iceberg?

There is a related problem about journalistic coverage that may not be apparent to most readers, but which disturbs informed professionals. Not only does the press tend to cover only the outlines of the news, these inside critics contend, but it also tends to focus on overt, noisy, dramatic peaks of events while failing to present an adequate picture of the more important subsurface forces that have led to these outward developments.

One critic has suggested that the press has transferred the police beat approach to the coverage of all news. A reporter on the police beat (assigned to cover news developments originating with the police) necessarily concentrates on the reports of crimes committed and arrests made; he rarely has the time or resources to probe behind the violent outbreak to trace the factors of environment or character that led up to the crime. Nor does he attempt to balance each report of a criminal development in the community by citing

[1] Quoted in *Newsweek*, "What's Wrong with the Press?" November 29, 1965, p. 56.
[2] The nearly encyclopedic New York *Times* is perhaps less vulnerable than any other American newspaper. But it is unique in world journalism.

statistics about the good behavior of most of the rest of the citizenry during the same time period.

It would not be realistic to expect a police reporter to approach his assignment in such depth; his job *is* to cover the peaks of events that break the surface. But in some other areas of news, covering only the peaks and ignoring the vast and significant bulk that lies below can lead to serious distortion.

The 1968 report of the Kerner Commission[3] was severely critical of the press for its preoccupation with reporting violence in the cities while failing to bring to public attention the festering problems that had brought on the riots and the burning.

Some close observers of the phenomenon of unrest among students on American campuses in the late 1960s contended that the press reports misrepresented reality by focusing only on the occasional outbursts of violence and ignoring the nature of the grievances that lay behind the demonstrations and seizures of buildings.

And in the area of foreign news reporting, American correspondents abroad have been accused of distorting the picture of the world for their readers by centering attention on coups and crises and providing little information about national movements and public attitudes.[4]

The response by some newspapers to this kind of criticism has been constructive. Their editors have begun to develop staff specialists who have had intensive grounding in the subject areas they regularly cover; seminars and short courses for working newsmen have been established in such fields as urban problems, poverty, and racism; correspondents for assignment abroad are being chosen not just for their mobility and resourcefulness but also on the basis of their background in international affairs, comparative governments, and economic development.

But such response has not been universal, by any means. Many newspapers, and even more electronic news staffs, continue to report the world, the nation, and City Hall largely in terms of the tip of the iceberg.

[3] *Report of the National Advisory Commission on Civil Disorders*, Bantam Books, New York, 1968 (paper). Also published in hardcover by E. P. Dutton.
[4] See Robert Sollen, "Wire Service Nationalism and Its Consequences," in the October, 1961 issue of *Nieman Reports*, a quarterly journal published by Harvard University's Nieman Foundation, and Malcolm Browne, "Viet Nam Reporting," in the *Columbia Journalism Review* for Fall, 1964.

"The prelevance [sic] of error"

The subtitle above appeared as the headline on an article in the *Columbia Journalism Review.*[5] The article took a wry, rueful look at the persistent nemesis of the mass media—the mistake, plain or fancy, human or mechanical.

Errors of all kinds, from trivial to catastrophic, find their way into the end products of the information media. They can be amusing and harmless typographical mistakes (From a wedding story: "The sacred cows were exchanged before the Rev. Francis King.") or they can be grave misrepresentations that damage careers and give rise to multimillion dollar libel actions.

All the persons involved with the gathering, writing, processing, and production of a newspaper story or a radio news broadcast do their best to avoid letting mistakes show up on the newsstand or on the air. But their best is not good enough, time after embarrassing time.

Some of the mistakes (including most of the inadvertent typos) can be chalked up to the high-speed pace at which news is gathered, written, and presented to the consumer. Despite the introduction of automated equipment, human hands and minds have a role at every step in the process. And even pros err when they hurry under pressure.

Gladwin Hill, chief of the Los Angeles bureau of the New York *Times,* put the newsman's case well:

Laymen, although they expect their newspapers to be on the doorstep every morning and their radio and television news reporter to chime in on the appointed second, are chronically unable to comprehend the time pressures involved in producing these results. Ask a college professor to write a 1,000-word treatise and he will say gladly—in a week, two weeks, a month. In the news business, it is a standard exigency to have to assemble, select, arrange, and indite the material of a 1000-word article *in the time it takes to type it.* One hour would be par for such an operation—several hundred times faster than the one-month schedule available to a college professor or a lawyer writing a brief. . . . In asking for short-order history, the public underwrites an

[5] Wilbur G. Lewis, "The Prelevance of Error . . ." *Columbia Journalism Review,* Winter, 1965, pp. 48–49.

implicit compromise: the completeness of information, the ruminations and judgments open to the scholar, simply are not humanly and mechanically possible when you are racing the clock.

No competent reporter trifles with accuracy, presents as unqualified fact information about which there is a reasonable doubt, or cites as an authority someone whose competence is questionable without indicating that questionability.

But there are limitations inherent in the compromise of short-order history. There is not time to delve into the lifetime reliability of the farmer who saw the airplane crash; readers are supposed to infer that his account is no more nor less dependable than would be that of the average farmer. The statements of public officials must be assumed, barring arrant implausibility, to be competent. If they are not, that is a problem for the citizenry to rectify; it is not something the press can reform before press time.[6]

Some critics of the press would not accept the whole of Mr. Hill's thesis on its face. They argue that the reporter and editor should take whatever time is necessary to eliminate the mistakes and check the reliability of the source of information. But, the journalist responds, completely error-free news would be stale news; the consumer has been accustomed to immediacy, and short-order history inevitably has flaws.

Whatever its cause, the error that finds its way into the newspaper's columns, or into the news broadcast, is doubly dangerous to the medium.

It may have tangibly painful consequences, as in a libel damage award to someone injured by the mistaken publication. But almost invariably it is costly to the newspaper or the broadcasting station in terms of lost public confidence.

Any reader, listener or viewer who spots an error—whether it injures him personally or not—is from that time on less confident about the accuracy and integrity of the news media. Over time, the cumulative effect can be the development of a credibility gap as potentially serious as the one that plagued President Lyndon Johnson through his second term.

Two Washington correspondents, writing in 1969, warned of the possible consequences.

---

[6] Quoted in Gladwin Hill, "The Press and the Assassination: Dispelling Some Illusions," *Frontier*, March, 1966, pp. 17–20.

Since a credible, fair-minded, responsible, fair-reporting press in all its forms is essential to democratic government, any wide and continuing credibility gap between press and public cannot fail to impair the functioning of our free society.[7]

If the gap indeed has been widening, it could be reclosed.

Newspapers that promptly acknowledge mistakes, and correct them, usually can regain the confidence of their readers. Editors who welcome and publish the reactions and comments of readers, whether in a letters column or an "Action Corner" feature, can establish rapport. Reporters who do their best to maintain an objective approach will be forgiven an occasional slip or omission.

But the reporter or broadcaster who refuses to admit the possibility of error, or is persistently sloppy, or deliberately deceptive in the handling of news, will suffer the consequences of declining credibility—and deservedly so.

With molasses-like speed

Another criticism of newspapers that strikes uncomfortably close to home is that they are stubbornly slow to change; they cling to old methods, and they do not recognize the altered patterns of reader needs.

It is a fact that the methods of typesetting and printing that were in use a half century ago are still being used in some sectors of the newspaper business. It is also a fact that some newspaper presses that were first put to work in Theodore Roosevelt's presidency are still grinding out papers today. It would be difficult to identify another major American industry in which methods and machinery of 50 or 60 years ago were still in use.

At a time when computers had become commonplace in much of business and industry, they were still limited to a tentative foothold in newspaper composing rooms and front offices. (John Diebold, a pioneer in automation, observed that "I've never seen an industry that will be more completely changed than the newspaper industry, and one that realizes it less.")

And many of the design and packaging characteristics of news-

---

[7] Roscoe and Geoffrey Drummond, "How Reliable Is Our News?" *The American Legion Magazine*, June, 1969, p. 9.

papers have been held over by habit or inertia from earlier eras, even though they may be outmoded today. The uncomfortably narrow newspaper column was first necessitated by mechanical limitations that no longer exist; the size and structure of headlines reflect a philosophy of display that has been rendered obsolete by the rise of competition from the broadcast media; the placement of the major story on most front pages continues to be dictated by a tradition that research findings tell us is directly at odds with the reader's pattern of eye movement.

But the resistance to change by the newspaper press has been of even greater significance in terms of content than in packaging and processing.

As the flow of news grew ever more complex during the first part of the twentieth century, and as our interest in the world at large broadened after America's emergence on the international stage in World War I, the newspaper reader found himself more and more bewildered. He needed help in his attempt to make sense of complicated issues and new concepts. The newspaper's response was to provide still more news, on the traditional pattern. The editorial pages continued to offer analysis. But the reader's needs were still not met.

Henry Luce and Briton Hadden sensed the opportunity, and *Time,* the first successful magazine of news summary, was launched. It was followed by several others, and it was only after all had been thriving for some years that the newspapers finally and reluctantly turned to the task of providing on their own pages the interpretation and backgrounding for which the reader had been thirsting.

The newspapers showed similar insensitivity and lack of imagination when they were faced successively by other kinds of competition for the reader's attention and favor.

The newspapers' primacy as an advertising medium was cut into first by the general circulation magazines, then by radio and finally, and most seriously, by television. When this happened, the newspaper's response tended to be defensive and imitative. It tried to fight its rivals on their ground, with their weapons. Editors added features and comics to match the magazines' entertainment appeal, more pictures to compete with television. But Roger Hutchins, former president of the University of Chicago and an eloquent newspaper critic, told a meeting of such editors that he disagreed with this strategy.

I do not believe that newspapers can do what comic books, picture magazines, motion pictures, and television can do in glorious technicolor. Since they can do this kind of thing better, why should you do it at all? You may say it is the only way to survive . . . it may be a way to die.[8]

Hutchins urged the editors to recognize that complete and fair coverage of the news was the product they had built on and the only basis on which they could survive. Newspapers, he said "should do as well as they can the things that they can do best, and they should leave to others the responsibility of entertaining the public."

Ben H. Bagdikian, another newspaper critic writing 15 years after Hutchins's admonition to the editors, provided evidence of that admonition's validity when he pointed out that the good newspapers, the ones that took the news seriously, were flourishing, while many others that had chosen different paths were failing.[9]

This same latter-day critic provided documentation of another aspect of the newspaper's failure to respond to changing patterns of reader needs by making the most of its special quality. He pointed out that in 1940 the average American newspaper had 27 pages; by 1965 it had 50 pages, but of the 23 additional pages 20 went to advertising and only 3 to news. Moreover, in net terms the reader was getting *less* hard news in 1965 than in 1940, since the type size used by newspapers had been increased (thus cutting down the number of words per page), and more white space and more pictures were being used than had been the case 25 years earlier. Yet in that same quarter-century span the flow of news had enormously increased in size and complexity, with the ushering in of the Atomic Age, the Cold War, the burgeoning of science, and the exploration of space.

Fortunately, there have been signs in recent years that the newspaper's traditional reluctance to change with the times is being overcome by new generations of editors and publishers. The shift to new, more flexible methods of production (offset printing and com-

[8] In a speech delivered to the annual meeting of the American Society of Newspaper Editors at Washington, D.C., on April 21, 1955.

[9] Ben H. Bagdikian, "The American Newspaper is Neither Record, Mirror, Journal, Ledger, Bulletin, Telegram, Examiner, Register, Chronicle, Gazette, Observer, Monitor, Transcript, nor Herald of the Day's Events. It's Just Bad News," *Esquire*, March, 1967, pp. 128 ff.

puter-assisted cold-type composition) accelerated during the 1960s. And there is more and more widespread willingness to add to newspaper staffs the kinds of substantively grounded writers who can give the reader the informed, in-depth treatment of news that he needs and wants.

Writing it white

A criticism of press performance that has been given increasing currency recently has to do with the mental set of reporters and editors when they approach news with racial overtones.

As a staff member of *Newsday*, Robert E. Smith, put it: "There is a white attitude in the daily press and in major broadcasting—innocuous, or insulting, or perhaps even inflammatory."[10]

He goes on to cite several tell-tale signs of this attitude:

1. *The we-they syndrome.* "Reporters, commentators and especially editorialists find it hard to realize that their audience is made up of people of many races and colors. Too often they talk of 'we' (white people) in relation to 'they' (black people). What they don't realize is that one-tenth or even one-third (in the case of some big-city newspapers) of that 'we' ain't white."

2. *The articulate syndrome.* White reporters or commentators persistently use such terms as "articulate," "clean-shaven," or "well-dressed" when making approbatory references to black persons, probably never realizing that implicit in such use of the terms is the assumption that most other blacks are inarticulate, bearded, and untidy.

3. *The first-name syndrome.* Sportswriters and sportscasters are particularly prone to this, according to Smith. They refer to black players by their first names, while using last-name references most of the time for white players. The subtle note of patronage underlying this practice grates on the sensitivity of blacks.

Racism in all forms is a malady affecting our whole society, of course, not just the mass media. But since these media profess to be channels of unbiased information for all of the public, they have a special obligation to rid themselves of all traces of the ugly ailment.

---

[10] Robert E. Smith, "They Still Write It White," *Columbia Journalism Review*, Spring, 1969, pp. 36–38.

"Whose bread I eat, his song I sing"

A final criticism of the press, that conflict of interest affects the impartiality of reporters and editors, is not often justified. But some of the time it is, and even that is too often.

Norman E. Isaacs, executive editor of the Louisville *Courier-Journal*, once wrote:

There is nothing in society that matches the importance of . . . [the newspaper's] function. The doctor touches just a handful of people. How many can a man see in a day? The minister? a few hundred in his congregation—once a week for the most part. We have in our hands such great power that when we use the word responsibility it ceases to be a cliché.[11]

Isaacs might well have added that the possession of such great power carries with it an obligation of integrity and incorruptibility not less than that of Caesar's wife. Whenever that incorruptibility is thrown into question, the standing of the press suffers.

There have been few major scandals touching the integrity of the working press in recent times.[12] But there have been enough isolated instances of shady practice, and there is sufficient evidence of borderline laxity with respect to certain news beats (notably sports, business, and travel), to establish a nagging unease in the mind of the critical observer of press performance.

A lengthy background article on conflict of interest in the press by a team of *Wall Street Journal* reporters opened with the following lead paragraphs:

In Boston and Chicago, newspaper investigations into suspected hanky-panky suddenly are aborted. In one case, a subject of inquiry turns out to be a stockholder of the paper and friend of the publisher. In the

[11] In *Nieman Reports*, December, 1968, p. 28.

[12] The case of Harry Karafin is an exception. A business writer for the Philadelphia *Inquirer*, Karafin was fired by his editor in 1967 after it was charged that he had used his position as an instrument of blackmail, threatening to run uncomplimentary stories about business leaders or firms in Philadelphia unless he got requested payoffs. The newspaper then investigated the case and forthrightly reported the results in a lengthy front-page story in its April 16, 1967 issue under the headline: "With Sadness and Regret, Inquirer Traces the Sordid Story of One 'Reporter.'"

other, the investigation threatens to embarrass a politician who could help the paper in a building project.

In California, a batch of small newspapers run editorials endorsing the Detroit position on auto safety. All are worded similarly. An incredible coincidence, this identity not only of opinion but of phrasing? Hardly, for all the articles are drawn from a single "canned" editorial emanating from an advertising agency in San Francisco.

In Denver, the advertising staff of a big daily wrestles with an arithmetic problem. A big advertiser has been promised news stories and pictures amounting to 25% of the space it buys; the paper already has run hundreds of inches of glowing prose but is still not close to the promised allotment of "news" and now is running out of nice things to say.

All this hardly enhances the image of objectivity and fierce independence the U.S. press tries so hard to project. Yet talks with scores of reporters, editors, publishers, public relations men and others reveal that practices endangering—and often subverting—newspaper integrity are more common than the man on the street might dream. Result: The buyer who expects a dime's worth of truth every time he picks up his paper often is short-changed.

All newspapers, including this one, must cope with the blandishments and pressures of special interests who seek distortion or omission of the truth. And no newspaper, again including this one, can ever be positive that every one of its staff always resists these blandishments and pressures.[13]

The blandishments take a variety of forms, and range from the relatively innocent to the plainly venal.

Item: A survey of 78 editors indicated that 31 permitted their sports writers to accept free transportation, hotel accommodations, and meals from the teams that they were assigned to cover; 46 editors said they did not permit such largesse. Of the same group of respondent editors, 56 said that their sports staff members received Christmas gifts (golf bags, cases of Scotch) from news sources, in some cases despite the paper's policy, and 26 said that their reporters were allowed to hold outside jobs, such as writing publicity for sports promoters.

Item: Universal Artists Corporation, producers of the film *Judgment at Nuremberg,* brought 300 movie critics and writers to Berlin

---

[13] "Conflicts of Interest, Pressure, Still Distort Some Papers' Coverage," *The Wall Street Journal,* July 25, 1967, p. 1.

for the premiere of the movie. Of the group, 110 came from North and South America, and were flown by Air France jets to Paris for a week's stop-over before the premiere itself.[14]

Item: In August, 1964, Chrysler Corporation flew more than 300 automotive reporters to New York City, put them up at the Waldorf Astoria, and showed them advance previews of the 1965 cars. The cost to Chrysler: $400,000.

Item: In October, 1965, Holiday Inns of America, Inc., and Grand Bahama Port Authority, a development group, brought 99 reporters and their wives to Freeport on Grand Bahama Island, in an effort to promote tourism there.[15]

Obviously, in these and in other similar cases, any reasonable person would be led to wonder how objectively the reporters involved could be expected to cover the news event that had been the occasion of such generous bounty.

As *The Wall Street Journal* inquired:

On some papers, courthouse reporters have been appointed by courts as estate appraisers. Are they in a position to write critically of the courts if the facts dictate it, considering they might be risking the loss of their outside income? For the same reason, how much objectivity in rail strike coverage could have been expected from the labor reporter of a sizeable East Coast daily—who until recently had an outside publicity job with a major railroad?[16]

Some editors and reporters insist that acceptance of favors from news sources, or even moonlighting in jobs closely related to their main assignment, does not necessarily result in doctored news. And they argue that without the subsidy of sports writers, or of travel reporters on junkets to far-off vacation spots, the paper would be unable to afford coverage of certain types of news.

To many critics of the press, this is not persuasive. Nor do all editors find it so.

Some newspapers refuse to permit their staff members to go on junkets of any kind, among them *The Wall Street Journal,* the Louisville *Courier-Journal,* the Providence *Journal-Bulletin,* and the Washington *Post.* The *Post* instructs all staff members in a policy

[14] *Editor & Publisher,* December 23, 1961, p. 15.

[15] Frederick C. Klein, "More Concerns Offer Newsmen Free Trips for Promotion's Sake," *The Wall Street Journal,* February 14, 1966, p. 1.

[16] *The Wall Street Journal,* July 25, 1967.

guide booklet that "Reporters aren't to free-load, free-ride or free-wheel."

The New York *Times* "always makes it plain we wish to pay, but we don't refrain from covering the news because we might have to accept a free meal or an occasional trip in the process," according to Clifton Daniel, one of the paper's editors.[17]

Those papers and those editors who insist on the most immaculate probity are on the safest ground, and they are the ones whose policies best serve the interests of the reading public. For where the integrity of the press is concerned, it simply is not possible to be just a little bit pregnant.[18]

---

[17] *The Wall Street Journal*, February 14, 1966.
[18] For more on newspaper performance, see John Tebbel's concise paperback, *Open Letter to Newspaper Readers*, James H. Heineman, New York, 1968.

CHAPTER FIVE

Are facts true?

Given the complexity of the communication processes utilized by the mass media, and taking into consideration the institutional, human, and mechanical frailties discussed in earlier chapters, what is the reader and viewer to believe about the reliability of the information served up to him by the daily newspapers, the TV newscaster, and the weekly magazine pundit? How factual are the "facts" reported to him, how dependable the judgments, how complete the picture?

For answers, it is necessary to probe still further into the ways in which news is gathered and written, and into the actions and motivations of the men and women who staff the channels of information. Some historical background may be helpful at this point.

To every man his soapbox

The men who developed the libertarian philosophy upon which the concept of a free press is based—John Milton in the seventeenth century, Thomas Jefferson in the eighteenth century, and John

Stuart Mill in the nineteenth century—were thinking in terms of ensuring a free exchange of information and opinion.

Milton argued in the *Areopagitica* that men would be able to recognize the truth and distinguish it from falsehood so long as there was an "open market place of ideas."

Jefferson envisioned the public interest being safeguarded in a society where there were numerous newspapers, free to express themselves without government censorship, and with every citizen able to read them and piece out an impression of reality from their various offerings.

Mill emphasized the need for every man to be able to express his opinion, so that others could benefit from the clash of views and refine their own understanding of the truth on the basis of such interchange.

As this philosophy developed, it rested on two basic assumptions:

First, that there would be numerous channels through which information and opinion could be disseminated;

And, secondly, that it would be relatively easy for the average citizen to obtain information and opinions from those channels *and* to make use of the same channels to pass his own ideas on to his fellows.

These conditions have not been completely met in any society, in any age. But during the early history of journalism in this and in other countries, there were periods when there did exist many channels—in the form of newspapers, newsletters, and irregularly issued pamphlets. And it was not too difficult for a determined individual to make use of such a channel to disseminate his views, since neither substantial investment nor specialized skill was required.

But as society became more complex and populations grew, the means by which men could communicate ideas and information to one another became costly enterprises and dwindled in number, as was noted in Chapter One. The channels of communication came under the control of a very few, and the conditions assumed by the architects of the libertarian theory of the press became more and more difficult to realize.

Thus, although the constitutional basis was not altered, the concept of press freedom had to undergo some internal modification. The notion of social responsibility was grafted onto it.

It was recognized that the free clash of ideas in an open market-place, as contemplated by the philosophers, was not very likely to take place automatically when the avenues of communication were under the control of a relatively small handful of persons. It followed, then, that those who did have the media of information under their control had not only freedom but also responsibility—a responsibility to society to employ these media in the public interest.

To be sure, this concept of social responsibility was not self-enforcing. No watchdog agency was established to keep the editors honest. But the idea was a powerful and pervading one, and it gave rise to some of the ground rules by which the media more and more tended to abide.

Objectivity: ideal or myth?

The ethic of objectivity as an ideal of reporting is one such ground rule. In the "free and open encounter" of ideas pictured by Milton and Mill, objectivity was not a necessary consideration. Amid the clash of various versions of an issue or event, the outlines of the truth would gradually become clear. But the new social responsibility theory contemplated a situation in which there might be only a few—or perhaps only one—version being circulated; in those circumstances it becomes vital that this single version be as near the truth as possible. The man who runs the only wheel in town had better run an honest one.

So during the first half of the twentieth century the ethic of objectivity made its way into most newsrooms, winning more wholehearted acceptance in some than in others. Most reporters and editors strove as best they could to discover and report the news in undistorted form, and to confine expressions of opinion to the editorial page.

Even the best-intentioned newsman would acknowledge, however, that objectivity is an unattainable ideal. (Bill Moyers, former press secretary for President Lyndon Johnson and later publisher for several years of the Long Island newspaper *Newsday*, once declared that "of all the myths of journalism, objectivity is the greatest."[1])

---

[1] As quoted in *Newsweek*, September 16, 1968, p. 67.

As our earlier examination of the communication process suggests, a completely undistorted report would not be likely to survive all the way through *any* channel, whether back-fence gossip or New York *Times*. But, newsmen have rationalized, if we keep trying for a truly objective news report we ought at least to come close.

That's a reasonable, a pragmatic stance. And if honestly lived up to, it would provide the consumer of the mass media product with some assurance that he was getting relatively unadulterated goods.

Or would it? Even before it had been fully enshrined, the ethic of objectivity had come under question from thoughtful men both inside and outside the news field.

Their concern was not with objectivity as a guide to newsmen. What they questioned was whether objectivity was *enough*. If a reporter or editor presented the news as faithfully as possible, with as little distortion as possible, had he met his obligation to society? Or should something more be expected of him?

After World War II a national Commission on Freedom of the Press conducted an inquiry into the ways in which the media of information functioned. Among their conclusions was this one: "It is no longer enough to report *the fact* truthfully. It is now necessary to report *the truth about the fact*." The commission members and others contended that unswerving adherence to the ethic of objectivity might actually result in misleading the public.

Suppose a reporter carefully and accurately reports what a cabinet officer says in a speech. The reporter has been true to the ethic of objectivity. But suppose that the cabinet officer was uttering deceptive falsehoods. The report of what he said may have been a factual report—but was it truth?

Elmer Davis, for many years a radio reporter and later director of the Office of War Information during World War II, said in a 1951 speech at the University of Minnesota: ". . . Objectivity is all right if it is really objective, if it conveys as accurate an impression of the truth as can be obtained. But to let demonstrably false statements stand with no warning of their falsity is not what I would call objectivity."

To meet such objections as those raised by Davis and the Commission on Freedom of the Press, reporters and editors began to develop a modification of the social responsibility concept. It was called, variously, "interpretive reporting," "backgrounding the news," or "explanatory writing." As James Reston of the New York *Times* put it: "You cannot merely report the literal truth. You have to explain it."[2]

The proponents of this new approach had no trouble documenting the points they made.

How interpretation helps

It was quite true that news sources had become sophisticated about managing the news—that is, presenting only those facts about an issue, a personality, or an event that would make the most favorable possible impression. Government officials, corporate spokesmen, public relations experts—all of them had become adept at exploiting news situations for special ends. If reporters and editors functioned only as hygienic, impartial channels for transmitting to the public the pronouncements, propaganda pitches, or half-truths put out by news sources, they would be guilty of the very offense that Davis had been warning about.

Moreover, the day-by-day, common garden variety of news had indeed been growing more complicated and difficult to understand, as Reston had suggested. The issues involved often stretched far beyond the experience of the average reader; clearly, he could use some help in placing the facts in meaningful perspective. Interpretive reporting offered one way of providing such help.

In the words of Lester Markel, then Sunday editor of the New York *Times:* "Interpretation, as I see it, is the deeper sense of the news. It places a particular event in the larger flow of events. It is the color, the atmosphere, the human elements that give meaning to a fact. It is, in short, setting, sequence, and above all, significance."[3]

Note the following lead from a Los Angeles *Times* story describing the scene in Watts two years after the disastrous 1965 racial rioting. The writer uses an anecdotal approach, naturalistic dialogue, and a cast of characters to add depth and meaning to the facts that he wants to present to the reader.

[2] At the 1948 meeting of the Associated Press Managing Editors Association.
[3] Quoted in the *Bulletin of the American Society of Newspaper Editors,* April 1, 1953.

By JACK JONES

Four thin young Negro men with "natural" hair drink wine near spilled trash cans in the sprawling Jordan Downs public housing project in Watts. "Ain't nuthin' changes," one of them says, adding an explosive four-letter word.

Another demands, "What the hell's the good of all them training programs? Ain't no decent jobs anyway."

At the Watts Manufacturing Co. on El Segundo Blvd., the single major new plant in the area, 26-year-old John L. Price works as a cabinet man after two years' "hard time" in prison for forcible rape and five years of joblessness.

"This is a beautiful place if you want to work," he says. "I love to work. Just give me half a damn chance and get off my back."

These differing attitudes point up the impossibility of measuring just how much two years of studies, federal grants, private industry efforts, redevelopment plans and endless discussion have begun to bleach the scars of a fiery August in South-Central Los Angeles.[4]

The approach taken by the writer in the above lead provides the reader with a more immediate insight into the story, and engages his interest more fully, than the following more conventional and strictly factual approach would have done.

Two years after the fiery riots in Watts, only a single new factory stands as a result of studies, private industry efforts, redevelopment plans, and endless discussion about ways to deal with the problems that led to the 1965 disorders.

A skillful interpretive reporter can add depth to a story and to the reader's understanding, not by resorting to fiction or opinion, but by presenting the basic facts in company with supplemental information, or in a helpful context.

Sometimes such interpretation involves personifying the elements of the news story, so that the reader can make an immediate identification with flesh-and-blood individuals rather than being obliged to grasp at abstract issues or forbidding statistics.

Consider the following opening paragraphs of a story published

[4] Los Angeles *Times*, Sunday, July 16, 1967.

several years ago in the Paddock group of suburban weekly newspapers in the Chicago area:

By WILLIAM L. DULANEY and CHARLES E. HAYES

The poor of Illinois—the bankrupt in hope, in courage, in purse,
and in purpose. More than a half million of them, each day
struggling for food, for shelter, for clothing.

Poverty is no respecter of age. Its most tragic victims are also
its most helpless—the very old and the very young.

The aged sit in numb despair, proud spirits now dimmed by
privation and loneliness. Life is over, without hope or promise.
There is nothing left but to sit in the shadows and wait.

In a basement room on Chicago's LaSalle street sits a 63-year-old
man without family or friends. Sick of body and broken in spirit,
he lives on a relief check of $72.28 a month. Bitterly, he notes
that if he "hangs on for another two years" he'll be eligible for
old age assistance—and an additional $4.72 a month.

An elderly man is crouched in a bare cubicle of a dank "men's
hotel" on Chicago's Northside. Could he spare some time to chat
a while? "I have nothing in the world but time."

In Highland, Ill., a white-haired widow is on her hands and
knees, stuffing rags into holes in the walls and floor to keep out
the coming winter cold.

In Venice, Ill., the 101-year-old son of slave parents is himself
a slave to the chains of poverty. He lives alone in a two-room tar-
paper shack. His sole income is a Spanish-American war pension
of $80 a month.

Illinois is spending $5.6 million a month on care for the aged.
Thousands of old people, alone and unwanted, survive on a monthly
pittance. Only 33 percent of the state's aged on relief are eligible
for social security. All confront the frustration of maintaining a
decent, independent standard of living on an income below, or
barely at the subsistence level.[5]

The writers of the story that began thus had managed to drama-
tize in personal terms the nature of the problem they were going to

[5] This was the lead paragraph in the fourth article of a series of six published in a group of 14 Chicago area weekly newspapers owned by Paddock
Publications, Inc., of Arlington Heights. The articles appeared on a weekly
basis between October 13 and November 17, 1960, under the bylines of
William L. Dulaney and Charles E. Hayes.

discuss—before they launched into the statistics, the cold, factual dimensions of the story. By the utilization of some of the techniques of interpretation, they had invested the story with an additional dimension at the outset and had made it more meaningful to their readers, as the advocates of interpretive reporting had urged.

Yet it should be noted that in one respect this new obligation—to interpret the face value of the news so as to bring out the half-obscured truth behind it—often confronted the newsman with a staggering assignment.

The search for truth had eluded philosophers for centuries. Now the reporter was on notice to come up with a definitive version before press time.

In attempting to respond to this charge, the newsman came up not only with personification, setting, color, and sequence, as Markel had urged, but also sometimes with opinion. In the effort to explain the meaning of the news, the reporter found himself straying over the boundary line established by the ethic of objectivity.

The proponents of interpretive reporting themselves recognized the hazard involved. In the same article quoted above, Markel went on to emphasize:

There is a vast difference between interpretation and opinion. And the distinction is of the utmost importance. Three elements, not two, are involved in this debate. First, news; second, interpretation; third, opinion. To take a primitive example:

To say that Senator McThing is investigating the teaching of Patagonian in the schools is *news*.

To explain why Senator McThing is carrying on this investigation is *interpretation*.

To remark that Senator McThing should be ashamed of himself is *opinion*.

This simplification perhaps helps to clear the air. But even in its own terms, it contains some disturbing ambiguity. How can one explain *why* Senator McThing is doing his thing without speculating on motives? And doesn't that veer into the realm of opinion?

As has been pointed out, even the best intentioned newsman had confronted a formidable enough task just in trying to adhere as best he could to the ideal of objectivity. Now, having done his objective best to obtain an accurate report of an event, he was asked to add an overlay of interpretation (but not opinion) that would reveal to his reader "the truth about the fact," as the Commission on Freedom of the Press phrased it.

There certainly are some newsmen (perhaps many) who are experienced, well-informed veterans and who could accept this kind of tightrope assignment and respond to it creditably, in a fashion that would truly serve the reader's interests and enhance his understanding of a difficult aspect of the news. If in the process such a reporter teeters on the ill-defined border between interpretation and opinion, his experience and respected standing provide his readers with assurance that the trespass will not be great.

It takes a steady hand

The cult of interpretive reporting is an appealing one, since it offers the writer an opportunity to express himself more creatively than he can in the role of a passive channel for the transmission of news. Thus many reporters—not only the seasoned experts—are tempted to try their hand at it, and some of them simply do not have the judgment or the informational background that would equip them to do a responsible job of explaining the meaning of the news.

Look over the following lead, written by a distinguished, highly respected wire service foreign correspondent and published in the front page news columns of a number of newspapers:

By WILLIAM L. RYAN
Of the Associated Press

BERLIN (AP)—Here is some plain, unvarnished news about Berlin, gathered from highly responsible sources:

The current Berlin crisis is over—but not for long. The crisis has yet to reach its peak. Any relaxation by the United States and the West, however much lull there might seem to be, would be regarded in West Berlin as extremely perilous. Whatever happens, a new Berlin airlift is regarded as impossible.

The United States has suffered a heavy blow in Berlin. For the time being, the Kremlin has what it wants. . . . People in close touch with overall strategy express belief that the Kremlin has been surprised that it got that much so swiftly and so easily.

In the space of just a few sentences the reader is asked to accept several points on faith—faith in the integrity of the wire service and in the judgment of the individual reporter involved. Consider the phrases: ". . . gathered from highly responsible sources . . . any relaxation . . . would be regarded in West Berlin as extremely perilous . . . a new Berlin airlift is regarded as impossible . . . People in close touch with overall strategy express belief . . ."

As far as the reader is concerned, these are all faceless, anonymous informants. For all he knows, they may not even exist. But Mr. Ryan's reputation is impressive, and his credentials are well established, so the reader presumably is willing to extend his trust. He assumes that the reporter really did consult the sources, and that they were indeed well posted. He accepts Mr. Ryan's flat assertions that "the crisis has yet to reach its peak . . . the Kremlin has what it wants," recognizing that these can only be speculations but that they are coming from a man whose expertise and responsible standing give him a right to be listened to.

So far so good. But suppose it hadn't been a Bill Ryan, an established expert, who had written that story. When the techniques of interpretive reporting begin to extend through all of the news columns, and when everyone from the gray-haired Washington correspondent to the police beat cub reporter gets into the act, the possibilities for trouble are numerous. How much trust is the reader justified in extending to newsmen who dilute the ethic of objectivity with the new doctrine of interpretation?

Even some editors do not believe that that trust should be extended very far. James S. Pope, an editor of the Louisville *Courier Journal,* once observed: "Objectivity is a compass for fair reporting, a gyroscope, a little secret radar beam that stabs you when you start twisting news to your own fancy; news-column interpretation, as interpreted by far too many of its practitioners, is a license to become a propagandist, an evangel, a Crusader under a false flag."[6]

Mr. Pope then went on to illustrate the kind of abuse he found objectionable: "Here's a recent lead on a story by perhaps the most respected practitioner of news-column interpretation in the country:

WASHINGTON—When White House secretary James C. Haggerty was asked today about Senators Stuart Symington and Hubert Humphrey calling for the resignation of Secretary of State Dulles, he replied: "It is remarkable what people will say to get their names in the paper."

[6] In a speech at the University of Michigan on March 24, 1959.

These are the extremes in the controversy over the consequences of Dulles' illness. *Most impartial observers* here do not think it is necessary to reach any decision now.

I have underlined three words, and I want you to think about them— and for heaven's sake avoid them. "Most impartial observers." It sounds like wondrous interpretation all right, but from On High. Actually those words are a masterpiece of interpretive gobbledegook. How many impartial observers has the census bureau counted in Washington? What does the phrase mean anyway, news wise, "impartial observers"? How many did the reporter interview to get his majority? Mainly, of course, he interviewed himself, which is the first technique to be learned by interpretive reporters. He did, the story reveals, talk to three Democratic senators. Now they are hardly impartial observers, but how much more factual to say "Three Democratic senators believe a decision on Mr. Dulles can wait."

Another distinguished newsman, Wes Gallagher, then head of the Associated Press, warned his colleagues in a general staff memo:

We should bear in mind a basic premise: There is no reason why the reader should accept the writer as an authority on any subject at any time, regardless of whether he is a specialist or whether his byline is well known. The only effective reporting and writing is that which convinces the reader by the recitation and logical presentation of facts. This requires that the reporter know his subject thoroughly and be able to explain it clearly.[7]

It is fortunate for the customers of the press that such editors and managers *are* concerned about the problems created by the vogue for interpretation. For the problems are built in; they can't be sidestepped altogether, only minimized by constant vigilance.

If the effort is not made to minimize the harmful side-effects of interpretation in the news columns, the damage to the quality of the news report may be substantial.

In an article in *Saturday Review,* former Hartford *Courant* editor Herbert Brucker considered the arguments being put forward by those who found the ethic of objectivity wanting and who sought to replace it with a more up-to-date approach:

What it comes down to is that there lurks within the drive against objectivity the revolutionary notion that the reporter should get into the

---

[7] From the *AP Log*, a newsletter for AP client newspaper editors, issue of December 27, 1963–January 3, 1964.

act he is reporting. The journalist's goal is deemed to be less to report the world than to change it. "Objectivity is the rationalization for moral disengagement, the classic cop-out from choice making," wrote the Washington journalist Andrew Kopkind in a review of James Reston's *Artillery of the Press*. If this is not a call for the reporter to get out of the press gallery and into the action, what is it? A companion exhibit is the passionate conviction of many college editors today who see the role of the student press as being no longer to report the university community, but to radicalize it. . . .

The problem of what to report and how to report it will never be resolved, because the line between fact and the subjective view of that fact remains elusive. Then, too, he who burns with zeal to correct the errors of one side risks error on the other. Still, we can do a good job of it—as long as we keep the flag of objectivity flying high. That will give a more honest and more accurate view of this imperfect world than trusting a latter-day Trotsky, or any other partisan on any side, to tell us what's what.[8]

It is probably true that most newsmen feel, with Mr. Brucker, that objectivity still has very real meaning. Most also regard interpretation as a delicate, demanding art to be practiced with care and only by those whose experience and judgment qualify them to undertake it.

Caveat emptor

But those facts do not relieve the reader of responsibility for exercising some discrimination in his acceptance of the mass media products that are served up to him each day. As we have noted, the quality is not uniform.

Every reader and viewer ought to find out enough about the particular newspaper he reads and the TV newscaster he watches so that he can form some judgment about how much trust to put in their reliability.

Comparing versions of a news event as reported through several different channels can help to reveal bias in a given medium. Where

[8] "What's Wrong with Objectivity?" *Saturday Review*, October 11, 1969, pp. 77–79. For two additional views on objectivity, interpretation, and the "new journalism" of advocacy, see J. K. Hvistendahl, "The Reporter as Activist: A Fourth Revolution in Journalism," *Quill*, February, 1970, pp. 8–11; and Nicholas von Hoffman, "The Four-W's Approach—So, Who Needs It?" *American Society of Newspaper Editors Bulletin*, November, 1969, pp. 12, 13.

such comparisons are not feasible, close monitoring of a letters-to-the-editor section, for example, may provide meaningful clues about whether a newspaper is giving fair coverage or is instead the target of frequent complaints about omissions or distortions.

And, finally, there are some kinds of abuses of the concept of interpretation that can be spotted on their face by the alert observer. Consider the following newspaper lead:

> DETROIT—Barbara Hoffa got married Saturday. Her father, President James R. Hoffa of the Teamsters Union, gave her away without batting an eye before a wedding crowd that packed the church.

At the time this story appeared, Mr. Hoffa had been under investigation by Congressional committees and was facing court action for alleged misuse of union funds. The press had been sniping at him for some time, and the habit of referring to him in denigrating terms had apparently become standard operating procedure.

The phrase "without batting an eye" is irrelevant to this story. If the reporter had wanted to indicate that the father of the bride was calm and unflustered, he could have used those terms. The expression he did use is a gratuitous piece of negative interpretation, designed to leave the reader with an unfavorable impression of the person thus described. Its use in this fashion should have put the reader on notice that the publication concerned was less than meticulous in its adherence to newspaper ethics.

As a general rule, however, most newsmen and news channels do try to be scrupulous about their use of background or interpretive material. And when such reportage is well done, its inclusion in the over-all information report is unquestionably beneficial to the consumer of news. It helps him to have a clearer understanding of the bewildering glut of facts in each day's flow of information. Interpretive reporting has added a new and valuable dimension to the service that the news media can provide us, but it must be *within* the context of the ethic of objectivity, not a substitute for it.

CHAPTER SIX

Ethics in the newsroom

The ethical problems posed by the objectivity-interpretation debate are a major cause of soul-searching by reporters and editors, but they by no means represent the only situations in which newsmen confront decisions involving ethics. Virtually every day of their working lives the men and women who gather, process, and package the news must make choices that in one way or another test their sense of fair play and their perception of values.

In facing these choices the newsman often must act as an individual, unsupported by the kind of clear-cut guidelines or the supervisory controls that point the way for persons in some other fields where ethical decisions are also a daily responsibility.

The judge, the doctor, the lawyer, the minister—all of these members of society deal constantly in problems with ethical implications. But there are codes of practice, and professional associations to police those codes, in most such fields.

A lawyer who violates the ethics of his profession finds himself accountable to the bar association, and possibly subject to loss of his right to practice; a doctor who oversteps the guidelines can expect to face similar admonitory or punitive action from the local medical society.

But there are no equivalent policing agencies to make certain that the newsman adheres to the ethical principles of his field. For the most part, he is left with his conscience.

There are associations of editors, and of publishers, to be sure. But they do not have any leverage over individual members. And the constitutional shield of the First Amendment bars the establishment of a governmental agency to be a watchdog over the performance of the various media of information.

So the reporters, editors, and newscasters—the gatekeepers—make their decisions as individuals responding to the historic traditions of the press and its responsibility to society.

By and large, their response is admirable. The majority of persons who have worked for a time in one or another journalistic role will testify that most of their coworkers take their obligations seriously. Though not monitored by the codes and agencies characteristic of other professions, they do indeed behave as professionals. They try their best to discover the facts and to relay them to their readers with as little distortion as possible. And they try to make ethical judgments in a spirit of sensitivity for the rights of individuals and with respect for the public service function of the press.

The cynical observer may find this thesis hard to believe. He can cite the truism about the corrupting influence of power and point to the undeniable power held by the gatekeepers of the press. In the absence of formalized codes and controls, why should journalists be immune to the temptation to abuse that power and forsake ethical standards?

They are not, of course, immune. And some do wrongly use their positions, as was noted in an earlier chapter. But the evidence is strong that most do not. One reason why they do not is suggested by a passage from Boris Pasternak's novel, *Dr. Zhivago:*

If the beast who sleeps in man could be held down by threats—any kind of threats, whether of jail or of retribution after death—then the highest emblem of humanity would be the lion tamer in the circus with his whip, not the prophet who sacrificed himself. But don't you see, this is just the point—what has for centuries raised men above the beast is not the cudgel but an inward music, the irresistible power of unarmed truth, the powerful attraction of its example.

Most newsmen would not put it so lyrically, but they would understand what Pasternak meant. Their response to the "inward music" is reflected in the decisions that they must confront at nearly every turn in their day's routine.

The occasions that pose problems of ethics for the newsman are so numerous and so varied in character that it would be impractical to catalogue all of them here. But anyone who hopes to understand the way in which the press functions should have at least some notion of the range and complexity of these problems so that he can be alert to the degree to which his local media are attempting to perform within ethical boundaries.

Are names always news?

Most crime stories confront the reporter and editor with one category of ethical decisions: how to strike a balance between the need to inform the public about an important sector of news in the community, while at the same time protecting as fully as possible the rights of persons caught up in such news.

For example, should juveniles be identified when they are arrested on criminal charges? Is it more important to publish their names in order to alert the community at large, or would it be better to leave out the identification and avoid stigmatizing a youngster publicly and thus jeopardizing his chances for rehabilitation?

And what about identifying the victim in a crime story? Is it a necessary part of the news? Should there be one policy with respect to, say, a burglary story, and another one with respect to a rape arrest?

Arriving at a decision in such cases as these may not be difficult. Most editors and reporters adhere to a policy of withholding from publication the names of juveniles, particularly when first offenses are involved. Almost universally, too, they do not permit the publication of the name of a victim of rape. In both situations, the sensitivity of individuals weighs more heavily than the public's right to know.

In the case of a burglary story, however, the decision will most often go the other way, on the ground that the identification of the home broken into is necessary to alert the neighbors and the community generally to a hazard.

But there are other situations in which the circumstances are more complex, and the identification of the paramount ethical values becomes much more difficult.

Consider the following newspaper lead. The names and place references have been changed, but it otherwise appears here just as it was originally published:

> RIVER CITY—A man whose career of lawbreaking was one of the most notorious in the state's history went free on parole Wednesday.
>
> John D. Doe, 41, shot a state policeman to death in 1947, led several prison break attempts here, set fire to the penitentiary flax plant and went over the wall in 1949.
>
> The FBI once called him a man of "wanton viciousness."
>
> But, said Warden Richard R. Roe Tuesday:
>
> "He has caused no difficulty at all in the six years I have been here."
>
> Doe turned over a new leaf after failure of his last escape attempt some eight years ago. For a time he taught in the prison school. He has been an aide in recent years to the prison psychologist. The warden said: "He has made a good adjustment."
>
> Doe, at the age of 16, began his criminal career with an armed robbery. Many crimes later, at 29, he gunned down a state policeman when the policeman halted him in a stolen car. . . .

The account went on to detail the man's criminal record, and toward the end of the story noted that Doe was hoping to find a job and begin a new life.

Two different lines of argument can be developed about that news story.

A reader concerned about the concept of rehabilitation of criminals could work up a lively indignation about the damage done by the story to the released convict's chances of making a new life. What hope has Doe got of finding acceptance in society if, as he emerges from prison, all the lurid details of his criminal past are paraded once again to refresh the public's memory?

How will he be viewed by a prospective employer if he arrives tagged as "one of the most notorious" lawbreakers in the state's history? How will he be welcomed by his new neighbors when he finds a home outside the walls? Isn't the likelihood great that he will, in desperation, eventually revert to his original pattern of criminal behavior, since it will be in that role that society pictures him?

Such a line of reasoning could be developed (and often is) about news stories reporting the release of criminals. But another, and also persuasive argument can be put together.

Balancing the scales

Such stories as the one quoted, this second thesis runs, are not only defensible but necessary in the public interest. Unless the press tells us about the background of persons being released from prisons, how are we going to be alert to a breakdown in the parole system? Shouldn't we be kept informed of the functioning of that system so that we know what kinds of persons are being turned loose on society, perhaps prematurely? How else could we learn whether hardened criminals are buying their way out by exploiting a corrupt parole agency? After all, that sort of thing has happened, and not only once or twice.

So how does the editor make his decision? Should he put the paroled convict's right to a fresh start above the public's right to know how one important aspect of the machinery of justice is functioning? Or should the scales tip the other way? Is there any way to balance them precisely on center?

Now look at this same kind of ethical poser, but in a different, and perhaps even more difficult context.

In 1959 a prominent St. Louis businessman, Frank J. Prince, the chief stockholder in the Universal Match Corp., made a gift of $500,000 to Washington University in St. Louis. In grateful acknowledgment, the university made plans to name a building after Mr. Prince. The St. Louis *Post-Dispatch* set a reporter to work to get a background story on the university's benefactor. During the course of his investigation the reporter discovered that Mr. Prince, now 71, had during his early life served three prison terms, adding up to nearly ten years, after being convicted of forgery, grand larceny, and issuing bad checks. After he had served his time he had begun life anew and in the intervening years had made a success as a legitimate businessman.

The reporter and his editors then faced a decision: should this part of Mr. Prince's life story be included in the paper's coverage, or should it be repressed? Was this something the readers of St. Louis had a right to know about a leading philanthropist of the community, or was it a chapter long past and properly forgotten?

The decision reached by the *Post-Dispatch* editors was reflected in the headlines that appeared over the story: FRANK J. PRINCE, UNIVERSAL MATCH OWNER, IS EX-CONVICT.

Time magazine, in its account of the episode, noted:

> The *Post-Dispatch* stories were factually accurate. Frank Prince did have a prison record. That record was known to many if not all of his friends and business associates. It was known to the Federal Bureau of Investigation, which had nonetheless cleared Prince for defense contracts. It had even been mentioned in Dun and Bradstreet. Indeed, among those closest to Prince, two of the few who did not know of his record were his wife and 24-year-old son.
>
> But were the *Post-Dispatch* stories relevant as news? By the paper's own accounting, Frank Prince had stayed in the clear for the last 25 years....[1]

Others joined *Time* in criticizing the newspaper's handling of the matter. The *Post-Dispatch* editor responded that: "I think the stories simply speak for themselves."

When does private become public?

A great many items in the flow of the news may involve decisions about whether or not to include reference to something in the past of a figure currently in the limelight. If a thrice-divorced woman marries again, should the wedding story mention her earlier alliances? Should a man who is now the leader of a powerful union be revealed as one who, twenty years earlier, had once held membership in the Communist Party? Or, to take a case that sounds too bizarre to be true but actually did take place, should a man who had made a successful career as the head of an extremist anti-Semitic organization be "exposed" as one whose parents and upbringing had been Jewish?

The New York *Times* in its Oct. 31, 1965 issue published a story revealing that a man named Daniel Burros, one of the leaders of the Ku Klux Klan in New York and a spokesman for that organization's racist philosophy, was of Jewish extraction. Burros had asked the reporter and his editor not to use the story because Burros had concealed his background from his Klan associates and contended that publication of the matter now would ruin him in his role as

---

[1] *Time*, February 22, 1960, p. 59.

leader of the organization. When the story appeared despite his plea, Burros shot himself to death.

Were the newsmen who made the decision here at fault? Should they have acceded to the Klan leader's request? Probably the majority of society would support the action of the newspaper, since the organization involved is generally abhorred and its tenets rejected by most Americans. Still, in commenting on the case, the *Columbia Journalism Review* was troubled:

> How much of a man's past becomes fair game when his current activity becomes public? In this particular case, the line marking the edge of public life was blurred, for what the practitioners clearly thought were reasons of public interest. But blurring should not be taken to mean that no such line exists, or that it can be crossed at will.[2]

If you want to ponder the complexities of the matter still further, consider how the issue might have looked had the circumstances been reversed. Suppose Burros had achieved leadership in a Jewish organization and in the process had passed himself off as a member of that faith. And suppose the newspaper had discovered that in fact he was not Jewish and had at one time been virulently anti-Semitic. What then should the paper have done? And how would the *Review* have analyzed the matter?

It is obviously not possible to lay down a convenient, precise formula for reaching decisions in cases such as the foregoing. An *ad hoc* balance must be struck, with the gatekeepers involved doing their best to respect both the rights of individuals and the right of the public to be accurately informed about matters that are justifiably the public's business.

Often such decisions revolve around human-interest values in the news. Some kinds of stories involving pretty girls, babies, animals, conflict—either actual or vicarious—are of great interest to most readers. Editors know this as a matter of common sense. They include in the daily news mix some such human-interest content, while reserving space also for other kinds of news that may be more significant and consequential but not so appetizing to the average reader.

But how does the editor identify the vague and shifting line that separates a legitimate emphasis on the human-interest values of a

[2] *Columbia Journalism Review*, Winter, 1966, p. 3.

story, from the unjustifiable, even sensational, exploitation of those values just for the sake of building readership? Consider an illustrative example:

In the early 1960s a shocking item of medical news was reported. A drug that had been widely used as a sleeping potion in Europe, and somewhat less so in America, was found to have drastic side-effects when used by expectant mothers. It resulted in the birth of grossly deformed children, armless and legless in some cases and with various other defects. Use of the drug, thalidomide, was immediately halted in this country and in Europe. But many persons were left with an agonizing dilemma.

Expectant mothers who had been using the drug now knew that their children almost certainly would be born with terrible handicaps. Some European mothers-to-be in this plight took advantage of the laws of their countries to obtain legal abortions. But at that time abortion was illegal in most parts of the United States except under extraordinary circumstances. All the elements of tragic and suspenseful drama were in the story.

These elements were highlighted in one particular case, that of Mrs. Sherri Finkbine of Phoenix, Ariz. Mrs. Finkbine was a young and attractive star of a children's television show in Phoenix, and she was facing the certainty that she would bear a thalidomide child. She petitioned the court in her home city for permission to undergo an abortion, but was refused. She then made plans to go to a European country in which such an operation would be legal.

Her story, coming at a time of national concern about the thalidomide revelations, was of great interest to readers. She was a public personality as a result of her television career and also because she had brought her case to the courts. What was legitimate use of this story, and where was the borderline of sensationalism?

There was, in fact, a whole spectrum. Some newspapers published brief, factual accounts of the case, soberly and sympathetically phrased, and positioned on an inside page. Others put the story on page one, but without any picture. Still others used both story and a standard, one-column portrait ("mug shot" in newspaper parlance). Some papers used a more dramatic press service photograph showing Mrs. Finkbine wiping away a tear as she waited at the airport to leave for Europe. And at the sensationalist end of the

spectrum were some few papers that gave the story wholly dispro-
portionate and tasteless treatment. One San Francisco daily, for
example, topped its first page with an eight-column headline in black
letters an inch and a half high: SHERRI OFF TO SWEDEN. And below
the headline was a three-column picture of Mr. and Mrs. Finkbine
at the Los Angeles airport, with the caption: "Flight to Abortion,"
followed by a detailed story that began on page one and was continued inside.[3]

Even the uninitiated would recognize that this last example constituted some kind of breach of journalistic ethics. But where, exactly, along the spectrum did the borderline fall? Obviously, a good
many editors arrived at a variety of answers, and the same sort of
variation is evident almost any day as the pattern of the news un-
folds in hundreds of different newsrooms around the country.

The use of pictures gives rise to numerous ethical problems for
both photographers and editors; the case of Mrs. Finkbine illustrates
only one of these.

A prize for what?

There is a perennial trouble area, for example, in photographs of
accident victims. If human-interest content could be measured with
some sort of geiger counter, such pictures would run the needle off
the dial. They contain elements of tragedy, heart-wrenching pathos,
drama, and death—and whether such interest is becoming or not,
all of us *do* have a deep and automatic interest in these elements.

A prize-winning entry in a national news photo contest one year
constituted a classic of this genre. At one side of the picture was
the body of a small boy who had drowned in a neighborhood swim-
ming pool, and bending over him in vain was an ambulance attendant. The neighbor in whose pool the boy had drowned was
seated in the background, hands clutched to her face in shock.
Watching, his legs stiff and his head bent tensely, was the little boy's
German shepherd. And at the far side of the picture were the victim's parents, clasped in each other's arms, the mother's face hidden,
the father's twisted in terrible anguish.

[3] San Francisco *Chronicle*, August 5, 1962, p. 1.

The picture had enormous dramatic impact, and it is easy to see why the judges awarded it the prize. But such a picture poses some profound and complex questions for an editor to answer.

By any measurement, the picture has great human-interest content and obvious news value. But it also constitutes an invasion of the privacy of several persons caught up in a searing moment they will never forget. Is the news value of the picture great enough to warrant intruding on such a moment, exploiting its ingredients for their effect upon the reader?

This is not a question to be answered easily. It requires—as do so many of the ethical problems that confront the newsman—some careful analysis.

The instinctive, humanitarian response would very likely be: Don't use it—don't fix that moment forever for the three stricken persons, don't traffic in their grief just to attract the reader's attention.

But the editor also has other considerations to weigh. Would the printing of the picture perhaps awaken some reader (or some dozens of readers) to the hazard posed to neighborhood children by his unfenced backyard pool? And would it thus perhaps result in the long run in preventive measures that might spare the lives of other toddlers and avoid a repetition of that tragic tableau in the photograph? Is the public interest better served by publication or suppression of the picture? Could a news story without the picture be counted on to have the same impact on readers who may not have realized their responsibilities as pool owners? Or would many overlook the news account if it were not accompanied by the picture?

A similar analytical evaluation goes on almost daily with one category of news pictures—those of auto accidents. Since the accident rate is high, such pictures are always available. How often should they be used? What considerations should dictate which ones should be used, and which tossed into the basket?

Safety experts are not in agreement whether a photograph of twisted wreckage, with a body sprawled by the roadside, has a sobering, deterrent effect upon drivers who may see the picture. Some feel that such pictures do make readers and viewers more aware of the need to drive defensively and employ seat belts. Others contend that the death shots and the recitation of accident statistics on holiday weekends only make other drivers more nervous and possibly *more* likely to be involved in accidents themselves.

When editors do use such pictures, it is usually with the purpose of promoting greater care on the highway, rather than to exploit morbidity.

In its 1967 Labor Day issue the Cleveland *Plain Dealer* ran a black banner headline across the top of its front page: "1,637,000 Killed in Traffic," and directly below it a five-column photograph of the mangled body of movie star Jayne Mansfield, lying in front of the wrecked car in which she had died earlier that year.

A nearby boxed message over the name of the paper's publisher, Thomas Vail, read, in part:

> With this page, the *Plain Dealer* is taking a bold journalistic step. For this one day, the front page is being devoted to one subject, traffic slaughter. Because we believe this may be a better way of communicating with our readers, we are willing to risk the stigma of being different. If people who didn't care before about traffic safety begin thinking about it, we know it will have been worth it.[4]

Whether this or other such uses of accident pictures actually does result in a lowering of the highway accident rate is arguable, as has been pointed out. But the purpose is defensible.

Far less defensible is the practice of some photographers and editors who attempt to wring the utmost of pathos out of accident pictures. One metropolitan East Coast paper ran three multicolumn shots of the same accident. One of them showed the body of the small boy who had died in the accident being cradled in his mother's arms, while the shocked driver of the car stood in the background. It was a distant shot, borderline perhaps but not indefensible under the wholesome warning theory.

But one of the other pictures used was a close-up of the mother's face as she looked up from her child's body. Her features were tortured, and tears ran down her cheeks. It was a powerful photograph—but its power was derived from the exploitation of the mother's grief. Ethical considerations had gone by the board when the decision to print that picture was reached.

[4] Issue of September 2, 1967, p. 1.

Photos by the Eugene, Oreg., *Register-Guard*

Other kinds of picture treatment can reflect even more blatant disregard of journalistic ethics.

Take a look at the panel of three pictures shown on the page opposite. They appeared in a small-city afternoon paper one day with the following feature cutlines at one side:

> Pat O'Malley, president-elect of the student body at St. Francis High School . . . didn't really get clobbered by a chunk of dirt. It just looks that way in this series taken Tuesday . . . at ground-breaking ceremonies for the future Marist Catholic High School. Tossing up the shovelful of earth is senior Urban Moore, outgoing student body president. The event Tuesday was attended by 60 persons—Catholic clergy and laymen, city officials, public school men and others. . . .

The series of feature pictures was made available by the newspaper to a wire service, which transmitted it to other newspaper clients. The pictures appeared the next morning in a nearby metropolitan daily with a quite different set of cutlines:

> "Here's Dirt in Your Eye" mishap turned dignified ground-breaking ceremonies for new Marist Brothers Catholic High School . . . into slapstick comedy. Outgoing student body president Urban Moore vigorously launched a spadeful of earth into the face of incoming student President Pat O'Malley (right).

It was not clear whether the new cutlines had been written by the wire service that had transmitted the pictures, or by the copy desk on the metropolitan newspaper in which the second version appeared. What. *is* clear is that someone along the way sought to doctor the original picture story to make a livelier and funnier feature. In the process, he deliberately distorted the facts.

Perhaps no great harm was done in this instance. But a newsman who will wink at so naked a breach of ethics in such a story may be equally lax in a more consequential matter. And a reader who finds traces of such ethical myopia in the information medium on which he relies has reason to question all else that it offers him under the label of factual news.

Still other kinds of borderline problems arise with respect to picture use in the news media. It has become a commonplace tactic for a photographer to maneuver himself or his subject around so as to catch a news figure against a background that is peculiarly appropriate, or perhaps wildly incongruous (a politician waving happily at a rally crowd while behind him looms an exit sign: "This Way Out"). Some such concocted juxtapositions are harmless enough; others can be cruel and damaging in their implications. At what point does defensible human interest shade over into tasteless and offensive distortion?

A similar kind of problem can develop with respect to headlines. As has been noted elsewhere in this book, the newspaper or magazine headline represents so extreme a distillation of the content of the story or article it introduces that some garbling of the whole message inevitably takes place. There are times, however, when the headline writer deliberately deals in some distortion for what may seem at the moment to be good reasons.

For a feature story he may write a headline that is a catchy play on words and is intended more to pique the reader's curiosity than to suggest the content of the story to follow. In the process he may let his ingenuity carry him beyond ethical bounds.

Consider the following brief wire service story:

FORT ST. JAMES, B.C. (AP)—Clement Joseph, 24, was electrocuted while playing an electric guitar in wet stocking feet, police at this northern British Columbia community said Tuesday.

The desk editor who processed the story for his paper put the following flippant headline on it:

Shocking Music

Momentarily amusing, perhaps, but is death—even a distant death—a fit subject for such treatment?

A New York tabloid account of a mentally deranged woman who fell to her death from a hotel window when she broke away from her husband's restraining hand was topped with the following head:

Spouse Loses Grip, Wife

Again, did the subject matter of the story lend itself to that approach?

Time after time in the complex, fast-paced process of bringing out a daily newspaper, or pulling together the material for a television newscast, the reporter and editor face decisions that call for ethical judgments. The illustrations cited are no more than a partial catalogue of the kinds of situations that the gatekeepers must deal with.

The degree to which ethical responsibilities are accepted varies from paper to paper and from newsman to newsman. This is inevitable, since as has been observed the decisions are usually individual ones, reached without formal guidelines and also without the scrutiny of any watchdog agency.

Considering these circumstances, the over-all record is reassuring, though by no means perfect. It *could* be even better if the readers and viewers showed more tendency to blow the whistle on abuses when they do appear in the news and information media. But first, of course, those readers and viewers must learn to recognize such abuses when they see them.[5]

---

[5] For additional discussion of the subject see William L. Rivers and Wilbur Schramm, *Responsibility in Mass Communication*, Harper & Row, New York, 1969.

CHAPTER SEVEN

A matter of opinion

Most of us turn to the mass media primarily for information or entertainment. In addition, however, whether we want it or not, most of these media also provide us with substantial helpings of opinion—sometimes openly labeled as such, sometimes slipped in under other guises.

In the newspapers, most expressions of opinion are clustered together on the editorial page, or in a multipage editorial section. These expressions may be those of the newspaper itself (in which case they appear as "editorials," usually displayed in the upper-left quadrant of the editorial page) or of national columnists, whose daily commentaries are distributed to many papers and whose views may or may not agree with those of the newspapers that include the column in their editorial offerings.

Some of the news and general circulation magazines also contain specific editorial pages, but others inject opinion between the lines of what purports to be news matter. And, of course, some magazines are wholly opinion journals and make no effort to represent themselves as anything else.

Over the radio and television channels, editorial expressions are not so often presented as such, but some newscasters have become adept at investing a news item with opinion overtones simply by the choice of a phrase, a change of voice inflection, or the strategic lift of an eyebrow on camera.[1]

In one way or another, all of the media of information make some kind of effort to mold the opinions and attitudes of their readers and viewers, as well as to inform them and entertain them. Sometimes the consumer who is the object of this effort is conscious of the intellectual massage to which he is being subjected; sometimes he is altogether unaware. Not often does he understand how it is being undertaken, or for what ends.

What are these ends? What is the purpose of the editorial or opinion function in the several mass communication media?

There are two sets of answers—one from the standpoint of the persons who own or staff the channels of communication, and one from the standpoint of the consumer.

From the owner's desk

As the publisher, the station owner, or the editorial writer sees it, the opinion function constitutes a significant service to the community.

Editorial expressions, by explaining the "why" facet of the news, can greatly expand the understanding of the reader or viewer. The editorial goes a considerable step beyond the level of interpretation, as earlier discussed, and ventures out onto the limitless plain of opinion. In so doing, it can help to put an issue, an event, or a personality into meaningful perspective more effectively than many columns of factual news summary or background report.

This role of the editor was described eloquently by Charles A. Sprague, editor of the *Oregon Statesman* of Salem, Oreg., a former governor of the state and for a generation the most respected voice in Oregon journalism.

---

[1] In the late 1960s the practice of presenting formal editorial commentaries on both radio and television began to spread, encouraged by the revision of Federal Communications Commission regulations that had earlier served as a deterrent to the expression of opinion on the airwaves franchised to the operators on behalf of the public.

What confronts the editor every day is the task of trying to make sense in the bedlam; to attempt to guide public opinion out of the confusing fog into the sunlight of clear thinking, if that is at all possible. The responsibility indeed is staggering.[2]

Secondly, editors and editorial writers will contend, the opinion function provides a means by which the channels of mass communication can exercise constructive leadership in the public interest.

This is a deep conviction with many of the men who control the news media of America. They regard it as a fundamental rationale for the existence of their enterprises.

Michael Bradshaw, editor of the Toledo, Ohio, *Blade*, once observed in a front-page article in his newspaper:

More time and thought, and in many cases, more money is devoted to . . . [editorial page] content than to any other page in the newspaper. Not because it brings in any money in circulation or advertising revenue, so far as our best cost accountant can see. It's simply, so far as I have ever been able to see in my experience, that the men who own newspapers don't consider their properties solely as business institutions but feel that the instrument in their hands is a vital part of our democratic processes.

This line of reasoning views the opinion function of the press as a kind of gyroscope for society. When emotion or fear sways public opinion toward irrational extremes that jeopardize fundamental values, the voices of reason raised by thoughtful, respected men in the communications fields can help to restore us to an even keel.

Supporters of the gyroscope concept point to periods when the stabilizing efforts of the press were felt. During the early 1950s, for example, when the late Senator Joseph McCarthy of Wisconsin was exploiting the fear of communism that then gripped many Americans, it was the newspapers, the magazines—and particularly television—that called attention to the irresponsibility and the character-assassination tactics the senator was using, and finally made the public aware that McCarthyism was as great a threat as the Red menace it purportedly sought to combat.

At a later period, when a parade of mobsters called before con-

---

[2] In a speech at the Editors' Conference at Stanford University, June 20, 1952.

gressional investigating committees repeatedly invoked the Fifth Amendment of the Constitution to help them evade questioning, a public clamor arose for the repeal of this troublesome "shield of wrongdoers." Again it was the press, among other voices in society, that reminded the public that the Fifth Amendment had been included among the provisions of the Bill of Rights as a profoundly important protection of the liberties of all citizens, and that to scuttle it now in order to make it easier to deal with a handful of hoodlums would be to throw out the baby with the bath water.

Certainly society has need of this kind of service from some agency. We need someone or something to act as a referee, gyroscope, or barometer—some voice that can cut through the smog of invective, emotionalism, and illogic that often characterize our national dialogue.

Most of the voices that are raised from various sectors—those of politicians, labor leaders, industrial magnates—have special interests to further. What is needed is someone detached but informed, not wedded to a special interest but clear-sighted enough to identify the forces at issue in a public controversy and remind us of basic values that must be preserved.

Many editorialists see themselves in this role, and some of them do indeed fill it with distinction.

There is a third reason why the opinion function of the mass media is important in the eyes of the owners and proprietors of those media: it is a means by which they can wield power.

Power has always been one of the reasons why men sought ownership or direction of the press or any part of it. Ambitious political figures have used party newspapers as mouthpieces. Chain owners have attempted to condition the community opinion of a dozen cities at once by using the gatekeeper control to keep some kinds of news out of the daily stream. And most proprietors of the press in every era have tried to wield influence through their editorial columns for causes that they sincerely (and often rightly) believed to be in the public interest.

The editorial page or column is the open-and-above-board, honestly labeled means of expressing the influence of the editors and owners, and those who respect the ethics of journalism employ this means rather than doctor the news columns to aid their causes or candidates.

What's in it for the reader?

Seen from the viewpoint of the consumer of the mass media products, the editorial function also serves several purposes, but not necessarily the same ones that have just been listed above.

Many readers turn away from the news columns perplexed and concerned, and consciously seek out the editorial pages, the columnists, or the news commentators in order to get some help in understanding what the day's forbidding tidings really mean.

They also look to the editorialists, though perhaps not so consciously, for another kind of help.

When you are turning over a controversial matter in your mind, and when your own conviction is still unformed, there is great value in testing your ideas against another's firmly expressed opinion. This is true whether the other opinion is one toward which your own thinking may be tending, or whether it is at the opposite pole. If you are trying to make up your mind about an issue and you encounter a vigorous editorial expression with which you can identify, it may provide just the impetus you needed to crystallize and formulate your own conviction.

But an editorial argument that is at the opposite end of the spectrum with respect to your tentative thoughts may be equally helpful. Having something solid and tangible to oppose may be exactly what you needed to marshal your own feelings about an issue or a personality.

The opinion section of the press can be of help to readers in both of these ways. In each case, the effect is to move the reader along in his own thinking process. Not often does a reader turn to a columnist, commentator, or editorial page and swallow whole the line of argument offered. Instead he views it through his own frame of reference, weighs it against his own thoughts and the information available to him from other sources, and moves toward a point of view with which he can identify.

A third service that the opinion component of the press provides to the consumer may be, from his standpoint, the most valuable of all. In the letters-to-the-editor column of the newspapers and magazines, and on the feedback talk shows on radio, the average citizen today finds just about the only channels available to him through which to get his ideas and opinions to the attention of his fellows.

In earlier times, when the structure of society was far simpler, the city forum or the town meeting gave every man a chance to speak his piece and state his views in the hearing of most of his fellow citizens. Even as the population grew, it continued for some time to be possible to print up a pamphlet or even start your own newspaper with the proverbial shirt-tail full of type and thus be sure of a wide audience for what you had to say.

But in America today, unless you are one of the handful of persons who control the media of information, or unless you have unlimited resources to enable you to buy newsprint space or prime time on the air, you have few opportunities to express yourself beyond the circle in which you regularly move.

The best and cheapest of those opportunities is to be found in the mailbag, people's corner, letter box—or however the readers' opinion section is labeled. The radio call-in shows are less satisfactory in that the audience may be limited and the effect more transitory than that achieved by a letter to the editor in a print medium.

The public forum service of the mass media of information constitutes an important safety valve and can be a useful corrective influence on both the media and public officials.

To achieve these purposes, however, the letters section must be conducted fairly. Readers' contributions must not be carved up by the editor's scalpel until the heart is cut out of them. A conscientious effort must be made by the editor to publish a representative proportion of pro and con letters received on an issue. Rarely can a paper or magazine afford to publish *all* letters received, so the practice usually is to publish some percentage of the total.[3] That fraction ought to be a fair cross-section of the whole, not stacked with letters that favor the side the newspaper's editorialists happen to be supporting.

When a letters section is well run it constitutes a true public service, and readers ought to cherish it as one of their few remain-

---

[3] The New York *Times* can find space for only 6 percent of the 40,000 letters it receives each year. On less prestigious papers, the percentage printed is much higher, and on small-city papers most of the coherent, nonlibelous, nonobscene letters that are received eventually break into print.

ing points of access to the vast leverage that is represented by the media of mass communication.

How well are they doing their job?

If you want testimony on how effectively the editorial or opinion function is being pursued by today's media of information, you can pay your money and take your choice of a wide range of judgments.

According to Alan Barth, himself an editorial writer for the Washington *Post*, the picture isn't bright:

> In most American newspapers, the editorial page serves no more than a ceremonial function. It is there because it was once recognized as the heart and soul of a newspaper. But too often it has become a mere adornment, perpetuated long after its purpose has been forgotten, as men continue to wear on the sleeves of their jackets buttons which do not open and which have become altogether devoid of utility.[4]

Yet Herbert Brucker, for many years editor of the Hartford *Courant*, contends that:

> . . . Good editorial writers, given a free hand, are the only means to that vitality that justifies newspapers in the unique special protection they have in the Constitution.[5]

These two opinions, while sharply dissimilar, are not inconsistent. There are a good many newspapers that take so timorous an editorial stance, and express it in such banal terms, that they deserve Mr. Barth's harsh words. But Barth's own newspaper, and a good many others, offer eloquent testimony to the continuing vitality of the editorial function in American journalism, and to the pertinence of Mr. Brucker's point.

There are editorial pages that make relentless exposure of the running sores of corruption in our society, that prod at the consciences of reluctant bureaucrats and indifferent electorates, and point out the ways in which we should be moving as a nation. The Washington *Post* has such a page, and so do the New York

[4] In a speech to an American Civil Liberties Union award meeting on May 6, 1964.
[5] In an article, "How to Write an Editorial," in *Saturday Review*, February 12, 1966, pp. 58–60.

Times, the Milwaukee *Journal,* the Louisville *Courier-Journal,* the St. Louis *Post-Dispatch,* and a dozen other great metropolitan journals. Some of the largest national magazines, notably *Life* and *Look,* have in recent years combined editorial and reportorial techniques in a one-two punch that is reminiscent of the best efforts of the muckrakers of the early twentieth century.

But it isn't only the major channels of communication that can demonstrate evidence of editorial vitality. Dozens of small city and community newspapers around the nation regularly bring to their readers thoughtful leadership and crusading zeal tailored to the problems of their own back yards. And sometimes their efforts extend far beyond those back yards. It was a community paper that set off the celebrated Teapot Dome exposé of the 1920s, and another a generation later that called national attention to the Billy Sol Estes scandal.

Yet with all this acknowledged, it is still necessary to note that there may be more to sigh than cheer about in the overall performance of the opinion function of the press.

There are too many small town papers in which the editorial page has atrophied to the status of Mr. Barth's jacket buttons; some have abandoned the effort altogether.

There are too many editorials published each day that constitute only a shallow, top-of-the-head sort of commentary; if analyzed, they test out as no more than a pretentious restatement of the news that has already been presented elsewhere in the paper, and thus represent no help to the reader's understanding, no stimulus to his thinking, and no leadership to the community.

There are too many writers and commentators whose most ferocious efforts are reserved for safe and distant targets like Red China or man-eating sharks, while home-grown crises that might involve influential local citizens are carefully skirted without comment.

And, finally, there are too many columnists and editorialists who have come to believe that their desks are situated on Sinai or Olympus, and hand down judgments and prophecies as though they were revealed truth, not subject to challenge by mere mortals among their readership.

The editorial sections of newspapers and magazines—and to the extent that they have gotten into the field, the commentary segments on radio and television—constitute a mixed bag of quality. The discerning consumer needs to pick his way, looking for the signs of excellence, and also for the tell-tale traces of third-rate imitation.

Which are the good guys?

It isn't always easy for the layman to sort out the signs. The most constructive and useful editorial pages aren't necessarily those that thunder the loudest or employ the most positive accents.

There was a time in American journalism when a single influential editor could count cadence and watch huge segments of public opinion march to his direction. Horace Greeley's editorial reiteration of the cry "On to Richmond!" in the New York *Tribune* was the decisive factor that brought about the first Battle of Bull Run in the Civil War. Joseph Pulitzer ("I want to address a nation, not a select committee") made his New York *World* a power in its day.

But there are few giants who tower over the field in this era. Syndicated columnists such as James Reston come as close to a modern day counterpart of the old editorial thunderers as we still have, but their influence is not of the same order. Today's consumer of the mass media hears a good many kinds of voices and remains skeptical of most of them. He is far less willing to be told how to vote, or how to think on a given issue, than his predecessors were in a time when the newspaper was the sole channel of information and the strong-willed editor a national personage.

In the *Saturday Review* article cited earlier in this chapter, *Courant* editor Herbert Brucker pointed out that in modern journalism:

We cannot persuade people against their will. A newspaper editorial has influence only if it articulates a public reaction that already exists, even though formless and not expressed in words. . . . The point is that editorial writers do not mold public opinion so much as give it voice. If an editorial says anything that even begins to impress people as arguing that black is white they simply shrug it off. They say to themselves, or possibly to their neighbors, "The old so-and-so doesn't know what he's talking about."

Does this mean, then, that the editorialists no longer have a significant influence on public attitudes?

Not necessarily. What Brucker was suggesting is that the editor or commentator today has to settle for a modest and cumulative kind of influence, rather than the dramatic, heavy-handed clout that a Greeley or a Pulitzer might have been able to wield.[6]

Such matters as the influence of an editorial page are almost impossible to render in quantitative terms. But a few researchers have tried, and some of their findings are instructive.

Two scholars at the University of Toledo conducted a study in which they attempted to identify in precise terms what effect the editorial page support of the Toledo *Blade* had on the outcome of a statewide or a local election. They found that the number of persons likely to translate the *Blade*'s endorsement of a candidate into a conscious, knowledgeable act of voting was from 4 to 12 percent of the voters in the case of a candidate for governor, and from 2 to 4 percent of the voters in the case of a candidate for the state senate. Applied to the 1966 elections, this meant that having the *Blade* backing meant from 5,500 to 16,500 votes in the gubernatorial contest, and from 1,500 to 3,000 in the local state senate race.[7]

Those figures do not sound very impressive on their face. But in weighing them the significance of the "swing" or pivot vote in any election must be considered. As the two Toledo University researchers concluded: "The power of the press in Toledo is real and important. This fact is particularly true since the politics of the area is competitive and many elections are decided by narrow margins."

To that might be added the point that the researchers were basing their findings on the persons who were able to say that the *Blade* position had a conscious effect on their vote. Presumably there may have been many other voters on whom the *Blade* editorials had a partial, or even peripheral effect that may have been decisive

[6] One editorial page editor, Joseph C. Jahn of the Suffolk *Sun*, Long Island, acknowledged that "I, for one, have given up trying to convert anyone, but if I can make a few people open their minds and think about the issues each day, I am succeeding, I think, in helping their mental processes percolate. A good editorial need not bellow the gospel to achieve its goal. . . . All it needs to do is throw out a few crumbs in the hope that they will be intellectually challenging enough to arouse curiosity." From Joseph C. Jahn, " 'A Little Light Shineth Forth,' " *Grassroots Editor*, November-December, 1968, pp. 24–26.

[7] Norman Blume and Schley Lyons, "The Monopoly Newspaper in a Local Election," *Journalism Quarterly*, Summer, 1968, pp. 286–292.

in the voter's final decision, even though he would not have been able to identify its impact if asked about it after the fact.

So the leverage of editorialists on public attitudes and decision-making cannot be assumed to have vanished with the days of the journalistic giants. It takes a subtler form today, but it still is evident, and politicians value and court it. Since editorial page opinion still does have power, it becomes important to all of us who are affected by that power to know how editorial policy is formed, and what factors have an influence on its development.

Who says so?

On very small papers, there's no mystery about how editorial policy is decided. The editor may also be the owner, the reporter, even the ad salesman. When he finds time to write editorials at all, they will likely represent no more than the reflection of his own understanding of the news, and since he wears so many hats he may not be able to spend much of his working day pondering the significance behind the headlines. There have been in every era some distinguished small-town editors (William Allen White of the Emporia, Kan., *Gazette* was one) whose perception was unusual and who could single-handedly contribute a meaningful analysis of the whole spectrum of the news. But that isn't easy to do on a small paper.

Going up the scale of papers in size, the development of editorial policy becomes more and more a joint or committee operation. Large metropolitan dailies have staffs of six to ten editorial writers whose whole daily assignment is to monitor the news flow and develop one or two editorials apiece on some issue of interest. Each of them usually serves as a specialist in some area of the news (foreign policy, economics, local government), but they typically meet daily in a general editorial conference to hammer out together the editorial position that the paper will reflect the next morning.

Magazines, if they use editorials, also use an editorial-conference approach to the development of a policy line.

There are obvious advantages in such procedure. When an editorial idea is thoroughly talked out in a roomful of pros who make it their full-time business to analyze the news and what it means, that idea is likely to emerge with most of the weaknesses eliminated.

A writer sitting off by himself in a secluded corner and building an editorial idea from scratch to finished draft without consulting anyone else may miss some vital points, or include some embarrassingly faulty logic in his line of argument. A newspaper hates to be caught going to the streets with a 100,000-copy press run containing an egregious error on, of all places, the editorial page, the showcase of the publication.

So the give-and-take of a full discussion in an editorial conference usually results in a tighter editorial than would be the case with an individual effort. It also, however, results in a kind of over-all, corporate gray tone to the editorial page, since the biting edges and sharply chiseled points that an individual writer might make in his first draft tend to be dulled and smoothed down during the course of an editorial discussion. There's a greater tendency to rely on such crutch phrases as "On the other hand," or "Yes, but . . ." and the like.[8]

Yet on balance, the reader is probably better served by an editorial page that is the product of an editorial conference approach. He benefits from the thinking of many seasoned and informed analysts, not just one. And if he wants a well-knit line of reasoning to sharpen his own thinking against, he will more likely get it from a panel of experts than from a single advocate.

One aspect of the corporate nature of editorial page comment is frequently a cause of irritation to readers. Most editorials are unsigned. They stand as faceless, institutional pronouncements.

This is deliberate policy; editorials cannot usually be attributed to the thinking and writing of one person, since several staff members very likely had a hand in them. Moreover, they are intended to represent the position of the paper as a whole, not of an individual staff member.

Yet we know from research studies that a reader responds more readily to a message from an identifiable individual source—a columnist whose picture appears alongside his writings, or a TV commentator who is alive on the screen as he expresses his viewpoint.

---

[8] For that reason, and others, the New York *Times*, with perhaps the largest editorial page staff in the business, does not employ the editorial conference approach. The editorial page editor instead consults individually with the various editorial writers, discussing the articles each will write and the policy lines that will be developed.

Recognizing the problem, some editorial page editors have attempted to give more personality to their pages by experimenting with signed editorials, or with occasional feature columns by individual editorial writers, complete with inset mug shots. Most editors still feel, however, that the image of institutional policy must be maintained.

What goes on the scales

It is usually easier to describe the process by which a newspaper or magazine staff goes about making policy than it is to identify the reasons *why* a given policy is finally decided upon as a result of that process. Readers often think they know why a publication comes out for a cause, or against it, or somewhere in between, but their guesses may not often be correct ones.

Most readers will respond, when asked, that "of course" the owner makes the policy for the paper, and the editorial writers are just hired hands who weave words to clothe his biases.

As a practical matter, the influence of ownership can be very strong and decisive, particularly on a small paper where the roles of owner and editor blur together. But on most larger papers the direct influence of ownership is diminished, in some cases almost to the vanishing point, even though the reader might find this hard to believe.

On major metropolitan papers the editorial writers may be the ones who set policy on most matters, perhaps getting direct guidance from ownership (through the publisher or the board of directors) only on such monumental questions as which candidate to support in a presidential election. In all lesser matters, the editorial writers may have a free hand to develop their analysis of the news on the basis of their own expertise and judgment.

It must be recognized, however, that any editorial page staff is likely to have a certain degree of ideological homogeneity simply because its members have been appointed to their positions by ownership representatives. Few conservative journals harbor resident radicals on their editorial staffs for purposes of leaven, nor is the reverse the case. So even if the owners don't send down regular and frequent directives on specific questions of policy, it may well be that they don't have to.

Readers also often assume that advertisers call the shots on editorial pages, but as has been noted in an earlier chapter such influence is rarely either effective or direct. It may have some osmotic effect, but even that probably is not great on most editorial page staffs.

If ownership influence is not often felt on large papers, and advertisers rarely exert much leverage, what forces *do* play a part in the shaping of editorial policy?

Sectionalism is certainly one potent factor, particularly in the case of newspapers, since nearly all are regional rather than national.

A congressman, if he is responding frankly, will acknowledge that he usually acts first as a representative of his district, second as a representative of his state, and third as a member of the national legislature. An editorial policy-maker has a somewhat similar blend of loyalties. As a detached analyst of the national scene he may be convinced that a hard-money policy would be best for the country. But if implementation of that policy would work a special hardship on the industries that are the economic backbone of his circulation area, he will very likely temper his advocacy.

There are some editors who—in some causes—will go directly against the grain of sectional interest. Ralph McGill of the Atlanta *Constitution* invited (and got) the wrath of his readers when he persisted in advocating racial integration in the schools. "Sometimes," he said, "you have got to walk out into the center of the ring and hit them square in the nose."[9]

But more often an editor will attempt to stay on a basis of reasonable discussion with his readers. He is aware that if he gets too far out of touch, or tries to advocate a position too greatly at variance with the interests of his readers, he may find himself waving the baton but with nobody in the parade.

This concern about not getting out too far ahead of the reader becomes an influential factor in the development of editorial policy. It may dictate the pace of an editorial crusade; even though the editorial writers may intend in the long run to press for wholesale reform, they may first advocate a lesser change, then wait to see whether that is accepted by the readers before pressing for more.

[9] Quoted in Eugene Patterson, "The South Loses a Forceful Voice," *Masthead*, Spring, 1969, pp. 15–17.

Another type of influence on editorial policy is an occupational factor. One editorial page editor once wrote: "The longer I'm in this business and the more I read the nation's newspapers, the more convinced I am that the great weakness of the American editorial page lies in its ivory-towerism. Too many editorials are written by people who don't know what they're talking about. The editor's reporting skills, if ever he had them, are set aside the day he gets a big desk and the services of a secretary."[10]

Some newspapers attempt to avoid the ivory-tower complex by assigning the editorial writers to occasional reporting assignments, so that they are reminded of the outside world from time to time.

Of all the factors that may have a role in shaping editorial policy, perhaps the one that weighs most heavily, most of the time, and in most editorial offices, is the effort to identify what course of action will be in the public interest. This is the basic purpose of the editorial writer—to explain, advocate, enlighten, all in the hope of bringing about some betterment of the city, the state, the nation, and the world. He does this within a context, to be sure. "Public interest" is an ambiguous term, and it is defined variously by editors and editorial writers. What may seem to be a sound course of action to the New York *Daily News* may seem a perfidious policy to the editorial writer of the more liberal Washington *Post*. And both papers may be altogether sincere in their advocacy. Only experience over time with a given paper's editorial policy will give the reader a basis for determining in what context "national interest" is viewed on that particular staff.

There are some other kinds of tests, however, that a reader or viewer can make in determining how much trust to put in the editorials of a particular newspaper, magazine, or network commentator.

The reader should be alert to the signs of superficiality—fence-straddling and the castigating of safe and distant targets.

He should be wary of the columnist or editorial writer who tries to serve up a sensation every morning, and who is not above magnifying issues out of proportion in order to meet his quota on a dull news day.

He should look for the kind of argumentation that is two-sided—

---

[10] Letter to one of the authors from Robert B. Frazier, editorial page editor of the Eugene, Oreg., *Register-Guard*.

that is, which examines the evidence both for and against before coming down on one side or the other. A one-sided argument, giving no hearing at all to the other side, is the mark of a propagandist.

He should watch, too, for the other devices of propaganda (catalogued in Chapter Fifteen); the editorialist who resorts to them is thereby acknowledging the weakness of his logic.

If a reader takes the trouble to make even simple analyses of the lines of argument thrust at him by the many voices that surround him, including the various organs of opinion, he can gradually learn which ones merit his attention and his confidence. He cannot afford, for his own sake, to view them all as being of equal legitimacy.

The purveyors of opinion in the mass media have a considerable service to offer to the readers and viewers they seek to influence, and only the consumer who knows enough to discriminate can make intelligent use of that service.

CHAPTER EIGHT

Not by words alone

Although man drew pictures before he developed an alphabet and reproduced them before he developed type, the first publications to come from printing presses when they were perfected in fifteenth century Germany consisted of words alone. Any embellishments were put there by hand after the printing was done. Prior to Gutenberg's experiments in type cutting and type casting, some pictures had been printed, of course, but they had first been carved out of blocks of wood. They were necessarily crude. It was several centuries beyond Gutenberg before intricate drawings and paintings could be reproduced in full fidelity.

It took until the middle of the nineteenth century before the camera was perfected. In 1872, in France, the principle of photography was applied to the reproduction of artwork. And photoengraving was born. By the turn of the century, reproduced pictures —photographs, drawings, and paintings—were commonplace in newspapers and magazines around the world.

So far, this book has concerned itself mainly with words and their effect on readers. This chapter will deal with nonverbal aspects of the news and opinion media, specifically: art.

What is art?

Like so many terms in journalism, "art" defies a clear-cut definition. In a narrow sense, it means drawings, paintings, cartoons, maps, and charts. Recent usage has broadened its meaning to include photographs. In an even broader sense, "art" means the over-all look of the pages: the design of the typefaces and the way they fit in with the pictures.

Art direction

When the reader follows a story down through a column on the newspaper's front page and onto another page inside, he does not notice—unless he's a typographer or a student in a class in typography—that the story is set, say, in 9-pt. Corona on a $9\frac{1}{2}$-pt. slug or that its headline is set in Bodoni Bold.[1] If the newspaper decides to experiment with unjustified columns or to change its headlines from Bodoni Bold to a sans serif face like Record Gothic, the reader may be vaguely aware of the change and a bit uncomfortable about it because it's different from what he's used to. But in a few days he will be perfectly at home with the new format, paying full attention again to what stories say rather than how they look on the page.

And yet, a publication must attend to the matter of which typeface or typefaces to use and how to arrange stories and other elements on a page. Type houses offer editors several thousand different typefaces, and each face comes with its own personality. Each face conveys its own mood. Some typefaces, because of their design, suggest urgency. Others elegance. Others power. Others dignity. How stories and headlines and pictures are arranged on a page can also have a psychological effect on the reader, an effect quite apart from what the stories themselves say.

Most publications help establish a personality for themselves by setting all stories in a single typeface and confining headlines to, at the most, two or three typefaces. Furthermore, they establish a basic format so that each issue has some resemblance to previous issues.

[1] Printers use "points" to measure type height. Seventy-two points equal one inch.

Magazines—some as long ago as in the early 1930s—have added art directors to their staffs to supervise the selection of typefaces, the design of the publication, and the assignment and use of artwork and photography. Newspapers—bound by tradition and facing deadlines that make difficult any serious attention to the subtleties of typography and design—do not, as a rule, employ art directors. They leave to their various editors the responsibility for making up the pages and working with the staff artists and photographers.

How pictures are reproduced

It's one thing to turn out a good print in a darkroom working from a photographer's negative. It's another to reproduce the print in a publication.

It's one thing to sit down at a drawing board and make a sketch in pen and ink. It's another to reproduce it.

To reproduce either a photograph or a drawing, a publication must see that someone takes a picture of the art and uses the negative to make an exposure on a sensitized piece of metal. The piece of metal, after it is further treated, becomes a printing plate.[2]

The reproduction of a photograph is a little more complicated than the reproduction of a drawing. A photograph has varying tones of gray. The printer's ink is black, pure black. He must create the *illusion* of grays. He does this by putting a screen (a piece of glass with crosshatched lines) between the lens and the film when he makes his negative. The light reflected by the picture goes through the screen and breaks down into a dot pattern. The plate made from this negative is called a *halftone*.

You can see the dots when you look closely at a photograph in a newspaper. Moving away from the photograph, you find that the dots blur into gray areas: dark gray where the dots are big and close together, light gray where they are small and farther apart. The dots are almost imperceptible in a photograph reproduced in a slick-paper magazine like *Life*. This is because the plate-

[2] What is described here, in very simple terms, is the process for making plates for letterpress printing, the kind of printing used by most large daily newspapers and by many national magazines. Two other printing processes— offset lithography and gravure—also require plates, but the processes for making the plates differ somewhat. For details, see Edmund C. Arnold, *Ink on Paper*, Harper & Row, New York, 1963.

maker uses a finer screen than he would use for a newspaper halftone. The finer screen makes possible greater detail. But a plate made with a fine screen must be printed on smooth paper; newspapers, printed on newsprint, can't use fine-screen halftones.

Color photographs require the same screening, but to reproduce them, a platemaker must make several plates. A color photograph requires several printings, one for each primary color and, for better printing jobs, an extra plate for black.

Perhaps you have subscribed to a small, community newspaper that runs halftones that seem sharper than those in a big daily. Chances are the newspaper was printed by a different process—by offset lithography rather than letterpress. Because the printing is done from rubber-covered rollers that deposit ink evenly on various surfaces, offset printers can reproduce fine-screen halftones on paper that letterpress printers would reserve for less detailed jobs.

By whatever printing process, photographs and paintings require halftone reproduction. Cartoons and ink drawings require regular— or *line*—reproduction.

In the most common of the printing processes—letterpress—platemaking adds considerably to the expense of publishing. A daily newspaper, for instance (most dailies are letterpress), invests $10 to $25 for one plate to print one photograph or drawing. This is why art from feature syndicates is so popular with editors. The platemaking has already been done. The syndicate has made "copies" of the plate by stamping it into sheets of special cardboard. When the newspaper gets its cardboard "copy"—the mat—it makes a casting from it (a simple matter) and prints from the casting.

But there is another more important reason why editors use syndicated art. Because many editors share in the expense, each gets big-name art at a fraction of what it would cost to buy it directly from the artist in its original form.

Stock art

Before the days of photoengraving, when woodcuts were all a newspaper could use to illustrate a story, readers could expect to see a picture in one issue that was the same as in an issue some weeks before. Let's say a fire broke out in a downtown building. Unfortunately for the editor, there wasn't enough time to make a new drawing and cut it out of wood. One fire looks pretty much like another, the editor reasoned, so why not use a picture of an earlier fire?

Publications still use stock art. Photo houses and art studios can provide by mail inexpensive "canned" illustrations for use by budget-conscious editors or advertising executives. The art is slick but predictable; it is, of course, more decorative than topical. And if the publication wants more elaborate art, it can buy already printed covers featuring full-color photography. When these arrive, the publication—it's usually a company magazine of some kind—prints its own name across the top of the picture and wraps the covers around sections printed locally.

Presto! An expensive looking magazine—until the reader gets inside.

Photographs or artwork?

Let a reader thumb through a publication, taking note of the art, and then, with the publication pushed to one side, ask him which items were illustrated with photographs, which with paintings or drawings. He probably won't remember. ". . . Research shows that on unaided recall, a high percentage of people do not even remember whether or not the illustration was created by an artist or a photographer. All they talk about is the subject matter," says an advertising art director, Stephen Baker.[3] And yet editors agonize over which to use in which situations.

Generally speaking, editors prefer photographs for nonfiction (news stories and magazine articles), drawings and paintings for fiction. But, as photographers have moved from literal recordings of what they see to experimental and creative photography, the distinction between the two kinds of art has diminished.

Much to the chagrin of illustrators, photography, because it is faster and, in most cases, cheaper, has overtaken artwork as the chief source for art in journalism, in magazines as well as newspapers. But the reader can still expect to see artwork used under these conditions:

[3] Stephen Baker, "Photo vs. Drawing: Is One More Believable?" *Advertising Age*, March 24, 1969, p. 94.

1. When the item to be shown is not in season. The editor wants to show snow, for example, but none is on the ground.

2. When conditions for taking pictures are not ideal. There's not enough light.

3. When the editor wants an exaggerated realism. It's true certain lenses can elongate or condense or otherwise distort, but a drawing or painting can still do the job more dramatically.

4. When the editor can't get a model's release. Under certain circumstances in journalism—and always when advertising is involved—the subject enjoys a right of privacy. If he is willing to be pictured, he signs a statement to that effect, often for a fee. An illustrator can create his own person, and that person can't object to his being used.

5. When the editor wants the person in a picture to look like no one in particular, when he wants him to be a composite.

6. When the editor wants a flat, decorative, or cartoony look.

If the reader can't tell how the picture was produced—through photography or through art techniques—he can look for a signature. If the work is signed, it most likely is a painting or drawing. Photographs usually carry credit lines set in type outside the picture.

Symbolism

Pictures can be realistic or abstract. As the communicator moves from the realistic to the abstract, he makes sure his audience is ready for the move. For, generally speaking, it takes a better educated—or at least a better indoctrinated—audience to understand abstraction.

The two journalists most devoted to abstraction are the editorial cartoonist and the advertising man. The editorial cartoonist takes familiar objects or legendary figures and makes them "stand in" for real people or events. He creates a situation or a scene, and asks the reader to pretend that real people are playing the roles. (See Chapter Nine.)

The advertising man abstracts when he uses symbols to represent products, services, ideas, or companies themselves. He calls his symbols "trademarks." They can be simplified renditions of objects easily recognized and clearly appropriate to the company—

such as CBS Television's eye; or they can be pieces of stylized art that have to be invented and shown again and again before the reader ever associates them with the sponsor—like Chrysler Corporation's "Pentastar."

What has a five-pointed star got to do with automaking? Obviously, it is arbitrary symbolism. It does suggest, vaguely, the heavens, and that's good: it does suggest "leading player," and that's good. But *any* company could use such an insignia. Chrysler developed it, only in recent years, to do a multiple job: it had to represent many divisions of the parent company, so it could not be literal. It couldn't be an abstraction of a car, for instance. Chrysler does more than make automobiles.

Symbols like the star are interesting because they mean different things to different groups of people. This is what makes their use such a challenge to the journalist. Adding one more point to the star, for instance, makes it stand for something entirely different from what the five-pointed star stands for. Take the umbrella. In the 1920s, thanks to the persistent efforts of an editorial cartoonist, Roland Kirby, it came to represent Prohibition. Kirby showed Prohibition as an old, skinny, crotchety man, dressed in black, and always carrying a folded up umbrella. Then, in the 1930s, the English Prime Minister, Neville Chamberlain, made a deal with Hitler for "Peace in our time"; because he had been photographed carrying an umbrella, the umbrella, at least in the hands of cartoonists, became associated with appeasement. In the 1960s an insurance company, not much worried about any earlier association with the symbol, adopted it as its trademark. To the readers of this company's advertising, the umbrella stands for "protection."[4]

Optical illusions

Everyone is familiar with graphic experiments in which the eye is tricked into accepting one line as being longer than another or one ball as being bigger than another. The lines are really the same length and the balls are really the same size; they just *look* different. You can "elongate" a line by adding supplemental lines that "pull" the eye out from the edges of the original line. You

[4] What things stand for in the minds of men everywhere, either through normal or through learned association, is thoroughly catalogued in J. E. Cirlot, *A Dictionary of Symbols*, Routledge & Kegan Paul, London, 1962.

can make one ball look larger than another by surrounding the one with smaller balls and surrounding the other with larger balls. By *comparison*, one ball looks bigger than the other.

You can take two squares, fill one with vertical lines and the other with horizontal lines, and one will look like a vertical rectangle and the other like a horizontal rectangle. The eye gets into the habit of moving in one direction—and it keeps moving.

Architects realize the eye is tricked by perspective and foreshortening, and so, in their designs, they *build in* error in order to make truth possible. Typesetters do the same thing. Spacing between letters, if perfectly consistent, results in an uneven appearance. Certain letters then, because of their shape, must be moved closer together; certain other letters must be moved farther apart.

Both photographic and drawing-board art are subject to optical illusions, intentional or accidental. Pictures are not always what they seem to be.

The fickle line

One of James Thurber's classic gags has a father and son looking at a photo album, the mother sitting in another part of the room, just listening. "That's an old beau of your mother's. He didn't get to first base." The gag is meaningless except for the expression on the mother's face. Were it an ordinary smile, the gag wouldn't work. Were it a frown, it wouldn't work either. Thurber used a cartoonist's favorite trick of combining a slight smile with a frown, an expression pretty difficult for a real person to work up. In a cartoon, where such an expression is possible, the effect is instantaneous: the look is evil incarnate. You just *know*, if the father and son do not, that the man pictured in the album certainly did get to first base or at least came close enough to make it a tough call for the umpire.

There is a less celebrated cartoon showing a little boy crying, standing next to a middle-aged man at the beach. The man is saying: "But I tell you, I don't have your miserable beach ball!" Again, if the man were ordinary looking, the gag would not come off. But the cartoonist has given him a pot belly about the size of a beach ball, and that small, curved line makes all the difference.

In each case, just the slightest twist in drawing is everything. A couple of tiny diagonal lines in Thurber's case; a half-moon line in the other.

Art and statistics

Nowhere in journalism is the placement of a line more crucial than in the making of a chart or graph. Charts and graphs have the feel of authenticity because they are, after all, based on statistics.

Cite statistics in support of an argument, and readers do not—can not—argue back. "Unquestionably, for the moment, numbers are king," observed *Time* in an essay on "The Science & Snares of Statistics." "But perhaps the time has come for society to be less numerically conscious and therefore less willing to be ruled by statistics." Benjamin Disraeli said: "There are three kinds of lies: lies, damned lies, and statistics." You can use a given set of statistics to "prove" almost anything. What, for instance, does the Chamber of Commerce claim, "Our average temperature is 70 degrees," really mean? That on most days 70 is how hot it is in that town? Or that half the time the temperature is over 100 and half the time the temperature is barely over freezing?

And how can readers be sure that, as reported, 40 percent of the population feels one way about a given issue and 60 percent feels another? Has the pollster provided evidence that his sample was truly representative? Was a large enough group reached? Did the pollster include all types in his sample: rich and poor, young and old, professional men and workers, men and women, swingers and squares, blacks and whites?

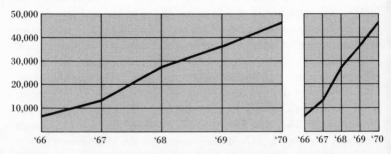

Which growth record is the more impressive, the one represented by the graph at the left, or the one by the graph at the right?

In his delightful *How to Lie with Statistics*, Darrell Huff criticizes the use of statistics not only in their raw form but also in their more dramatic form: graphs. He shows readers that in line graphs, bar charts, and pie charts, it is possible to create any impression the chartmaker wants to create, regardless of the statistics he works with.

In a line graph, where the upward trend is not convincing enough, all the chartmaker needs to do is to press the two outside verticals in toward the center, keeping his unit scale the same. (In a line graph, the sequence of time runs along the bottom, the number of units up the side.) The more the chartmaker compresses the extremities, the steeper he makes the angle of rise.

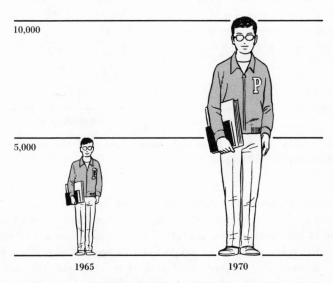

Is the figure representing 1970 only twice as big as the figure representing 1965?

In a bar graph, the most common lie occurs when the chartmaker changes the ordinary bar to a pictograph. In a case where he wants to show growth in enrollment at a university, he makes a drawing of a student (you can tell it's a student by the no-nonsense expression on the face, the glasses, and the books he's carrying) one inch high. That represents 5,000 for the year 1965. Right next to that he makes a similar drawing, this time two inches high. That represents 10,000 for the year 1970. But is the second drawing really only double the first? Of course not. Any person twice as tall as another person is also considerably wider and considerably bigger around. If the figures are drawn at all realistically, the second figure is *much more* than double the first figure. The effect, if not a lie, is certainly misleading.

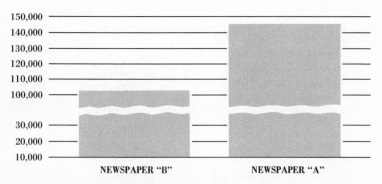

Does Newspaper "B" have only about one-half the circulation as Newspaper "A"? Look again.

An error almost as common in the making of bar charts is to cut out part of the center sections of bars when there is not enough space to run them in their entirety. Both—or all—bars are affected. But obviously, you change proportions as well as size when you take the same-size section out of a short bar that you take out of a long one. You may mean to show only that one bar is taller than the other, but you also change proportions.

The photographer as journalist

The photographer plays an increasingly important role in the dissemination of news and opinion. On newspapers, news-oriented magazines, and trade journals, he is a full-time employee, going out on a story just as a reporter does. On many publications, he is a combination man; he writes stories and takes pictures, too. For general circulation magazines and advertising agencies he takes pictures, usually, on assignment as a free lancer.

Like writers on the staff, he subjects his work to editing.[5] He typically submits a generous supply of contact prints, from which the editor—or his art director—makes selections. Out of scores of prints submitted, only two or three may be picked. The photographer then supplies carefully printed enlargements—glossies—for reshooting by the platemaker.

A writer need not be there when a news event takes place; he can gather his information later from eye witnesses or from participants. Sometimes a photographer can operate in the same way, re-creating the event for picture-taking purposes. But accident and tragedy cannot be re-created, and when these occur a publication cannot show them unless its photographer happened to be on the scene or got there soon afterwards. In many cases, an amateur photographer—or one not ordinarily associated with the publication—steps forward. A Dallas dress manufacturer, who happened to have a movie camera focused on President John F. Kennedy when he was shot, sold his eight mm color film to *Life* for $50,000. In 1969, a former army combat photographer sold, for a reported $40,000 with several publications bidding, 18 color photographs of an alleged massacre of residents of a South Vietnamese village by American troops.[6]

The photograph became a powerful social force during the Depression years of the 1930s when photographers brought out more vividly than writers could the plight of the dispossessed and the unemployed. And many of today's photographers are less interested in simply recording what they see than in influencing people to courses of action or in creating works of art.[7]

[5] Not always with good humor. Photographers almost to a man object to word-oriented persons having the final say on visual matters.

[6] There was some question about whether or not, having taken the pictures as an army photographer, he had the right to sell them, but that was another matter.

[7] See Cornell Capa, ed., *The Concerned Photographer*, Grossman Publishers, New York, 1969, book containing the work of photographers who use their photographs to fight social evils.

The best photographs don't look as though they are posed, even though they often are. This photograph, used to illustrate an article in the student magazine at San Fernando Valley State College, had to be shot and reshot some thirty times before the photographer, Gina Urbina, got exactly the effect she wanted. She wanted to show community reaction to hippie dress. The bus stop is adjacent to the campus at Northridge, Calif.

From left to right

Photographs in journalism sometimes tell a complete story. The photograph of Hitler dancing for joy after one of his victories in World War II did not need words to explain it. And you just knew, when you saw that photograph of General Eisenhower reacting to the news of the firing of General MacArthur by President Truman, that Ike was saying: "I'll be damned." The photograph in the late 1960s of the South Vietnamese national police chief shooting a prisoner at close range was shocking enough by itself. So was the picture in 1970 of the girl on her knees beside a mortally wounded student at Kent State University.

But most photographs need a few words to place them in context. Especially, people pictured need to be identified. Newspapermen call the words that go with photographs "cutlines," because the photographs are printed from "cuts" or plates; magazine editors call them "captions."

Cutlines often do not add enough to an understanding of the photograph to make them worthwhile. The photograph shows an army general pointing to a map, and the cutlines begin: "General A. B. Blank points to a map of. . . ." Obviously. Perhaps the trouble with cutline writing in many cases is that the photograph, to begin with, is not worth running and certainly not worth writing about. The clichés of journalistic writing show up in cutlines, too. A Northwest newspaper not long ago showed a body wrapped in a blanket, tied, lying in a wooded area. The cutlines read: "This body of an unidentified woman wrapped in gray blanket and sheet, bound with rope, was discovered Friday just off Evergreen highway six miles east of Washougal. Foul play is suspected." Foul play is *suspected?*

And sometimes cutlines and captions completely mislead the reader. You had to be more than a little sophisticated to see through *Esquire*'s cover hoax of March, 1969, when the magazine, a master of the put-on, showed four photographs, taken from a distance, of a man in a white robe standing at the side of a pool with two colleagues. All looked startled, as though they had just spotted an intruder. The caption read: "Howard Hughes: We See You!" It wasn't the elusive Hughes after all, as *Esquire* later freely admitted.

Do photographs lie?

The typical reader puts more credence in a news story than in a short story. He's more willing to believe a biography than a novel. After all, facts are facts. But do the facts add up to the truth? Isn't it possible for a piece of fiction to tell more about man and his problems than a literal report, accurate as it may be?

Photographs as used in journalism are a little like news stories: apparently literal, accurate, factual. Readers believe them. After all, a precision instrument was used to produce the picture. What the film recorded was exactly what was going on in front of the camera.

Or was it?

Russell Wiggins, the former Washington *Post* editor, considered this question in an address to journalism students at the University of North Dakota in early 1969. "It has been said that the camera does not lie. But the camera does lie. It is a notorious, compulsive, unashamed and mischievous liar."

He added: ". . . Readers . . . have difficulty in understanding that the camera is a congenital liar, condemned to prevarication by the mechanical limitations of a contrivance that could only tell the whole truth if it were equipped with lenses as all-encompassing as the very eye of God."

Editor & Publisher, the trade journal for newspapermen, after reporting the talk, asked for reaction from photographers and found that, to nobody's surprise, they were outraged. "Wiggins reflects the current non-think of the journalism profession," a teacher-photographer fired back. Another photographer complained that Wiggins "impugns the motives, honesty, and integrity of every photographer. . . ." Someone else questioned how an editor "can say a camera lies when it is a machine with no brains." ". . . An honest picture can be made dishonest by the direction of some editor, by his cropping, by what he has written or failed to write in the picture caption," countered another. "Many of the so-called camera lies that Wiggins referred to were not camera lies but interpretations made by the viewer," said another.[8]

[8] Don Maley, "Photojournalists Blur Charge: Camera, A Machine, Isn't a Liar," *Editor & Publisher*, March 29, 1969, pp. 11 ff.

It was not the first time the camera had come under attack. "The camera . . . is . . . the great lie of our time . . .," wrote Malcolm Muggeridge, trying to suggest that caricature was more believable than photography.

As is ever the case with deceit, the camera's deceitfulness varies in direct ratio with its plausibility; because it has the reputation of not being able to lie, it lies the more effectively. In this sense, "good" photographs are more harmful than bad ones, and the greater the photographer the greater is liable to be the lie projected.[9]

It is easy to understand photographers' response to this kind of criticism when you consider the rough time photographers have had establishing their place with the media—especially with newspapers. Columnist Heywood Broun once wrote: "Some of my best friends are newspaper photographers. . . . And yet I feel that when one or two are gathered together for professional reasons you have a nuisance, and that a dozen or more constitute a plague." Nor have photographers enjoyed the same rights reporters enjoy. Since the days of explosive flash powder, judges, citing Canon 35, a directive drawn up by the American Bar Association, have kept photographers out of courtrooms, and do so now in spite of the fact that pictures can be taken in natural light with inconspicuous 35 mm cameras.[10]

While some of the attacks on the camera do seem overdrawn, it is clear that, whoever is at fault—the camera, the photographer, or the editor—photographs do sometimes give readers a wrong impression. They may make a factual statement that is valid at the time the photograph was taken, but the fact as pictured may be completely out of context. A familiar example of this is the photograph of the man holding up his freshly caught fish; if he holds it out toward the camera, it will, of course, look considerably larger than it really is. Foreshortening puts the fish "out of context"—sets up a false scale by which the viewer measures size.

[9] Introduction to David Levine, *The Man from M.A.L.I.C.E.*, E. P. Dutton & Co., New York, 1966, pp. 5, 6.

[10] To circumvent Canon 35, newspapers historically have sent sketch artists to cover important trials. But in the James Earl Ray trial in 1969, Judge W. Preston Battle even drew the line there: no sketch pads. "It would be disconcerting to the participants to know they're being sketched," he said. That didn't bother one artist, Howard Brodie, who said: "It's better to draw by memory—you're really forced to observe."

Photos by Stan Bettis

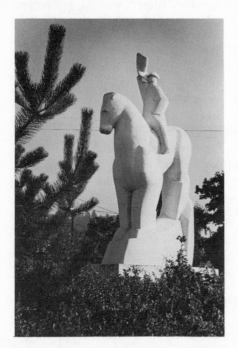

Two ways of showing a statue that was erected at the entrance to a small city. Which photograph would a writer choose to illustrate a s t o r y about urban blight? W h i c h one would a Chamber of Commerce manager choose for the cover of a brochure about his city?

Photographs can lie at three different stages:

1. *When they're taken.* The photographer can use special lenses to distort distances between items in a picture, creating an unnatural scale. He can use filters to exaggerate cloud formation and make a scene more beautiful than it really is. He can take the picture from an unnatural angle to make the subject appear to be bigger or smaller than it really is. He can take the picture at just the right time to make a man look stupid or profound, depending on the photographer's or his newspaper's bias. Or maybe the timing is unintentional. Still, stopped with his mouth open in the middle of a word, any speaker can be made to look ridiculous.

A friend of one of the authors once took a picture of the then junior senator from Wisconsin, Joseph McCarthy, sitting with a group of female hockey players. One of the girls had her hand resting on her exposed thigh. Because of the angle of the picture, it looked as though the hand belonged to the senator. Now the senator was an obnoxious political figure and the photographer would have enjoyed playing some small role in ending the senator's career. But to submit this for publication clearly would have been unfair to the senator, and probably even libelous.

Once during the 1952 political campaign, a photographer, shooting from a low vantage point, got a picture of Adlai Stevenson, the Democratic candidate for president, sitting on a chair with his legs crossed. The focus was on the sole of his shoe, which happened to have a hole in it. The photograph was widely printed, to the delight of the Democratic party, actually, because it at last gave their candidate, brilliant but a little too much the intellectual, the common touch: as happens to any man, his shoes had worn out and he needed to have them resoled. Stevenson supporters thought enough of the shot to use a shoe sole with a hole as a lapel pin in the 1956 race, when Stevenson ran again. It was a cute device but probably not a very accurate symbol for that solvent statesman.

2. *When they're adjusted.* Much can be done in the darkroom to change the mood of a print as it is being made from a negative. The light source can be stepped up in one part of the print, held back in another. To change a print more spectacularly, a retouch artist can paint over it, by hand or with an airbrush, and make it say something quite different from what the photographer intended. For instance: a public relations organization representing the lum-

ber industry has a photo it wants to use in a booklet on fire prevention. It is a dramatic shot, but a logger in the foreground is smoking a cigarette (cigarettes are a major cause of forest fires) and
he's not wearing a hard hat (companies like to point to their safety
measures in woods operations). Ideally, the cigarette should disap-
pear and a hard hat should appear. No problem. A retoucher can
airbrush out the cigarette and paint a hat on the logger. If the
photograph were to be run in a newspaper, the job wouldn't even
have to be done very carefully. Retouching for newspaper reproduction can be rather crude because the photograph will be converted
to a coarse-screen halftone which will not record the imperfections.

Retouching can be done on the negatives as well as the prints.
And certain changes in the photograph can even be made by the
platemaker. For instance, it is a simple matter to make a man face
left when in the original photograph he may be facing right.

It is also possible to take two or more prints and combine them
or to make a single print from two negatives. The history of politics
brings out a number of examples. A henchman for Joseph McCarthy
in the early 1950s once pasted an unsavory character next to one
of McCarthy's political enemies, made a copy print, and passed
the photograph off as a true depiction of the two in conversation,
capitalizing on the guilt by association suggested by the scene.

Finally, it is possible to edit a photograph by "cropping" it—cutting away a part that is not wanted. Sometimes the editor does this
to improve the composition. Sometimes he does it to change the
shape of a photograph so it will fit the space that has been provided
for it. But sometimes he does it to change the meaning of the photograph. A classic case involves the one-time executive head of the
Republican Party of Oregon, Wendell Wyatt, who later won a seat
in Congress. Senator Wayne Morse, the maverick Democrat, was
running for reelection. Wyatt had found a photograph of Morse
lecturing to a partially filled Senate chamber. Eager to help the
man who was running against Morse, Wyatt, in putting together a
campaign folder, included the photograph in question but trimmed
it to show nothing but the Senator and some empty seats. The implication was that Senator Morse was ineffectual, that nobody listened to him. Wyatt's excuse was that the photograph was too big
and that he had to get rid of part of it so it would fit into his
folder. But a Morse supporter in a letter to the editor of the *Oregonian* pointed out that as an ex-journalism student Wyatt surely real-

ized that it was possible to reduce the entire photograph to fit the space.

3. *When they're used.* An editor can control what photographs say through his selection of which ones to run and where and how to run them. He doesn't happen to like Nixon, let's say, and he has two stock photographs of the man: one focuses on the ski-jump nose and shows clearly the somewhat sinister five o'clock shadow. The other shows the face from his best angle and in a flattering light. Which photograph represents the truth?

When it appeared that John F. Kennedy would be the Presidential nominee of the Democratic Party in 1960, *Human Events*, a right-wing publication, stepped up its campaign to make Barry Goldwater the Republican nominee. It devoted one of its front pages to a comparison of the two men. The editor had to select photographs from among many that were available. The one he chose of Kennedy showed him sitting in a rocking chair. The one he chose of Goldwater showed him smiling broadly, in uniform, waving from the cockpit of a plane. Was this an accurate comparison of the two potential candidates?

Sometimes it's a question not of which photograph to run but whether the editor should run the one photograph that is available. Should an editor run a photograph taken for one occasion to illustrate a story about a later occasion? The subject is smiling broadly, and yet the story deals with tragedy. Is the photograph, then, true?

Motion pictures

Add motion and sound to the already considerable impact of pictures and you have the most powerful mass medium of all.

Thomas A. Edison produced one of the first motion pictures when he recorded the inauguration of William McKinley following the election of 1896. Others began experimenting with short takes of dances, prize fights, parades, and other events, and soon "nickelodeons" opened in most cities. Citizens for a nickle could enjoy the novelty of going to a darkened theater and watching an hour-long series of short films. *Harper's Weekly* in 1907 noted that nickelodeons were spreading "as thickly as saloons."[11] A few saloons installed screens and projectors of their own, just as bars installed

[11] Erik Barnouw, *Mass Communication*, Holt, Rinehart & Winston, New York, 1956, p. 17.

television sets years later when TV threatened to keep people home.

One of the earliest films with a plot was *The Great Train Robbery*, a seven-minute-long film produced in 1903 by one of Edison's assistants. The first motion picture of consequence came in 1915 with the release of David Wark Griffith's *The Birth of a Nation*. Integrated sound didn't come until the mid-1920s; *The Jazz Singer* in 1927 featured for the first time dialogue that could be heard while the picture was being shown. Color came in the mid-1930s.

The critics ignored the movies at first, looking on them as a fad and fare fit only for the lower classes. In 1915 the U.S. Supreme Court ruled that movies were not entitled to the protection of the First Amendment, and from that time until recently, pictures produced for theater showings faced various forms of censorship at the local level. But in 1952, reversing a lower-court ruling that found *The Miracle* sacrilegious, the Supreme Court said: "We have no doubt that motion pictures, like newspapers and radio, are included in the press whose freedom is guaranteed by the First Amendment."

With several states setting up censor boards, the industry in the 1920s drew up a code that saw to it that criminals in the stories never went unpunished and sex scenes were never explicit. By then, the movies had become acceptable entertainment for the middle classes. In the 1950s and 1960s the industry, prodded by an invasion of foreign films, greatly liberalized its code. In 1968 the industry abandoned its code altogether, setting up instead a set of ratings to help patrons decide what level of sex and violence they and their children could tolerate.[12]

Between the coming of television in the late 1940s and the beginning of experimental film-making in the 1960s, the feature-film industry appeared to be dying. Theaters by the hundreds closed their doors. One theater got a call one night asking what time the feature started, and the cashier answered: "What time can you get here?" Only the drive-ins seemed solvent, and for reasons probably independent of the motion pictures they showed. The cartoonist Robt. Day in *The New Yorker* showed a lot of cars at a drive-in with the picture on the screen upside down. One projectionist was saying to the other: "O.K., pay me. Ten minutes and nobody's said a word."

No longer concentrated in Hollywood, much more experimental

[12] See Richard Schickel's article, "Movies, Morals, and the Young," *The Progressive*, September, 1969, pp. 23–27.

than before, much more sophisticated, the motion-picture industry in the 1960s showed new signs of life. There was a new emphasis on photography as an art form. "In these cinematically knowledge-able times," wrote Hollis Alpert in the *Saturday Review*, "much more recognition is being given to the film craftsman. The photog-rapher's status is beginning to approach that of the kingpin, the director."[13] "What has happened this year [1969] in movies is roughly what happened five or six years ago in the pop music field —the artists have gotten control of the art," wrote Roger Ebert in *Moderator*.[14]

The new film-makers blend reality with fiction. In *Medium Cool*, for instance, actual scenes of the riots that took place in Chicago during the 1968 Democratic Convention became an integral part of the story. A crew filmed *The Rain People* against a real life back-ground in a trip across the country. Hollis Alpert sees a new film audience "ready and waiting to welcome almost anything that does not have the look of the Hollywood pap of the past."

From 1967, the time of *The Graduate*, films have dwelt on purity-of-youth themes. In both the notable movies like *Easy Rider* and their third-rate imitators, the heroes are always free spirits. This is nothing new: the main characters in the cowboy and gangster movies were free spirits too. What is new, as Craig Karpel points out in *Esquire* (August 1970), is the relationship between the sub-ject and the customer. They are one and the same. "Imagine if there had been lines of cowboys stretching around blocks waiting to pay $3 to see *The Virginian*, gangsters to see *Scarface*."

Some critics saw the wave of youth films in the late 1960s and early 1970s as exploitive rather than innovative. And the pre-occupation with perversion bothered even the most open-minded of the movie-goers. Ralph Graves, managing editor of *Life*, on seeing *Myra Breckenridge*, said, "At some point we should make an effort to draw the line—not in censorship but in disgust."

Frances Taylor, writing for the Newhouse News Service in 1970, reported that most youth movies were box office flops. So were the

---

[13] Hollis Alpert, "The Film of Social Reality," *Saturday Review*, Septem-ber 6, 1969, p. 43.

[14] Roger Ebert, "Personal Flicks Head toward Visual Revolution," *Oregon Daily Emerald*, March 10, 1970, pp. 8, 9. Reprinted from *Moderator*, Decem-ber, 1969.

"scrubbed" movies for family audiences. The film industry, she concluded, needs new material or it will lose its audience completely. Films, she said, need "content and characters that . . . people can relate to and care about."

Newsreels

Although the motion-picture medium became primarily a storyteller rather than a news-disseminator, a minor industry grew up to make and distribute what came to be known as "newsreels." Unfortunately, these films were universally bland and trivial, concentrating on ship launchings (the bottle never seemed to break), bathing-beauty contests, fashion shows, sports events, and animals acting up in the zoo.

With the coming of television after World War II, both national and local newscasters utilized newsreel techniques, but the newsreel as a separate entity all but died. A few companies continued to produce them until the late 1960s, but theater audiences considered them as nothing more than popcorn breaks between features.

Documentaries

In 1935 *Time* magazine brought the newsreel and the feature-film idea together in a series of short films called *The March of Time*. This series, which played for several years in major theaters, differed from the ordinary newsreel in that its producers, not satisfied with spot-news coverage alone, *reenacted* events, using in some cases the original participants, in other cases paid actors. It also treated events that up until then had been considered controversial. The series also had a point of view. It was to the newsreel what *Time* magazine itself was to the newspaper.

Going a step beyond *The March of Time*, a number of organizations began using films as instruments of propaganda. The New Deal philosophy of Franklin Roosevelt came through clearly in a government-sponsored film, *The Plow That Broke the Plains*, and later in *The River*. And when World War II broke out, this government, as well as all others caught up in the fighting, turned to motion pictures to ready their citizens and soldiers.

Thus, documentaries were born.

The Academy of Motion Picture Arts and Sciences has defined documentaries as films "dealing with significant historical, social, scientific or economic subjects, either photographed in actual occurrence or re-enacted, and where the emphasis is more on factual content than on entertainment. . . ."[15] But because the fictional techniques of the feature film are incorporated into documentaries, facts give way to something a little broader: truth—or truth as the film-maker sees it.

The documentary owes much to the feature film and much to the newsreel: it borrowed its techniques from both. But it owes more to television, because, as A. William Bleum points out in his *Documentary in American Television*, television gave it its financing and its mass audience.

The two men who did the most to make the documentary part of American television were Edward R. Murrow[16] and his colleague Fred Friendly.[17] Murrow had been the most listened-to voice of World War II, broadcasting from both Britain and America. Unlike most radio personalities, Murrow, with his rich voice and deep concern, was able to make the switch easily to television. *See It Now*, the documentary program he and Friendly did for CBS beginning in the mid-1950s, for the first time in the new medium examined important, controversial issues and took stands. One of the programs took a hard look at the then greatly feared Sen. Joseph McCarthy, who saw Communists everywhere in government—or said he did. Using skillfully edited film clips of the Senator in action and providing appropriate comment, Murrow contributed substantially to the Senator's eventual downfall.

Taking a note from *See It Now*, NBC offered its *White Paper* series and ABC introduced *Close-Up!*

Understandably, these and other estimable documentary shows were network produced. None of the stations could hope to produce programs so well-thought out, so well-researched and written, so well-financed. But even at the local level, some stations have begun

[15] Quoted by A. William Bluem in *Documentary in American Television*, Hastings House, New York, 1965, p. 33.
[16] See Alexander Kendrick's biography: *Prime Time: The Life of Edward R. Murrow*, Little, Brown and Company, Boston, 1969.
[17] See Fred Friendly, *Due to Circumstances Beyond Our Control . . .* , Random House, New York, 1967.

to turn out films in the tradition of Murrow and his fellow journalists.

The growing interest in causes spilled over to the makers of feature films. After several decades of escapism, the pictures playing in theaters after World War II increasingly explored social issues. They dealt frankly—sometimes shockingly—with racism, anti-Semitism, drug addiction, juvenile delinquency, and mental illness, among other problems.

The documentaries have their critics. Even the famous Murrow show on McCarthy came under some attack, and not only from right-wingers. Some liberals thought that the use of television in this way threatened anyone with controversial ideas who, lacking the charisma of a public performer, could not fight back.

The viewer of a documentary finds himself at the mercy of the producer and his crew. If the producer can be trusted, fine. If he has ulterior motives, he can make frightening inroads with his art. In addition to all the other chances for exercising his bias, he can edit film to change the sequence of events, and the reader is never the wiser. One of the most artful deceptions in film editing came with *Operation Abolition,* a documentary produced by putting various unrelated film clips together to "prove" that opposition to San Francisco hearings of the House Committee on Un-American Activities, as it was then named, was directed by Communists.

The film-maker can put his special imprint on what he reports by tricks of lighting, camera angle, focus, musical background. The way he changes from one scene to the other—abruptly or through "dissolves"—makes a difference, too. So does the narration that accompanies the film.

This is not to say that the average documentary or photograph is any more a lie than the average story or article appearing in a newspaper or magazine. But, like words, pictures do not always tell the truth. A man can use a camera—just as he can use a typewriter—to mislead a reader. He may do it intentionally. He may do it accidentally. The wise reader or viewer uses his critical facilities when looking at pictures, just as he does when reading a column of type.

CHAPTER NINE

Back to the old drawing board

In the early 1940s, when America was involved in an all-out war, Peter Arno did a cartoon for *The New Yorker* showing a military plane crashing into the earth, probably just after taking off on a test run. Angry and disturbed, high officers and maintenance men are seen rushing over to where the plane has crashed. An ambulance speeds over, too. Walking away from it all, looking a little foolish, carrying his plans, is the little man who obviously had designed the plane. He says, "Well, back to the old drawing board." Arno's cartoon is one of the classics among gag cartoons; his gag line, because it expresses so beautifully man's inability to react fully to life's tragedies, has passed into general usage. Another one of Arno's gaglines made *Bartlett's*.

Arno himself (he died in 1969) was probably the world's best-known gag cartoonist, a specialist within a speciality. He and men like him serve as the clowns of journalism. But they do more. With their barbs and contortions, through both under and overstatement, they chip away at man's pretensions. The typical cartoonist instructs and influences even while he entertains.

His work traditionally moves in one of three directions: gag cartoons, the special province of the magazines; comic strips, the province of newspapers; or editorial and political cartoons, also the province of newspapers.

We start with the gag cartoon, the newest of the cartoon forms. We move then to comic strips. We end the chapter with a discussion of editorial cartoons.

GAG CARTOONS

Only on Wednesdays

Every Wednesday within a few-block radius in Manhattan where many of the nation's major magazines are headquartered, scores of solemn-looking men with portfolios under their arms trudge from office to office hoping for a kind word from an editor. They are the nation's gag cartoonists, the most dogged of the freelancers, gambling that one or more of their rough sketches will make it.[1] Sometimes an editor will buy the sketch "as is"; sometimes he will ask the cartoonist to redo it in a tighter style; most of the time he will say "Sorry."

The cartoonists are not exactly sure how Wednesday came to be market day. Maybe it was because editors had too much to catch up with early in the week and they had to make a deadline or get away late in the week. Anyway, every gag cartoonist knows Wednesday is the day; and in some offices, coffee is served. Hundreds of other gag cartoonists mail their gags in, but most of these people are nonprofessionals or barely professional; and they concentrate on the smaller magazines.

On the Wednesday rounds, the first stop is *The New Yorker*, where the pay per cartoon is $300 to $400. Few magazines pay more, and none brings the cartoonist as much prestige. For the cartoonist, everything is downhill from there. He may end his Wednesday visits in the office of one of the sleazy men's magazines and unload what he can't sell elsewhere for as little as $10 per drawing.

The competition is rough. For each issue *The Saturday Evening*

---

[1] Peter DeVries devoted one of his comic novels to the hangups of a gag cartoonist. See *The Tunnel of Love*, Little, Brown and Company, Boston, 1954.

Post used to pick about 30 cartoons from about 4,000 submitted. And now that market is gone.

Still, "Every year a crop of new talents rises. The public's appetite for their work is apparently insatiable—as it should be. Their cartoons have become an indispensable staple of our periodical journalism." This is how critic Stephen Becker feels about it.[2]

To the real cartoon connoisseur, gag cartoons represent the ultimate in the cartoon art. A gag cartoon is to be savored, not just looked at and read. The subtleties of the art are considerable. Note that the whole point revolves around a single line printed underneath the cartoon, and everything within the drawing must substantiate that point. The gag cartoonist keeps his cast of characters down, his setting simple. He must make it clear at once, without benefit of balloon, just who within the drawing is doing the talking.

Sometimes he can put his gag over without a single word below. He does his gag in pantomime.

Unique among the cartoonists, he has no particular axe to grind. His objects of ridicule, when they are there, are hard to pin down, because he deals less in personalities and issues, more in general statements about mankind. He's never happier than when, in the words of Stephen Becker, he is "jabbing away constantly at our shams and illusions," in the end touching upon some social truths.[3]

Gag cartoonists come onto their gags in a number of ways. Sometimes they dream up a scene and then try to think of a gag line to fit. Sometimes they start with the line and then try to imagine a scene that will make it funny.

Most gag cartoonists buy ideas from outside sources. They pay the writer 25 percent of what the cartoon earns and keep 75 percent for themselves. Only the cartoonist signs the cartoon.

It has been said that the novelist has only a few basic plots to work with. Similarly, the gag cartoonist has only a few basic ideas. The setting, the props, the characters change; the words in the gag lines vary; but the ideas stay the same. Perhaps you will recognize them:

1. *The cliché.* Most journalists avoid the cliché. Not the cartoonist. He can take a cliché and let a character act it out literally

[2] Stephen Becker, *Comic Art in America*, Simon and Schuster, New York, 1959, p. 154.

[3] *Ibid.*, p. 127.

and get a laugh. Virgil Partch (Vip) is a master of this kind of gag. Vip shows a man lying dead on the sidewalk while a companion, unaware of the tragedy, turns to watch a cranky woman walk by. He says: "Boy! If looks could kill, eh, Steve?" Dana Fradon makes a slight change in a cliché in a *New Yorker* cartoon dealing with deteriorating telephone service. An executive leads a caller to the door and says: "Don't try to call me. I'll try to call you."

If you'd like to be a gag writer or cartoonist, see what you can do with these cliché lines:

> "Mind if I smoke?"
> "You'll only encourage him."
> "You're putting me on!"
> "Been waiting long?"
> "Am I getting warm?"

2. *That's life*. This includes any gag that depicts life as it is, so that the reader will identify with it, and say, in effect: "Ain't it the truth!" Tom Henderson in *The Saturday Evening Post* shows a lazy, unshaven man reading the paper, the phone on a table at his side. His wife has just picked up the receiver after rushing in from in front of the house where she's parked the car. She's dropped groceries all the way in and knocked over a chair in her rush to answer the phone. She's saying: "Yes, he's here."

3. *Ridiculous situation*. The opposite of "That's Life." It just couldn't be that way! Jerry Marcus in *True* shows a worried woman driver with her husband sitting beside her. In back of her is a line-up of cars: a tow truck, a police car, and an ambulance. The husband says: "Relax, it's probably just a coincidence."

4. *Out of character*. Sweet little old ladies act like gangsters. Kids talk like grownups. Ministers sit in bars with worldly ladies. Mulligan in *The New Yorker* shows a perplexed man and wife looking at a painting of a haggard, hungry woman holding a baby with a frightened child at her side. The scene is stark, desolate. The painting is signed "Norman Rockwell." The man says: "Well, there must be more than one Norman Rockwell in the world."

5. *In character*. People act out their roles to the point of absurdity. B. Tobey in *The New Yorker* shows a young man smooching with a girl on a park bench. With his free hand, and without looking, he's reaching into a bag of popcorn and feeding a flock of pigeons and squirrels. An older couple is walking by, and the man says to the woman: "Now, there's a warm human being for you!"

6. *Understatement.* This is a favorite theme for the cartoonist; and British cartoonists have no corner on it. Jim Stevenson in *The New Yorker* shows an art expert examining a fine painting while the owner looks on. The expert has rubbed his finger across the painting; his finger is wet with paint. He says: "Well, this initial test suggests that the authenticity of your Rembrandt may be questionable."

7. *Exaggeration.* The opposite of understatement. Chon Day in *The Saturday Evening Post* shows a tired, middle-aged man asleep on a couch. His wife, a little portly, and a lady visitor are talking. The wife says: "He's had a bad back ever since he carried me over the threshold."

8. *Ingenuity.* When man solves some problem in an unusual way, readers—even readers of gag cartoons—appreciate it. Rodrigues in the *Saturday Review* sets up a situation in which a father tries to tell his side of the story to the rebel generation. He's fat, balding, middle aged, well dressed; he stands on stage at a run-down coffee house, strumming a guitar. Hippie types sit watching him, frowning. He's singing: ". . . Oh, my kid's twenty-three and he don't like to work/Oh he don't like to work/When I was twenty-three I worked very hard/Oh, I worked very hard . . ." You could classify it as "out of character" too.

9. *Stupidity.* This kind of a gag especially satisfies the reader, because the cartoonist always lets the reader know something a chief character in the cartoon doesn't know. The reader feels superior. Jerry Marcus again, this time in *The Saturday Evening Post*, shows a middle-aged couple already in bed, looking bored. Another couple, obviously visitors, stand nearby. The man, hat in hand, says: "Well, we really must be going."

10. *The letdown.* Some definitions of humor suggest this is the real core of humor. The reader is led to believe one thing, then finally disappointed. Jim Stevenson again, in *The New Yorker*. A guru sits in front of his high mountain cave. Around him are signs scrawled on the rock: "Smile and the world smiles with you, cry and you cry alone"; "Early to bed and early to rise makes a man healthy, wealthy and wise"; "A penny saved is a penny earned"; and so on. A disappointed, slightly hippie-ish couple has just arrived. The girl says to her male companion: "Something tells me we've come to the wrong guru." Again, classification can never be exact. This gag could serve as an example of "Understatement."

COMIC STRIPS

Is anybody laughing?

A child of the William Randolph Hearst-Joseph Pulitzer circulation battles of the 1890s, comic strips—or "the funnies"—quickly became the most popular diversion in the mass media. Other media came along—the movies and the electronic media—to offer entertainment in an even more palatable form, and for a time interest in the strips waned except among the very young and the poorly educated. Still, that was a big enough audience in itself to keep strip syndication profitable.

When in the 1950s the syndicates began circulating strips that were truly comic again to replace or supplement the adventure strips, interest stepped up, and not just among people who moved their lips when they read; today the audience for this fare includes the young and the poorly educated, as always, but also the more sophisticated reader.

But comic strips today enjoy nowhere near the single-minded following they enjoyed in the early part of the century. Gone are the days when a cartoonist like Chic Young could offer $50 for a name for Blondie's new baby and get 400,000 entries, as once he did. It is hard to imagine it today, but once, when New York newspapers were on strike, the mayor himself took to the air to read the comic strips aloud for the benefit of the city's deprived youngsters.

We mean to include, in our discussion of the comic strip, the cartoon panel, the form the strip took originally. A few panels, like Robert Ripley's "Believe It or Not" and Jimmy Hatlo's "They'll Do It Every Time," survive, but panels-in-sequence—comic strips—are much more numerous, much more popular.

America's first "comic strip," *The Yellow Kid*, introduced before the turn of the century, was really more a panel than a full-fledged strip. Distinguished mainly by the extra press run of yellow to color in the Kid's cloak, the feature proved such a circulation builder that its creator, Richard Outcault, was lured back and forth between New York's *World* and *Journal* by successive increases in salary, finally settling with the *Journal*. The *World* hired another artist to continue its version of *The Yellow Kid*. Not only did both papers scramble for novelty in cartoons; both laced their news stories with sensation, causing an editor of a third paper to lump all of that kind of journalism together as "yellow," a term still useful today.

Drawn originally for adults, the early strips concerned themselves with the communities of "foreigners" making up America's Eastern Seaboard cities. These people were the strips' chief readers. If they weren't insulted by the humor in *Jiggs* and *Happy Hooligan* (for the Irish), *The Katzenjammer Kids* (for the Germans), *Alphonse and Gaston* (for the French), *Abie the Agent* (for the Jews), and *Black Berries* (for the Negroes), they should have been. Racial humor in some of the strips carried over until the 1950s, by which time readers were mostly children. Prof. Curtis D. MacDougall of Northwestern University observed:

The Negro is always the shuffle-footed Uncle Tom, the Chinese always has a long pigtail and speaks in pidgin English, and the Englishman invariably is a dignified appearing nobleman who doesn't quite understand what's going on around him. Since the comics are among the first pictures that a young child sees, during the most impressionable years, the lasting effect of this form of journalistic "art" is properly a matter of concern.[4]

Another kind of strip, dealing with the emerging middle class, concentrating on the family, took its place alongside the racial strips. The first was *The Gumps* (1917), described by Pierre Couperie and Maurice C. Horn, comic strip historians, as "hopelessly mediocre," featuring characters drawn "with a total lack of talent" and dialogue that was "sickeningly ordinary."[5] Another was *Gasoline Alley*, the first strip to allow its characters to mature, marry, and have babies to grow up and serve as new characters for later episodes. Both of these, and several others, were the brainchildren of Captain Joseph Medill Patterson, founder of the New York *Daily News*.

Chester Gould introduced real violence to comic strips when he launched *Dick Tracy* in 1931. "I was disturbed by the fact that the Prohibition gangsters in Chicago and other cities were repeatedly beating the rap," he remembered late in life. "I thought it would be a good idea to have someone just shoot these fellows down. When

4 Curtis D. MacDougall, *Understanding Public Opinion*, Macmillan, New York, 1952, pp. 637–638.

5 See their exhaustive study, *A History of the Comic Strip*, Crown Publishers, New York, 1968. Translated from the French.

they were caught red-handed, why bother with a trial and all that baloney?"[6]

The advent of *Dick Tracy* spelled the virtual end of "comic" strips; most of them by the 1930s had turned into adventure strips. One that remained genuinely "comic" was George Herriman's *Krazy Kat*, perhaps the only strip in those days (1916–1944) that appealed to intellectuals.[7] But when Herriman died his strip died with him. His humor was too subtle, his drawing style too individualistic to be continued under anyone else's direction.

By the end of World War II, the strips were in disarray. The adventure in them could hardly match the real life adventure of the war. Television came along to compete. And people didn't seem much in the mood for the strips' original fare: slapstick humor. It was in this setting that Walt Kelly came up with *Pogo*, which some considered the successor to *Krazy Kat*. According to Couperie and Horn, Walt Kelly was "the first [comic strip artist] to deal with the great moral, social, and political questions of his age." He won "the respect and admiration of the intellectuals, thereby contributing to the rehabilitation of the comic strip."

And just in time. Sex and violence had infiltrated the adventure strips, and parents, preachers, and educators mounted campaigns against publishers. Especially outspoken was psychiatrist Frederic Wertham with his alarmist book, *Seduction of the Innocent*. The comic book industry drew up a code and editors did a little more policing. But what saved comic strips was the new wave of humor and good fun represented by *Pogo* and then *Peanuts*, *Beetle Bailey*, *Miss Peach*, *B.C.*, and *The Wizard of Id*.

Scholars show renewed interest in the comics, and art lovers take them more seriously than before. The Smithsonian Institution

[6] Daniel Greene, "The Titans of the Funnies," *The National Observer*, September 12, 1966, p. 24.

[7] In an unsigned review of George Herriman's *Krazy Kat* (edited by Woody Gelman, Joseph Greene, and Rex Chessman and published by Grosset & Dunlap, New York, 1969), *The New Yorker* for March 14, 1970 (p. 156) said, "*Krazy Kat* is visibly the ancestor of much of our best comic art: Ignatz Mouse hurling his bricks at Krazy clearly becomes Lucy endlessly betraying Charlie Brown in 'Peanuts,' and there are clams with legs that anticipate 'B.C.,' a creation-by-drawing that obviously inspired Crockett Johnson's 'Harold and the Purple Crayon,' and a world of animal characters that must have influenced 'Pogo.' It may even be that Coconino County was the forebear of Faulkner's Yoknapatawpha County, and that *all* our arts derive from Herriman's fertile genius."

features a Cavalcade of American Comics. The Louvre in Paris stages an International Exhibition of Comic Art. Under sponsorship of the Italian Ministry of Public Information and the University of Rome, Italy hosts an international comics convention. Boston University's Communications Research Center runs a three-year study of the cultural effects of the comic strips.

"One survey after another indicates the funny papers are the most-read part of the daily newspaper," a *National Observer* writer reports.[8] Syndicate officials estimate readership is pretty evenly divided between children and adults.

One can understand the strips' continued appeal to nonintellectuals; what is more noteworthy is the interest in the strips among intellectuals. Some may be slumming. Some may regard the strips as high camp. But some obviously have a real affection for them. Al Capp can be forgiven his hyperbole when he says: "Comic strips are the best art being produced in America today. I judge them by the same standards I apply to Daumier or Michelangelo. And by those standards comic strip art is damned good."

It was the comic strip that inspired a whole new movement in the fine arts: Pop Art. And cartoons have been put to work in ways that have surprised their creators. Charles Addams's famous gag cartoon showing a skier who has passed a tree, one of his tracks going around the left side, one around the right, has been used by psychiatrists to test the reasoning of their patients. The caricaturist Al Hirschfeld, who does those sketches of show business personalities for the Sunday New York *Times*, always hides the name of his daughter, Nina, in his drawings; the U.S. Air Force has used them to train students to find "Nina" as rapidly as possible and thus increase their skill in instant map reading.

There is an honesty in the strips not found in other arts. The strips have not been "electronically enhanced for stereo," let's say; their music is more country fiddle and harmonica than electric steel guitar. But let a given strip catch on too well with the masses, and let its creator cash in on its popularity; then disillusion sets in. In the words of critic Richard Schickel, the artist's discoverers are

no longer compelled to clip his cartoons and pin them up on the office bulletin board, quote them at parties, and discuss their hidden depths with fellow cultists. . . . Too many people have come to have a vested

8 Daniel Greene, *loc. cit.*

interest in taking the whole business [of popular culture] entirely too seriously. In the process we are beginning to forget that, whatever the excellent and amusing qualities sometimes achieved by the popular artists, such qualities are always incidental to his basic function, which is to make money. Very simply, the popular artist must be "sold out" from the beginning. His glory lies in the fact that he occasionally rises above his origins.[9]

Why syndicates?

The strips do not originate with the newspapers that run them but rather with feature syndicates.

Editor & Publisher 44th Annual Syndicate Directory (1969) lists close to 300 syndicates in the United States and Canada, ranging from the largest, King Features, to one-man operations offering single features. Together, these syndicates offer daily and weekly newspaper editors about 225 different cartoon and comic panels, 275 comic strips, and 65 editorial cartoon features—these plus the hundreds of columns on astrology, books, bridge, business, fashion, food, health, politics, religion, science, sports, travel and women's interests.

The typical cartoonist draws each strip about six weeks in advance of publication. He need not—probably does not—live in New York, where his syndicate is headquartered; rather, he mails his strips in, usually in sets of six or seven to cover a full week's series. The syndicate takes care of making the plates and circulating the mats to subscribing newspapers, who pay for the feature on the basis of their circulations. A small daily gets a strip at a cost considerably less than what a big paper pays. The syndicate offers the feature to the newspaper on an exclusive basis: that is, it agrees to withhold the feature from any other newspaper in the paper's circulation area. This explains why most successful comic strips have imitators, circulated by competing syndicates, to service papers which have been denied the original.

In some cases, the cartoonist, in a dispute with his syndicate, leaves it for another. Unfortunately, his contract is so written that he leaves his feature behind, too. When Roy Crane left Newspaper

---

[9] Richard Schickel, "Smaller Peanuts, Bigger Shells," *Book Week*, December 27, 1964, p. 9.

Enterprise Association for King Features, someone else took over his *Wash Tubbs.* He started a new one: *Buz Sawyer.* Milton Caniff had to leave *Terry and the Pirates;* he started *Steve Canyon.* In recent history, only Al Capp was able to take his strip with him when he changed syndicates.

Of the net income from the strips, the syndicate usually takes half, the cartoonists the other half. A few cartoonists have tried to beat the system by syndicating their own stuff. But without the syndicate's resources behind them and without the sales staff, they soon learn that half of a lot of money is more than all of almost nothing.

Techniques of the comic strip

The comic strip is part novel, part art, part theater. Its creator serves as playwright, set designer, and director. He's also in charge of casting. Casting is what made Chester Gould so successful: who can forget (shudder) "Pruneface," "Shoulders," "Gargles," "Flattop," "Influence," "Mumbles," "Nothing Yonson," "B.O. Plenty," "Gravel Gertie," and more recently "Mr. Bribery"?

The cartoonist picks the camera angle and decides for each panel whether it should be a close-up or a long shot, whether it should be in detail or in silhouette. He must find room, somehow, for balloons to carry the conversation, and in a correct order. (The use of balloons for conversation, incidentally, goes all the way back to fourteenth-century woodcuts.)

The cartoonist has his own shorthand. By a kind of general agreement among his fellow cartoonists, he uses a solid outline to indicate regular conversation, a bubbly outline to represent thinking.

To turn up the volume, the cartoonist does his letters in bolder strokes than usual. To get away with characters swearing in a family newspaper, he resorts to jumbled consonants interspersed with stars and other typographic dingbats.

His shorthand to indicate action is familiar enough to everyone: irregular parallel lines with puffs of smoke for speed; a line of Zs for sleep; a light bulb for inspiration; special outlined words, like "Pow!" and "Wham!," to step up the pace. Roy Crane, first with *Wash Tubbs* and later with *Buz Sawyer,* is the acknowledged master of action in the strips.

The cartoonist prides himself that some of his manufactured

words creep into general usage: words like "heebie-jeebies," "twerp," "Buster." When he's not making up words or expressions, he's giving new life to old ones: "Good grief!" He leaves other lasting imprints. Al Capp made "Sadie Hawkins Day" an almost universal high school celebration. With his "Great Pumpkin," Charles Schulz gave Halloween a new dimension. His "Charlie Brown" and "Snoopy" served as code names for the command and lunar modules of Apollo 10 in mid-1969. Chic Young has the "Dagwood Sandwich" to his credit. An early human-interest panel-cartoonist, Clare Briggs, had a pipe tobacco named after him.

Everything in black and white

If cartoonists have one thing in common it is their allergic reaction to pomposity. Let him see a stuffed shirt and any cartoonist— gag cartoonist, comic strip artist, editorial cartoonist—will move at once with his pen to deflate it. His is a one-sided art. He has neither time nor inclination to present his case in full context. Everything to a cartoonist appears black and white.

No other journalist gets away with the cartoonist's use of stereotypes. To a cartoonist, anyone with close-set eyes can't be trusted. Anyone with buck teeth is stupid. Anyone with a receding chin is weak willed. Any pretty girl is busty. And busty girls are not very bright. A gynecologist, Dr. Erwin O. Strassmann, professor at Baylor University's College of Medicine, in 1964 corroborated this notion through a research project, and cartoonists around the world were probably thinking: "I told you so." "The better the brain, the smaller the breasts and vice versa," Dr. Strassmann told *Newsweek*. But "The idea just doesn't stack up with my observations," countered Dr. Charles M. McLane of Cornell University's Medical College.

In cartoonland, everyone seems to have an oversize head and oversize hands and feet. The big head makes sense when you realize how important facial features are to the cartoonist. He needs room to dot his eyes, place his eyebrows, attach his nose, open up his mouth. The big hands give him a chance to do things with fingers. And big feet are, well—they're just funny.

Cartoonists move rather freely from one cartoon form to the other. Understandably, the big pull has been toward the comic strip, where the money is. Mort Walker *(Beetle Bailey)*, Charles Schulz *(Peanuts)*, Buford Tune *(Dotty Dripple)*, Johnny Hart *(B.C.)*, Frank O'Neal *(Short Ribs)*, and Mell Lazarus *(Miss Peach)* all started out as gag cartoonists. Virgil Partch *(Big George)* and Jack Tippett *(Amy)* still do gags. Frederick Opper *(Happy Hooligan)*, Clare Briggs *(When A Feller Needs a Friend)*, Billy De Beck *(Barney Google)*, Fontaine Fox *(Toonerville Trolley)*, Jimmy Murphy *(Toots and Casper)*, H. T. Webster *(The Timid Soul)*, and Walt Kelly *(Pogo)* all made the switch from editorial cartoons. But only one cartoonist of note, Rube Goldberg, moved from the comics to editorial cartoons, and in his new role he won a Pulitzer Prize.

A surprising number of cartoonists started out as reporters or newspaper desk men: Harold Gray *(Little Orphan Annie)*, Dik Browne *(Hi and Lois)*, Alfred Andriola *(Kerry Drake)*, Allen Saunders *(Steve Roper* and *Mary Worth)*, Dick Brooks *(The Jackson Twins)*.[10] From their media bases, they branched off into cartooning.

Like all creative artists, cartoonists at work draw on their own experiences, express what they know and feel. Some observers even insist that when a cartoonist draws a character, he really draws himself. What Charles Schulz does in his *Peanuts* strip serves as an example. Those who know him personally see Schulz in every Charlie Brown episode. ". . . All the things that are said in the strip are things that I would normally say," Schulz told *Psychology Today*, "and you would find out if you were around me for a week that this is just the way I talk all the time when I am with people that I know very well or with whom I feel comfortable."[11] Among the "Peanuts" characters, perhaps only Lucy does not fairly represent her creator. "I have to watch myself, of course, so that I am not Lucy-ish and sarcastic. This strip gives me an outlet because there was a time in my life when I didn't know that sarcasm was not a good trait to have, and I have overcome this. Having a comic strip is a marvelous outlet for the various frustrations in one's life."

Perhaps, among creative artists, cartoonists have more than their share of frustrations. Most of them must write as well as draw, and

[10] See "The Inside Story of the Creators of the Comics," *Editor & Publisher*, March 9, 1963, pp. 13 ff.
[11] Mary Harrington Hall, "A Conversation with Charles Schulz," *Psychology Today*, January, 1968, p. 19.

this combination of talents, though common enough, does not seem authentic to other creative artists. Says Al Capp: "Writers don't take you seriously because you draw. Artists don't take you seriously because you write."[12]

"Cartooning is a *fairly* sort of a proposition," says Charles Schulz. "You have to be fairly intelligent—if you were really intelligent you'd be doing something else; you have to draw fairly well—if you drew really well you'd be a painter; you have to write fairly well—if you wrote really well you'd be writing books. It's great for a fairly person like me."[13]

Looking back on his dealings with cartoonists when he was editor of the British *Punch,* Malcolm Muggeridge said:

. . . as a body of men they [cartoonists] were, I discovered, inclined to be morose, abnormally sensitive, and surprisingly solemn, to the point that they seldom laughed even at their own jokes. Just as war was too serious to be left to soldiers, so, I used to reflect, humor was too serious to be left to cartoonists. On the other hand, they were kindly, gentle and blessed with a curious kind of innocence that is seldom found in writers. I found them, by and large, lovable rather than likable.[14]

The "Peanuts" phenomenon

Unlike most name comic strip artists, Charles M. Schulz does all the work himself, including lettering in the balloons. He calls himself "the fastest letterer in the West" and can't imagine any cartoonist leaving that part of the assignment to someone else. "Not doing your own lettering is like Arnold Palmer having someone else hit his nine irons for him."[15]

He takes two days to draw six daily strips and a third day to draw the Sunday strip. In the time that remains, he tries to answer personally the 400 to 500 letters that come in each week.

Schulz started *Peanuts* in 1950 after a brief career as a free-

[12] Henry Lee, "Good Grief! A History of the Funnies," *Signature,* July, 1969, p. 22.

[13] Quoted by Barnaby Conrad in "You're a Good Man, Charlie Schulz," *The New York Times Magazine,* April 16, 1967.

[14] Malcolm Muggeridge in the Introduction to David Levine, *The Man from M.A.L.I.C.E.,* E. P. Dutton & Co., New York, 1966, p. 7.

[15] Mary Harrington Hall, *op. cit.,* p. 67.

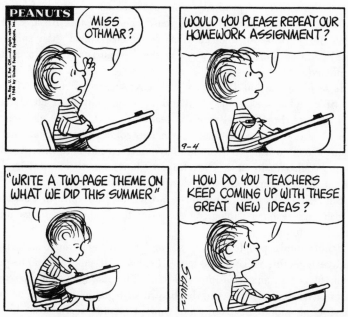

Reproduced through the permission of United Feature Syndicate

lance cartoonist and instructor for a correspondence art school in Minneapolis. The strip took off quickly; by 1969 some 1,000 dailies in the United States and Canada and another 100 papers in 41 foreign countries were running it.

That was only part of the story. By 1969 some 200 different products had been marketed bearing the *Peanuts* imprint. Shoppers could choose among dolls, sweatshirts, greeting cards, wrist watches, key chains—even a new "Snoopy" brand dog food. By 1969, 55 million copies of books growing out of the strip had been issued by a half dozen publishers. One, Determined Productions, San Francisco, literally built its business around *Peanuts* characters, starting with the *Happiness Is a Warm Puppy* book in 1962. The World Publishing Company, New York, in 1970 brought out *Charlie Brown and Charlie Schulz*, written by Lee Mendelson in association with Charles Schulz. Several TV specials, films, musical comedies, and record albums, all favorably reviewed, had drawn even more attention to the strip. Advertisers had used Peanuts characters to help sell a variety of products, from automobiles to loaves of bread.

In 1970 Schulz and his wife Joyce opened, at Santa Rosa, Calif., what Jerry Hulse of the Los Angeles *Times* called "the spiffiest [ice] skating parlor ever put together." Tourists refer to it as "Snoopyland."

It seems clear that *Peanuts* is the most successful comic strip of all time. What makes the strip unique is its appeal to all classes and all ages. For the less cerebral reader, *Peanuts* is cute and sentimental. For the thinking reader, it makes some profound statements about life. Two different scholars have devoted books to interpreting what *Peanuts* really says. One, Robert Short, sees theological implications.[16] Another, Jeffrey H. Loria, sees psychological insights.[17]

But Schulz does not consciously preach a philosophy in *Peanuts*. If scholars read psychological and even theological meanings into the strip, fine.

Schulz thinks people need to strive for more emotional maturity, and perhaps this is The Message in *Peanuts*. His approach is to put adult fears and anxieties into children's conversations. Consider the chief characters. There's Charlie Brown with his pathological desire to succeed and to be liked; and Snoopy, trying to be what he is not; and Lucy, representing the domineering female; and Linus, who needs, above all, security. All this hits home.[18]

Writer Barnaby Conrad came to this conclusion about the strip:

Charles Schulz feels the loss of his dog Spike today as deeply as—or more deeply than—he did a quarter of a century ago, just as he feels the loss of his childhood. Happily for the readers, he is able to translate this long memory and deep feeling into words and pictures. It seems to be universal, either because we had a childhood like that, or wish we had. There's a little Charlie Brown in all of us males and, Lord knows, we've all known, and maybe even married, Lucy van Pelt, a girl who shouts: "I don't want any downs—I just want ups and ups and ups." Certainly there's been *someone* in each one

16 See *The Gospel According to Peanuts*, John Knox Press, Richmond, Va., 1964, and *The Parables of Peanuts*, Harper & Row, New York, 1968.

17 See *What's It All About, Charlie Brown?* Holt, Rinehart & Winston, New York, 1969.

18 Charles Schulz on Lucy: "Little girls at that age are smarter than little boys and she knows it better than most little girls. But she's not as smart as she thinks she is. Beneath the surface there's something tender. But perhaps if you scratched deeper you'd find she's even worse than she seems."

of our lives ready and eager to pull away the football just as we're about to kick it.[19]

Propaganda in the strips

Creators of the early strips merely amused their readers or offered them momentary escape. Beginning in the 1930s, a few of the cartoonists began sounding off on political and social matters, as their fellow cartoonists on the editorial page had been doing since the days of Thomas Nast.

At first, the cartoonists used their art to promote causes rather than fight injustices. Some strips propagandized for the various professions, including the military. *Terry and the Pirates* and later *Steve Canyon* did a job for the Air Force. *Buz Sawyer* and the lesser-known *Thorn McBride* did a job for the Navy. The Army never did get its spokesman on the comic pages, unless you want to count *Beetle Bailey*!

Medicine got its *Rex Morgan, M.D.* So appreciative was the American Medical Association that in 1954 it gave Dr. Nicholas P. Dallis, the psychiatrist who created and wrote the strip, a special citation:

Through an entertainment medium of widespread appeal he has contributed immensely to public education on many medical subjects and alerted Americans to the dangers of medical quackery. The character of Dr. Morgan has come to typify the modern doctor, a man of high principles, intelligence and integrity, devoted to the service of his patients, and yet a truly human, compassionate individual.[20]

But a cartoon, including a comic strip, ridicules much more effectively than it praises. When it ridicules, readers—certain readers—become outraged. Editors, if they are on the other side of the issue, begin to question their own judgment in selecting the feature from among the many available to them.

In 1935 in Huntington, W. Va., the editor of the *Herald Dispatch* left blank the space where *Little Orphan Annie* ordinarily appeared and ran instead this note: "Deleted! For Violation of Reader Trust." In the opinion of the editor, Cartoonist Harold Gray had become

[19] Barnaby Conrad, *op. cit.*, p. 44.
[20] "Cartoon Crusader," *MD*, February, 1963, p. 187.

too much the propagandist. The strip had shown Daddy Warbucks, the lovable capitalist, promoting a new product, "Eonite." An evil competitor hired some liberal politicians to brand Warbucks—to make him "the most hated man in the country. . . ." In an aside to the reader, the competitor said: "I'm using these liberals because they don't know any better. . . . They are misguided rabble rousers and misleaders of the masses." Labor leaders were shown joining in the fight against Warbucks, but workers finally turned against these leaders and tarred and feathered them.

Nor was it the last time the strip delivered itself of an attack on liberal ideals. Ben H. Bagdikian, who reports frequently on press performance, noted in 1962 that Little Orphan Annie had been "fighting democracy, social welfare, high taxes, universal suffrage, reform, education, culture, and human love for years."[21]

In an interview late in his life Gray with disarming good humor dealt with the continuing criticism of his strip. "A publisher once told me that 'Annie' should be on the editorial page," he said. "I told him that some of the funniest stuff I ever read was in editorials, so why not put them on the comic pages?"[22]

Mental health became his favorite target shortly before he died. In 1965, readers saw Daddy Warbucks railroaded into an insane asylum. Angered over the strip's attitudes on this subject, the Hartford, Conn., *Courant* suspended it for two weeks. The Dallas, Tex., *Times Herald* continued to run it, but in a front page editorial referred to its "irresponsible propaganda." But, the paper said, "in the belief that even misguided Orphan Annies are entitled to a viewpoint without censorship, this newspaper will reluctantly continue the objectionable episode."

Pogo is another strip with a strong point of view, but on the other side of the political spectrum. The strip's creator, Walt Kelly, a former editorial cartoonist, would never be content to be simply an entertainer. In 1954, before most journalists felt safe in attacking the excesses of Joseph McCarthy, Kelly incorporated the senator in a character called Simple J. Malarkey, and a number of papers were outraged. The Orlando, Fla., *Sentinel* dropped *Pogo*, saying comics should be funny, not preachy.

21 Ben H. Bagdikian, "Stop Laughing: It's the Funnies," *The New Republic*, January 8, 1962, p. 14.
22 Daniel Green, *loc. cit.*

Even more repugnant to some papers in the South was the strip's attitude toward integration. The Richmond, Va., *Times-Dispatch* threw the strip out after Albert the Alligator, in one of the panels, said: "You open up a school, next thing you know all kinds of ignoramusses is coming in. . . . They meets yo' daughter . . . splits an orange with her, poof! They're engaged, married, an' livin' in the attic." So did the Charleston, S.C., *Evening Post* throw the strip out, at least until the sequence on education was over.

In 1964, when Kelly was concerned about the prospects of Barry Goldwater's becoming president, he created "Typo," who looked remarkably like Goldwater. He also satirized the John Birch Society, which became the Jack Acid Society. Knowing that a number of editors would be upset, this time he created an alternate sequence for those editors who would not use the original. That so many editors chose the alternative series disgusted Kelly. He told a writer for *True:* "Anybody who worries about what a comic strip says worries about who their mothers are!"

Following Vice President Spiro Agnew's late 1969 speech attacking the TV networks for their alleged liberal bias (see Chapter Thirteen), Kelly introduced in his strip a large dog with the unmistakable features of the Vice President. In one sequence the dog enters into a discussion of air pollution, but it turns out he's thinking about pollution of a different kind: "It's a national disgrace. All due to the irreducible provincialism of the commentators."

Kelly saves some of his satire for the left. In 1962 a Japanese newspaper dropped the strip temporarily after the Soviet Embassy there pointed out that a Russian-talking pig looked remarkably like the then Premier, Nikita Khrushchev.

Li'l Abner is another strip that can be counted on to stir up audiences. For a long time, its creator, Al Capp, was the antithesis of conservatism. Today, Capp chooses the New Left as his primary target. Capp ridicules unreason wherever it may be found. He once told *Playboy,* "I am against primitive singing, primitive guitar strumming and primitive political solutions." Lately he has taken out after campus rebels and protesters.

An early confrontation for Capp occurred in 1947 when the Pittsburgh *Press* omitted his strip because, the editor said, it made the United States Senate look ridiculous. In the strip, senators wouldn't vote for a bill to broadcast their proceedings because, as one senator put it, "You realize what monkeys we'll sound like if the folks back home can actually hear us on the air?" Senator Phogbound wouldn't join in the fight against the bill unless the senators agreed to vote money for a $2,000,000 university to be named for him. "That's a high price," said Phogbound, "but it isn't my money—it's just the taxpayers' money."

In one recent sequence, when the Yokum family offered to help their even more poverty-stricken relatives, the Deep Misery Yokums, and when Li'l Abner and his family had to move out of their own house, finally, because of the filth and indolence of their relatives, some in Washington read this as an attack on the "War on Poverty," which indeed it was.

Many prominent political figures and entertainers have found themselves, thinly disguised, playing a role in *Li'l Abner*. To some, the role isn't very funny. When Capp heard of Joan Baez's anger over his "Joanie Phoanie" sequence, he pretended to be astonished that she would see any resemblance between herself and "a character who hates her country, won't pay taxes and whines and gripes all the time." Some years earlier, Liberace thought he saw himself in "Loverboynik," a "dimpled darling of a piano player," to use Capp's words, and threatened to sue. *Time* asked Capp what his defense would be, and Capp said it would be that there was no resemblance whatsoever between Loverboynik and Liberace because Loverboynik could play the piano rather decently. Capp heard no more about the suit.

The introduction of propaganda into the comic strips makes the editor's job considerably more difficult. The editor feels he has a right to pick what he wants to go into his paper; and, just as with a piece of writing by a staff member, he can cut out part of a comic strip or leave it out altogether. The cartoonist feels that because a comic strip is a personal thing and because it has his name on it and his reputation is at stake, no one should tamper with it. Al Capp used to argue with editors: if you don't like the strip, drop the franchise and let some other paper pick it up.[23]

Perhaps by now the argument is academic. Editors pay less attention to propaganda in comic strips these days, partly because the strips are, in their opinion, not quite so important as they were

[23] For more on Al Capp see Arthur Asa Berger, *Li'l Abner: A Study in American Satire*, Twayne Publishers, New York, 1970.

and partly because all journalists, even reporters, are freer than they once were to inject self into their work.[24]

And now color

Comic strip artists have been among the last of the journalists to recognize the revolution in race relations. Up until recently they practiced what one writer calls "comic strip apartheid."[25] More to blame than the artists were their syndicates, who feared offending readers. If a Negro played a villain's role, syndicates believed, pressure groups would complain; if he played a hero's role, newspapers, especially in the South, would surely cancel.

But that has changed. The syndicates are now convinced that integrated strips are salable, and there has been a rush to get on the bandwagon.

Several of the standard strips have introduced black characters. Charles Schulz, for instance, added Franklin to his cast. By the early 1970's, a half dozen strips were featuring Negroes regularly.

Wee Pals by Morrie Turner was one. Patterned somewhat after *Peanuts, Wee Pals* is a multiracial strip with gentle humor. "If there's a philosophy," says Turner, "it is that we can all get along together."[26]

A less well-known strip—only five papers had signed up for it by early 1970—is *Butter and Boop,* which deals with the lives of ghetto children.

The most widely publicized black strip to date is *Friday Foster,* launched in early 1970 by that master syndicate that has circulated so many of the best-read strips: the Chicago Tribune-New York News Syndicate. *Friday Foster* is "the story of black Americans reaching out for a piece of the action," but it is written and drawn by whites. The heroine is a beautiful photographer and model.[27] The strip suggested itself to writer Jim Lawrence (he does

---

[24] To better understand the comic strip as a social force see David Manning White and Robert H. Abel, eds., *The Funnies: An American Idiom,* The Free Press of Glencoe, New York, 1963.

[25] Jack E. White, "Color and the Comics," *Columbia Journalism Review,* Winter, 1969–70, p. 58.

[26] *Ibid.,* p. 60.

[27] Don Maley, "Adventure Strip and Column Feature Blacks," *Editor & Publisher,* December 6, 1969, p. 69.

continuity for two other strips) when he was reading the Newark *Evening News.* "I was running my eye down the page, and I suddenly said to myself, 'God, here's a page full of nothing but white faces! And Newark's a town that's well over half black! It struck me as very wrong.' "[28]

EDITORIAL CARTOONS

"The ungentlemanly art"

Since it developed as a modern-art form—and it goes back to the days of Honoré Daumier in early nineteenth-century France— the editorial cartoon has taken one of two tacks: either it has expressed an opinion, vividly, dogmatically, even crudely; or it has solidified some event in the news, presumably making it clearer for the reader. The latter tack is the more recent. It grew out of America's penchant for objectivity in news reporting; with this clarifying kind of cartoon, a cartoonist need not commit himself. Nor need he do much thinking. Clearly, the trenchant editorial cartoon—the editorial cartoon in its original form—is much more memorable.

Furthermore, to be remembered, the cartoon of opinion must criticize, not praise. The British cartoonist David Low made the observation in his autobiography:

On the face of it one would not say the attitude of political caricaturists was one of admiration or even goodwill. The traditional terms of their expression are perhaps better adapted to censure than to praise. Admiration is for the poets. A satirist perverted to hero-worship becomes pathetic and sickening. His approval can best be expressed by leaving its object alone.[29]

Possibly Don Hesse, editorial cartoonist of the St. Louis *Globe-Democrat,* gave the best description of editorial cartooning in the title of an article he wrote for the *Quill:* "The Ungentlemanly Art." Stephen Hess and Milton Kaplan picked it up, acknowledging its source, and used it as the title of their admirable history of Ameri-

---

[28] "The Talk of the Town," *The New Yorker*, March 21, 1970, p. 33.
[29] David Low, *Low's Autobiography*, Simon & Schuster, New York, 1957, p. 204.

can political cartoons.[30] It *is* ungentlemanly of Bill Mauldin, formerly of the St. Louis *Post-Dispatch* but now of the Chicago *Sun-Times*, to show Khrushchev standing there with one shoe off and stuffed into his mouth. But how in one small panel could the cartoonist better make his point?

The cartoonist and his editor

Editorial cartoonists in most cases work directly for a newspaper, although, if they are good enough and if other papers and magazines begin to reprint their stuff, they, like comic strip artists, can be syndicated. Papers with circulations of more than 100,000 generally employ their own editorial cartoonists; papers with smaller circulations get their editorial cartoons from a syndicate. Among the big-city dailies, only the New York *Times* gets by without its own editorial cartoonist (the *Times* doesn't run comic strips, either); but for its "The Week in Review" section on Sunday it reprints the work of cartoonists on other papers.

Most newspapers allow on their editorial pages the work of syndicated columnists whose points of view may be antithetical to their own. But editors want their editorial cartoonists to preach the same dogma they preach, probably because they feel readers identify the editorial cartoon with the staff-written editorials. Occasionally, an editorial cartoonist disagrees with his paper's editorial stand—with its endorsement of political candidates, for instance; in that case, the cartoonist does his work on some other subject or maybe, as the Washington *Post*'s Herblock has done, takes a vacation during the campaign.

"Quite obviously, no newspaper can operate under a system of anarchy," says Arthur B. Poinier, editorial cartoonist for the Detroit *News*. "The cartoonist is a member of a team. If he is not in basic agreement with the fundamental premises upon which the paper's policy is built, he should be working somewhere else, and he has no right to demand that his paper print cartoons which violently oppose the paper's own policies."[31]

[30] Macmillan, New York, 1968.
[31] Arthur B. Poinier, "The Editorial Cartoon," letter to the editor of *Editor & Publisher*, May 3, 1969, p. 7.

The idea

Some of his fellow journalists get the impression that the editorial cartoonist just knocks out a cartoon and he's free for the day. Not so, says Karl Hubenthal, editorial cartoonist for the Los Angeles *Herald-Examiner*. "Four hours of think time and four hours of drawing is the general work pattern. Add to that the hours of reading, researching and waiting for editors to get off the phone, and you have a full work day by anyone's standards."[32]

The editorial cartoonist works with the editorial writers like this: he sits in on their daily editorial conference, and, knowing then what subjects the editorials will tackle and what stands they'll take, he works up several rough sketches of ideas. The editor looks them over and picks the one he thinks shows the most promise, and the cartoonist does a finished drawing. His cartoon appears in the paper the next day.

Editors and editorial writers seldom supply the idea itself. "It's been my experience," says Hubenthal, "that editors are much too literal-minded to be good idea sources. When one suggests 10,000 Chinese crossing the Viet Nam border, he actually means draw 10,000 Chinamen all marching. It doesn't occur to him that one big figure would tell the same story and be more effective doing it."[33] And be a lot easier to draw.

What editors sometimes forget is that the editorial cartoon is a figure of speech in graphic form. It does not make its point directly; instead it resorts to analogy.

Let's say the cartoonist wants to show that the oil interests, thriving on their special depletion allowance, are not acting in the best interests of the country. He can't very conveniently draw them "not acting in the best interests." How could he? So he puts a fat man in an oculist's office, sits him down right in front of an eye chart, and labels him "Oil Interests." The first line on the eye chart is a big dollar sign. "Oil Interests" is looking at that and smiling. The second line, almost as big, is "U.S. Welfare." A worried Uncle

---

[32] Karl Hubenthal, "Editorial Cartoons: The Role They Play in a Modern Paper," *California Publisher*, September, 1965, p. 22.
[33] *Ibid.*, p. 23.

Sam points to it and asks "Oil Interests": "Can you see the second line at all?" (A Herblock cartoon.)

Putting the idea across

Editorial cartoonists use labels to make their analogies and captions outside the cartoon to hammer home the point. They seldom use balloons any more inside the drawing.

The caption can be either (1) the cartoonist's comment about the cartoon, further explaining it (often unnecessarily) or (2) a bit of conversation coming from one of the characters in the cartoon, in which case quotation marks are added. The conversation caption is more popular these days and is evidence of the effect of gag cartoons on editorial cartoons.

Sometimes the idea is so natural and appropriate it needs no explanation. The cartoonist doesn't bother with labels or caption. Mauldin's famous obit cartoon on the assassination of President Kennedy serves as an example. It simply showed the Lincoln Memorial's statue of Lincoln, another martyred president, with his head bowed.[34]

As an aid to quick communication, the editorial cartoonist has developed a varied array of symbols, and every newspaper reader by this time understands them. The most familiar is the gangly, bewhiskered character called Uncle Sam, by now so outdated that some cartoonists, including Bill Mauldin, no longer use him. Scholars think Uncle Sam is the original Samuel Wilson (nickname: Uncle Sam) of Troy, N.Y., who, during the war of 1812, furnished beef and other supplies to the government. About as familiar are the elephant and donkey, symbols of the Republican and Democratic parties either invented or resurrected by Thomas Nast.

Caricature, of course, is another important tool of the editorial cartoonist, and it is another term in journalism likely to give the student trouble. Originally, it was the word for what we today call the "editorial cartoon." Librarians still file books dealing with cartooning under the heading "caricature." To most cartoonists,

---

[34] Raymond B. Rajski collected most of the Kennedy obit cartoons in *A Nation Grieved,* Charles E. Tuttle Company, Rutland, Vermont, 1967, but he didn't include Mauldin's, probably because he couldn't get permission to reprint it.

however, "caricature" is only that part of the cartoon that shows a figure and face so exaggerated that it makes the subject hideous; yet you can at once recognize him. Before the days of photo-journalism and television, a cartoonist found it necessary to put a label on each figure telling who he was, even though the caricature was right on target. Now, provided the cartoonist is good enough, he doesn't have to label; everybody has seen photographs of the person caricatured and recognizes him.

Generally speaking, the more amateurish the editorial cartoonist, the more labels he uses. Bill Mauldin and Jim Berry—the latter of the Newspaper Enterprise Association—are two editorial cartoonists who work almost entirely independent of labeling.

But even when the idea is sound and the labels clear, readers are likely to miss the point. LeRoy M. Carl, assistant professor of journalism at Temple University, found in a survey of readers in three northeastern cities, that a substantial majority read entirely different meanings into cartoons from what the cartoonists intended. One cartoon showed "Jim Crow" blackbirds flying north. More persons thought it meant "northern migration of Negroes" than thought it meant "increased northern bigotry." Commented Professor Carl: "The assumption has been made by many that editorial cartoons are easy to understand—easier than the written word. Some of the cartoonists . . . have indicated a complete unawareness of the communications barriers between them and their public."[35]

Cartoons then and now

Nostalgia, someone has said, is not as good as it used to be. Take the editorial cartoon. Some of us remember it as a vital force in American life. We remember—or at least we have been told—that editorial cartoons like those of Thomas Nast and Homer Davenport could bring robber barons to their knees and change the fortunes of political administrations. They *said* something, those cartoons, at least those that survived to be reprinted in the history books. "But," says Karl Hubenthal, "look at their daily output over the years and you will be absolutely astonished at the stacks of puerile pap they [early editorial cartoonists] ground out . . . every

[35] LeRoy M. Carl, "Editorial Cartoons Fail to Reach Many Readers," *Journalism Quarterly*, Autumn, 1968, p. 535.

one of them. There is a greater percentage of really good cartoonists working in this country today and a lesser percentage of trite cartoons being produced than at any time in the history of journalism."[36]

Perhaps. But if the examples from 140 editorial cartoonists gathered together by John Chase as a project for the Association of Editorial Cartoonists[37] is representative, one wonders whether Karl Hubenthal might be engaging in a bit of hyperbole. The examples, without meaning to, show that what passes for editorial cartoons are in the main banal and predictable. Of course, Chase's book came out in 1962. Some press scholars since then have noted a renaissance in editorial cartooning, citing a number of younger artists moving in to take their places beside Herblock and Mauldin. Still, the editorial cartoonist's function "is not to produce masterpieces for all eternity (although an occasional classic is inevitable) but to make a brief, effective impression on public opinion, and then to pass on to the next day's work."[38]

The reader should expect in the work of some of the lesser editorial cartoonists an amateurishness not found in gag cartoons and comic strips. While the gag cartoonist must crack a national market where competition, we have seen, is stiff, and the comic strip artist earns his berth with his syndicate either because he is something of a genius or because he has endured a grueling weeding out process, the editorial cartoonist represents local talent. Nor does the editorial cartoonist earn the money of the comic strip artist.

Some of the editorial cartoonists working for newspapers have made arrangements to have their work syndicated, among them Herblock, Mauldin, Paul Conrad of the Los Angeles *Times*, Hugh Haynie of the Louisville *Courier-Journal*, and Pat Oliphant of the Denver *Post*. A few editorial cartoonists work directly with the syndicates.

If the editorial cartoon is not so effective as it was at the turn of the century it may be because its setting has changed. Then little else competed for the reader's attention: no radio squawked, no television blared. Films were in their infancy. Magazines did not dazzle the reader with their pictorial excellence. In those days, the

---

[36] Karl Hubenthal, *op. cit.*, p. 29.
[37] See *Today's Cartoon*, The Hauser Press, New Orleans, 1962.
[38] Stephen Becker, *op. cit.*, pp. 112–113.

cartoonist could afford to clutter his drawing with many labels, much shading, many asides. He covered a lot of ground. He knew his readers would not just glance at his work; they would study it and talk about it over their morning coffee.

Today the editorial cartoonist must make his point quickly, almost as a billboard does a selling job on the passing motorist. The reader can't be bothered with more than a quick glance. Actually, simplification of the cartoon, with the cartoonist using broad brush and crayon strokes rather than fine pen shading and stripping the cartoon of its labels, has, in some observers' opinion, improved the cartoon. Strength and simplicity are what set Herblock and Mauldin apart from other cartoonists. "People say there aren't many good political cartoonists anymore, and that's true," observes Al Capp, "but two of the few we have—Herblock and Bill Mauldin—are better than any *ever* were."[39]

---

[39] The reader who does not see Herblock's and Mauldin's work can refer to the many collections available. By Herbert Block: *The Herblock Book, Herblock's Here and Now, Herblock's Special for Today, Straight Herblock,* and *The Herblock Gallery.* By William H. Mauldin: *What's Got Your Back Up?, I've Decided I Want My Seat Back,* and *Some Day, My Boy, This Will Will All Be Yours.* Two earlier Mauldin books feature his war cartoons.

CHAPTER TEN

The slicks

The word "magazine," from the French *magasin*, means "store." The place where explosives are kept aboard ship, the cartridge chamber of a gun, the flat metal container for Linotype matrices— these are magazines. The early magazines of journalism (*Gentleman's Magazine* in England in 1731 was probably the first publication to use the term in its title) were "stores" containing essays, stories, reviews, news, poems, and other items to delight and instruct the reader.

Editors refer to their magazines as "books," and indeed magazines enjoy a close alliance with the book publishing industry. Some of the early quality magazines—like *Harper's Weekly* and *Harper's Magazine*—were by-products of book publishers. That influential and irreverent magazine of the 1920s, *American Mercury*, was published by the book publisher Alfred A. Knopf. Lately, a number of magazine publishers have gone into book publishing: Time-Life, for instance, and Cowles Communications (publishers of *Look*). Whether or not a magazine is owned by a book publisher, or owns a book publishing firm, its stories or articles often end up in book form.

Example: Truman Capote's celebrated "non-fiction novel," *In Cold Blood*, was written in installments for *The New Yorker* and published later by Random House.

And magazines have some qualities in common with newspapers. Like newspapers, magazines inform readers as well as guide and entertain them. Until the coming of TV, in the more general magazines the entertainment function predominated. At one time the ratio of fiction to nonfiction was five to one. Now the reverse is true. Newspapers have competed with magazines by launching magazines of their own. Outstanding is the Sunday magazine section of the New York *Times*, which uses national and international news as a peg on which to hang its articles. *West*, the locally edited magazine of the Los Angeles *Times*, comes close to matching its eastern counterpart in quality, but *West* is more oriented to the local scene. Keeping newspapers on their toes are some 60 independent city magazines, like *Philadelphia, Washingtonian, San Diego*, and *Los Angeles*—magazines of controversy for an intelligent and high income minority. Included in the Sunday editions of some newspapers are national syndicated magazine sections, like *Parade* and *Family Weekly*.[1]

Magazines differ from newspapers in that everything in a single issue must appeal to every reader. A typical issue may have only half a dozen stories and articles; if just one of them is beyond his interest, the reader is likely to feel cheated. A newspaper, with its hundreds of items daily, can run any number of them for the benefit of only a few readers.

It is impossible to count all the magazines published. "In America, it appears, if three or more people get together their first act is to form a committee and their second is to launch a publication; generally it is a magazine," observes Prof. Roland E. Wolseley of Syracuse University.[2] No subject is too esoteric. Calvin Trillin, tongue in cheek, in a review in *Life* (May 30, 1969) claimed he was coeditor of *Beautiful Spot, a Magazine of Parking*. If by "magazines" we mean bound publications (distinguishing them from newspapers) of eight or more pages issued on a regular basis

[1] Following the death of *This Week* in late 1969, *Parade*'s circulation jumped to more than 16,000,000, crowding *Reader's Digest*.

[2] Roland E. Wolseley, "The American Periodical Press and Its Impact," *Gazette*, Vol. 15, No. 1, 1969, p. 3.

(weekly, biweekly, monthly, bimonthly, or quarterly), an estimate of 20,000 in this country alone seems reasonable. No one directory—not even N. W. Ayer & Son's *Directory of Newspapers and Periodicals*—lists them all, no one trade organization represents them all.

The Magazine Advertising Bureau, which is concerned with magazines of a general nature, says, on the average, 87 copies of magazines reach each American home each year. Broadly speaking, the better a person's education, the more magazines he reads. A college graduate buys or subscribes to twice as many magazines as a high school graduate, four and a half times as many as a man with only a grade school education.

One way to consider magazines is to separate them into *general circulation* and *specialized* categories. Under *specialized* go the professional and trade journals (like the *Journal of the American Medical Association* and *Iron Age*) which contain largely news, advice, and reports of research; the company magazines (like *Ford Times* and *Caterpillar World*) designed to do a public relations job either for employees or outsiders, or both; the struggling literary quarterlies; the journals of opinion; magazines for hobbyists—the list is endless. It is hard to imagine an area of interest that does not have its own magazine.[3]

The smaller magazines force the bigger magazines to upgrade content. A few of the company magazines, for instance, are more brilliantly edited, more handsomely produced than most of the slicks. *Kaiser News* is one. Prentice-Hall, the book publisher, in 1967 brought out the highly praised volume, *The Dynamics of Change*, which was a compilation of materials from six issues of the magazine. *Lithopinion*, a quarterly published by Local One, Amalgamated Lithographers of America, is another house organ of awesome quality. Unfortunately, the ordinary reader does not have access to these magazines.

This chapter deals primarily with *general circulation* magazines (or "slicks"), few in number compared to specialized magazines but high in total circulation. They go out on a subscription basis, but, unlike specialized magazines, they also sell on newsstands. Such sales are important, because advertisers feel that people who buy single copies of a magazine are more responsive—at least to adver-

[3] See James L. C. Ford, *Magazines for Millions: The Story of Specialized Publications*, Southern Illinois University Press, Carbondale, Ill., 1969.

tising—than people who get the magazine delivered to them. One promotional campaign points out to media buyers in advertising agencies that the reader of *Family Circle* has got to go out of her way to get the magazine. The implication is that while she is out, she buys; and having bought the magazine, she'll read it when she gets home.

Note the distinction between *circulation* and *readership*. *Circulation* figures are clearly measurable: the number of copies sold either through subscription or on the newsstand. The figures are watched over by the Audit Bureau of Circulations, an organization set up by advertisers, agencies, and the media to keep circulation claims honest. Magazines further try to measure—though these figures are less reliable—the *readership*, which presumably is always higher. A copy gets passed along in a family or to friends and neighbors. Two, three, or more persons read each copy.

Magazines make some attempt to measure, too, the *amount of time* each reader spends with the magazine. Claims by magazines in this area amused the late Charles W. Morton, himself a magazine editor and writer. He didn't think reader time could be measured; but even if it could, what would it prove? He said, "The question of whether Magazine X possesses unusually slow readers or is offering unusually slow reading matter is not dealt with, but meanwhile chalk up another coup for Magazine X."

Impact of magazines

While it is impossible to measure precisely the impact of magazines on our society, it seems reasonable to conclude that the impact, at least on the middle classes, has been substantial. Looking back on magazine development, Theodore Peterson of the University of Illinois concludes that, as an editorial medium, magazines were "inclined to perpetuate the ideological status quo."[4] As an advertising medium, they "played a significant part in raising the material standard of living in the twentieth century."[5] Major magazines gave readers pretty much what they wanted, Peterson observes, skirting controversial issues so as not to offend either

[4] Theodore Peterson, *Magazines in the Twentieth Century*, 2nd ed., University of Illinois Press, Urbana, 1964, p. 445.
[5] *Ibid.*, pp. 442, 443.

readers or advertisers. They left experimentation to the little magazines, who had less to lose.

The big magazines were, in Peterson's phrasing, "highly imitative." When a subject caught on, all the magazines came forward
with their versions. They had an almost naive faith in the advances
of science. They preached the line that *anybody* can do *anything*,
provided he uses the appropriate techniques. The women's magazines provided the illusion that complete fulfillment was guaranteed
for those who are married.

Yet some of these magazines operated some of the time in the
vanguard of public opinion. The big, national magazines led the
way toward social reforms shortly after the turn of the century.
The "muckrakers," as they were called, pressed for honest government, better regulation of industry, safer food processing, and other
measures. In his *Magazines in the Twentieth Century* (pp. 448–
451) Peterson draws up a list of seven contributions made by magazines.

1. Magazines in the twentieth century were responsible "in some
measure" for social and political reforms.

Peterson gives credit to a 1959 *Saturday Review* article for
moving the Federal Trade Commission to file a complaint against
a pharmaceutical company for some of its advertising and for the
resignation of a Food and Drug Administration executive. James
Playsted Wood in *Of Lasting Interest* points out that a series of
Reader's Digest articles by Lois Mattox Miller and James Monahan
in the 1950s first alerted Americans to a possible link between
cigarettes and cancer. Robert Root in his *Modern Magazine Editing*
offers some evidence that a *Saturday Evening Post* article played
a major role in President Johnson's decision to start his "War
on Poverty," and an article by William Styron in *Esquire* prompted
a Connecticut legislator to introduce and help pass a new law
on capital punishment. *Newsweek* (Aug. 19, 1968) acknowledged
that Missouri Senator Edward V. Long's 1968 primary defeat was
"generally ascribed to the impact of a series of *Life* magazine
articles. . . ."

2. They put issues and events into perspective, adding a dimension not offered by the newspapers.

3. They fostered "a sense of national community." They created
a bond among peoples. For instance, they made the techniques of

southern cooking nationally known; they helped spread the idea of ranch-type houses from the West eastward.

4. They provided low-cost entertainment, from stories in the pulp magazines to stories in quality magazines by important and thoughtful writers.

5. They offered instruction in the art of daily living: how to raise children, decorate the home, etc.

6. They provided education in man's cultural heritage. They explored the past through historical articles and biography. They helped us better appreciate art. Peterson reserves special praise here for *Life*. "*Life* alone was perhaps the greatest disseminator of art that mankind had ever known."[6]

7. Magazines brought variety to the lives of readers. Each magazine sought out its own audience and tried to serve it with special interest articles. ". . . The typical magazine was not edited for just 'everybody'." This gave readers innumerable choices at the news-stand.

Magazines and Madison Avenue

Magazines in the United States date from Andrew Bradford's *American Magazine* (it lasted three months) and Benjamin Franklin's *General Magazine* (it lasted a little longer: six months), both started in January, 1741. Not many of the early ones survived. The impetus for magazines came in the next century with the development of high-speed presses and, more important, a rapid, long-haul transportation system to provide nationwide marketing of brand-name products. The Congress, to encourage dissemination of knowledge, gave magazines an added boost when it passed on March 3, 1879, the act that set up cheap second-class rates for periodicals.

Advertising agencies refer to general circulation magazines as *consumer publications* because of their singular importance as vehicles through which makers of popular products can reach consumers and potential consumers with appeals to buy. Such magazines exist, it is fair to say, *primarily* because they are excellent advertising media. Without revenue from advertising, these publications, with their high production costs, would have to price themselves right out of business. What subscriber would be willing to

[6] *Ibid.*, p. 450.

pay $30 or more for his subscription, say, to *Look?* Advertising agencies, then, through their decision as to which ones will deliver the most responsive audiences to their clients, largely decide which magazines shall survive and which shall die. To name some of the recent expendables: *Country Gentleman, Pathfinder, Household,* the original *Coronet, Collier's, American Magazine, Woman's Home Companion, American Boy,* the original *Show, Show Business Illustrated, The Reporter, The Saturday Evening Post.*

Advertising agencies also determine how big a particular issue shall be. To make a profit, a general circulation magazine should be about two-thirds advertising. Anything less than one-half is dangerous. Just before Christmas, issues are fat because advertisers want in on the consumer buying-spree. Immediately after Christmas and in mid-summer the issues are thin; it really doesn't pay to publish. Indeed, some magazines double up on issues then.

To better serve the advertisers, magazines in recent years have gone in for *regional* and *demographic* editions. Now it is possible for an advertiser to buy space in only those copies that go to certain parts of the country—to advertise *regionally.* It is also possible in some magazines to advertise only to certain *classes* or *professions. Time,* for instance, has four demographic editions: one going to doctors and dentists, one going to students, one to teachers, one to businessmen. This means an advertiser of a specialized product can pay a lower rate and reach only persons who clearly are interested in the product. In most cases, it is only the advertising that is different in regional or demographic editions; but a few of the magazines also change editorial content.

Magazines offer a further service to advertisers: split runs, by which it is possible for an advertiser to run two different ads in a single issue in order to determine by counting coupon returns or through some other procedure which ad is the more effective. Magazines also offer advertisers certain merchandising services, such as "seals of approval," reprints of ads in attractive poster or brochure form, and dial-a-number information on where advertised merchandise can be purchased.

The big ones: weeklies and biweeklies

When *The Saturday Evening Post* announced in 1968 that it was cutting its 6.8 million circulation by more than half, readers not familiar with the economics of journalism could only shake their heads in disbelief. Why would a magazine want to do it? Wasn't a magazine's main function to build a huge circulation so it could charge high rates to advertisers? What about the circulation wars of the 1950s, when magazines, competing with television for mass audiences, cajoled, begged, twisted arms, and made sweet deals to gain more and more subscribers, when their circulations went up from three to five to eight million and beyond?

The truth was that the *Post* had been unable to match the circulations of *Life* and *Look* (each with about eight million). Nor were advertisers willing to go with an also-ran when for just a few dollars more they could buy space in the bigger books. The *Post* had to move in some other direction.

What the *Post* action really showed was that the magazine world had undergone a rather dramatic change. The age of specialization had caught up with it. There had always been specialized magazines, of course (the trade journals, religious magazines, science magazines, literary quarterlies, etc.); but now even *general circulation* magazines were operating in narrower fields, digging deep rather than wide. They were appealing to readers with similar, intense interests. Readers wanted such treatment. More important, advertisers demanded it.

The *Post*, after decades of domination over middle-class America, could not, in mid-twentieth century, adjust to a new society.[7] It revolutionized itself, both in content and format, in the early 1960s; but the change only alienated a hard-core, old-line following without convincing advertisers and younger readers that the magazine mattered. So now the *Post* was dropping all pretenses of serving everybody; it was directing itself to a select group of "with it" readers. "Our circulation is at an all-time low" bragged the magazine in one of its ads to advertising agencies. "Why? Because *The Saturday Evening Post* has made a publishing decision based squarely on marketing considerations. By reducing circulation, *The Saturday Evening Post* now delivers the better part of 3,000,000 customer-families precisely in the A and B markets where advertisers account for the bulk of their sales."

Essentially it bought off rural and small-town subscribers by

[7] *The Saturday Evening Post* claimed Benjamin Franklin as its founder, but magazine historian Frank Luther Mott showed the claim was far-fetched.

switching them to other magazines, giving them refunds, or not inviting them to resubscribe. It was not the first time a magazine had voluntarily given up readers. *Farm Journal* earlier had pruned its nonfarm subscribers because implement manufacturers and others felt they were wasting their money advertising to them. *True Confessions* and *Motion Picture* eliminated all regular subscribers to go strictly to newsstand circulation. But, because it was such an important American institution for so many years, the *Post* move stirred the country. In one of his columns Art Buchwald dealt with an imaginary family whose subscription was cancelled. "If this gets out we'll be ruined," cried the man of the house, a lawyer. "They seemed like such nice people," one of the neighbors remarked later. The bank refused the man a loan; the gasoline company failed to renew his credit card; clients deserted him. His child came home from school with the tale: "They said my father was a *Saturday Evening Post* deadbeat." The family at last moved to another town and resubscribed under a different name, but the father lived in fear he would one day be found out. Observed Buchwald: "When you're dropped by the *Saturday Evening Post*, you have no choice but to live a lie for the rest of your life."

But the *Post*'s attempt to change from a mass to a class magazine came too late, and with its Feb. 8, 1969 issue the magazine gave up. "The *Post*'s frenzy of rejuvenation was really a dance of death," observed *Time*. Stewart Alsop, who had left the *Post* when he saw it dying, observed in a column in *Newsweek:* "It was television that killed the *Post*, though television had a good many willing little helpers, in and out of the Curtis Publishing Co."[8]

Its remaining circulation went over mostly to *Life*, which then surged ahead of *Look*, but *Life* was having problems of its own.

The Wall Street Journal on April 15, 1969 reported that hard times had come to Time, Inc.—especially to *Life*. Circulation was still impressive, but ad linage was down. Jerome S. Hardy, *Life* publisher, said: "We have to get a hell of a lot more competitive. . . ." The magazine gradually became more the muckraker; it

---

[8] For insiders' looks at the last days of *The Saturday Evening Post* see Otto Friedrich's *Decline and Fall*, Harper & Row, New York, 1970; Matthew J. Culligan's *The Curtis-Culligan Story*, Crown Publishers, New York, 1970; and Martin S. Ackerman's *The Curtis Affair*, Nash Publishing, Los Angeles, 1970. See also the novel by Clay Blair, Jr.: *The Board Room*, E. P. Dutton & Co., New York, 1969.

even became somewhat anti-Establishment. With more book, play, and film reviews, it became more culture-oriented. George Hunt, then managing editor, said: "The mass media today is TV; *Life* is a select magazine."

It was *Life* that exposed the Mafia in a series of hard-hitting, well-researched articles. It was *Life* that uncovered Supreme Court Justice Abe Fortas's questionable association with the Wolfson Foundation. It was *Life* that brought to the public's attention the misuse of political contributions by Ohio Governor James A. Rhodes. "It occurs to us," editorialized the Washington *Post* on May 5, 1969, "that *Life* is performing a service of the highest order. . . ." Yet the magazine still saw fit (November 7, 1969) to devote a cover and inside feature to disproving a rumor that one of the Beatles was dead and, a little earlier, to run a feature reenacting Jackie Kennedy's encounter with a photographer (did she use judo on him—or did he slip and fall?).

Meanwhile, *Look*, a biweekly that had edged ahead of *Life* in the 1960s with its more sophisticated dress and its more sensational features, like the excerpts from William Manchester's *Death of a President*, was doing some muckraking of its own. In its September 23, 1969 issue it ran an article linking San Francisco's Mayor Joseph Alioto to the Mafia.

In an ad directed to media buyers in advertising agencies, *Look*, earlier in the year, had said proudly that "Whys guys finish last." "You can tell at a glance *what* is happening," the ad said. "But it takes a lot longer to find out *why* it's happening. This is why *Look* gets extra attention. Virtually alone among major media, *Look* focuses on the important reasons behind major events and trends. As a result, readers spend twice as much time with an issue of *Look* as they do with the next magazine in the field—which is *what*-oriented." The "next magazine in the field" was, of course, *Life*, although the ad didn't actually name the magazine. Media buyers would know.

But the distinction is overdrawn. The two magazines are more alike than their overzealous space salesmen will admit. Both were born in the mid-1930s, although there had been an earlier *Life*, a snobbish humor magazine for the upper classes. The new *Life* (the Henry Luce organization picked up only the name) was supposed to be a sort of illustrated *Time*, and even today, issued more frequently than *Look*, it is news oriented. *Look* deteriorated into a sort of barber-shop peep show in the 1940s, but began a remarkable climb after World War II.

Life tends to stress the sciences and history, *Look* the social sciences and some of the areas covered by women's magazines. But it would be impossible to look at a hard-hitting manuscript with great political or social impact, and say, categorically, "This is a *Life* article," or "This is a *Look* article." Each magazine comes up frequently with a blockbuster, either of its own development or from the pages of a to-be-published book.

Life has greatly influenced the development of photojournalism; what it has done with photography has been widely imitated by other magazines. Its format was adopted by *Ebony*, started in the mid-1940s "to emphasize the brighter side of Negro life and success." *Look*, especially since Allen Hurlburt took over as art director (he has since moved to a higher executive position with Cowles Communications, *Look*'s publisher), has greatly influenced the design of other magazines, especially their typography.

In 1970 *Look* cut its circulation to 6,500,000 to concentrate on the 60 most profitable urban markets. "The numbers game is over," said Gardner Cowles, chairman of Cowles Communications. "Goodbye, *Look*, Good luck wherever you go . . . ," said *Grit* in a two-page ad in *Advertising Age. Grit* suggested that it was the only general publication still edited for rural readers—people who make up "over 20 percent of the national market."

In early 1971 *Life* also cut its circulation. Among major magazines only *Reader's Digest* seemed to talk big numbers.

In a class by itself: Reader's Digest

With its 18,000,000 circulation (this does not include foreign editions) *Reader's Digest* ranks as the largest of all U.S. magazines. James Playsted Wood in *Of Lasting Interest* calls it ". . . possibly the most influential magazine in the world."

Started in 1922 by DeWitt Wallace and his wife under the most austere conditions, the *Digest* grew rapidly, inspiring many imitators. But few lasted long enough to give the *Digest* any serious competition.

DeWitt Wallace's original idea was to take articles from other magazines, boil them down, and present them—about 30 each issue—in a simple, convenient format. Gradually, as some magazines began withholding reprint rights and Wallace found too few articles coinciding with his own rather conservative ideals, he began developing articles on his own, "planting" them in other publications, and then picking them up for reprinting. Then the magazine started running originals along with the reprints.

The magazine does not now fit fully the "digest" designation. One of the nation's most attractive if hard-to-crack markets for free-lance writers, the *Digest* is swamped with contributions. For one department alone, the "First Person" story, editors go through an average of 1,900 manuscripts a month.

One of the best-known articles ever published anywhere was a *Digest* original that Wallace assigned to J. C. Furnas in 1935. "—And Sudden Death," with its vivid descriptions of mangled bodies and twisted automobiles, made a strong plea for safe driving. Reprints went out everywhere. Probably no other magazine article had been so widely promoted. In updated versions, the article continues to appear from time to time in other publications.

Middle America's renewed interest in the flag, used as a protest against the protesters, could be traced to the *Reader's Digest*. The February, 1969 issue included a stick-on flag and an invitation to use it on car and home windows. The magazine, in answer to requests, distributed another 50,000,000 flags following the initial press run of 18,000,000.[9]

Up until the 1950s, the magazine was able to get along without advertising. Today, as an advertising medium, the *Digest* ranks high. People generally not only have faith in the *Digest* itself; they have faith in its advertising. What misgivings Madison Avenue has about the magazine center on the age level of its readers, who fall mainly in the over-50 category.

In *Little Wonder,* an amusing and disrespectful book about the *Digest,* John Bainbridge cited three reasons for the success of the magazine:

1. The articles are simple. Any high school student can understand them.

2. They are dogmatic. Bainbridge, in 1948, when he wrote the

[9] "Ensign of Reassurance," *Time*, July 11, 1969, p. 17.

book, suggested the dogma was becoming more pronounced. He cited someone as saying the *Digest* was suffering from "hardening of the articles."

3. The articles are optimistic. *Through science and hard work, we can solve any problem* is a recurring theme.

David Oglivy, the advertising man who put an eyepatch on the man in the Hathaway shirt, has praised the *Digest* for its mastery of the technique "to present complicated subjects in a way that engages the reader." He calls the magazine a crusader. "They [the editors] crusade against cigarettes, which kill people. They crusade against billboards, which make the world hideous. They crusade against boxing, which turns men into vegetables. They crusade against pornography. They crusade for integration, for inter-faith movement, for the Public Defender system, for human freedom in all its forms."

He adds: "Some highbrows may look down their noses at the *Digest*, charging it with superficiality and over-simplification. There is a modicum of justice in this charge; you can learn more about the Congo if you read about it in *Foreign Affairs Quarterly*. But have you time?"

The popularity of the magazine does not extend to intellectuals who, able to side with the magazine on some of these crusades, nevertheless distrust it, partly because they prefer all articles in their original form[10] but mainly because they detect a bias against, among other things, government programs to solve social and economic problems. And of course they do not accept Oglivy's contention that complicated issues can be explained, successfully, in simple terms.

The quality magazines

The authors of this book acknowledge readily that much material of quality appears on the pages of the big slicks. With all their resources, *Life* and the others offer readers some of the best-re-

[10] Interestingly, the intellectual who ridicules a *Reader's Digest* reader for settling for a digested version of a magazine article may himself settle for a review of a book and quote from that review, never bothering to read the book itself. Starting in late 1969, intellectuals had their own *Intellectual Digest* covering 300 publications like *Antioch Review* and *American Scholar*. Its editors promised "Many of the articles will be published in full."

searched, best-illustrated, most worthwhile, most brilliantly written articles on both historical and contemporary subjects available anywhere. This section puts certain other magazines under the "quality" heading only because their articles are more consistently significant. At the least, the "quality" magazines appeal to a generally better educated audience.

We start with one that is unique: *The New Yorker*, not edited, as they say, for the lady in Dubuque. Patterned in some respects after the British *Punch* and started in 1923 by Harold Ross as a magazine for The City, *The New Yorker*, after a few years of uncertainty, rose to become one of the most successful magazine properties of all time. And yet, it has purposely held its circulation at about a half a million, 16 times less than that of any of the big ones.[11] But what a select half-million!

For all its affluence, *The New Yorker* has always been a socially conscious publication. And without being stuffy. This is the magazine that regularly gave us such writers as James Thurber, E. B. White, and Robert Benchley. It was one of the first magazines to devote a whole issue to a single subject: John Hersey's story on Hiroshima.

Journalism professors go to the reporting in *The New Yorker* for examples of the art of interviewing at its finest. They like the hard-to-find combination of accuracy and a casual style. English teachers point to the stories, although perhaps not as often now as formerly, as models to go by.

The "profiles" have greatly influenced all magazines in their handling of personality sketches. There is a relaxed quality about them. Writers interview enemies of the subject as well as his friends; and sometimes a writer doesn't interview the subject at all.

The look of the magazine is remarkably subdued. Editorial matter seems to be wrapped around the ads as a means of separating them from each other. Any graphic beauty in the book comes from the full-color ads. This is one reason advertisers are comfortable in *The New Yorker*. They fight no visual competition.

Nor does the magazine have any sacred cows. It ridicules anyone, anything—including its own advertising. Readers seem to

---

11 By the late 1960s *The New Yorker*, threatened by an aggressive and lively newcomer, *New York*, had become more innovative and promotion-minded.

particularly enjoy the cartoons and the back-of-the-book fillers such as "Most Fascinating News Story of the Week," "Words of One Syllable Dept.," and "Our Own Business Directory."[12]

The magazine recently has become more militant. A 1970 editorial on President Nixon's sending of troops into Cambodia sounded like something out of *The Nation* or *The New Republic*.

Two other magazines easily belong in the "quality" category: *Harper's* and *The Atlantic*, similar in content and evenly matched in circulation. They are allied in the sale of advertising space, but they are independent otherwise. Westbrook Pegler used to call them "Doubledome" and "Deepthink."

Harper and Brothers, the book publishing concern, launched a monthly magazine in 1850 to keep its presses busy when they weren't being used to print books and to serve as an advertising medium to sell them. It would be correct to say that *Harper's Magazine* was in its beginnings a house organ (company magazine). *Harper's Weekly*, the illustrated journal featuring the work of Thomas Nast, among others, was launched seven years later.

The monthly publication devoted itself primarily to the work of English authors, as did the parent company, and in those early years the magazine was primarily literary. Only in our century did it change its emphasis to nonfiction.

While *Harper's* is New York-based, *The Atlantic* (founded in 1857) is a Boston magazine, and the New England influence, once marked, is still felt. Also more journalistic now than literary, it remains more concerned with literature and the arts than *Harper's*, which tends somewhat to emphasize the social sciences. Neither magazine is afraid of controversy.

A few years ago Luke E. Hart, a Supreme Knight of the Knights of Columbus, wrote in to *Harper's* to complain about the magazine's using an article by Richard H. Rovere. Hart complained that Rovere had earlier written a book critical of Senator Joseph McCarthy. "A person who could write such a book," he said, "should not be allowed to write anything else for decent people to read. . . . I am

---

[12] The three biographies of Harold Ross tell much about what gave the magazine its unique character: Dale Kramer, *Ross and The New Yorker*, Doubleday & Company, Garden City, N.Y., 1951; James Thurber, *The Years With Ross*, Little, Brown & Co., Boston, 1959; and Jane Grant, *Ross, The New Yorker and Me*, William Morrow & Co., New York, 1968.

going to give serious thought to the question as to whether we should not discontinue entirely the publication of advertising [by the Knights of Columbus] in *Harper's*." Unshaken, the magazine pointed out that "placement of advertising in *Harper's* is decided entirely by the business department" and "advertisers rarely try to influence *Harper's* editorial policy, and never succeed in doing so." The Knights withdrew their advertising from *Harper's,* and the magazine is off the Knights' schedule to this day.

The *Saturday Review of Literature* evolved in 1924 from a literary supplement to the New York *Evening Post*. In 1952, carrying articles on a variety of topics along with its book reviews, the magazine dropped the "of literature" from its name. Of special interest to the readers of this book is the once-a-month special section in the back of the magazine on communications. This could well serve as an up-to-date textbook for a journalism class. The section rotates with sections on music, education, science, and environment.

Magazines by sex

Men have their stag affairs, women their Stanley parties. So why not segregate the magazine audience?

The first newspapers and some of the first magazines did this automatically—by excluding women. Everything was written from the man's point of view. The women couldn't vote, anyway; there was no need to keep them informed or to mold their opinions. Gradually, separate sections evolved in which women found advice on such topics as how to better run the home. In the mid-1800s came their first important magazine: *Godey's Lady's Book,* which, after half a century of eminence, gave way to the *Ladies' Home Journal,* then a Curtis publication. Late in the 1950s, when circulation battles among women's magazines reached a fever pitch, the *Journal* fell behind *McCall's*.

The upsurge of *McCall's* was remarkable. Way behind in the circulation race, in the mid-1950s it had adopted the idea of "Togetherness," attempting to serve the entire family. But this theme, merrily punctured by columnists and cartoonists, soon withered; and a new editor, Herbert Mayes, in 1958 turned the magazine completely around. It took on a new sophistication, both in content and format; soon it was number one among women's magazines. Like *Ladies' Home Journal,* it broadened its interests to include politics and social problems. What magazine paid $1,000,000 for the late Robert Kennedy's manuscript on the Cuban missile crisis? Not *Life* or *Look*; it was *McCall's*.

Not that the women's magazines had completely given up their alliance with trivia. More than other media, they lent dignity to the astrology craze of the late 1960s, treating "as established fact the notion that stars and planets influence people's lives." A *Ladies' Home Journal* article provided, in its words, "a completely original way for you to discover your secret self, and the influence of stars on your life."[13] Several of the women's magazines ran regular horoscopes.[14]

In *The Lady Persuaders* (1960) Helen Woodward documented a case against the women's magazines that they relied rather shamelessly on veiled but sensationalized sex—"sex with a false face," she called it—in the frightening late 1940s (TV was coming on the scene) and the frantic 1950s, with such titles (from the *Ladies' Home Journal*) as these: "Chastity and Syphilis," "I Love My Husband's Best Friend," (doesn't that belong in *True Confessions?*) and "I'm Tempted to Have an Affair." And the magazine had the gall, Helen Woodward wrote, to run this article: "The Smut Peddler Is After Your Child"! She credits *Good Housekeeping* and the grocery store-circulated women's magazines (*Family Circle* and *Woman's Day*) with staying above the battle.

Women's magazines returned to an emphasis on sex at the end of the 1960s, as what magazine did not? As one writer put it:

Even the most casual study of women's magazines—from *Seventeen* at one end of the age scale to *Ladies' Home Journal* at the other—reveals an almost frantic attempt on the part of editors to get with the sexual revolution, the new permissiveness, call it what you will, that manifests itself these days in advertising, motion pictures, television, and best-selling novels with sex and perversion as the themes.[15]

Perhaps the best illustration of this trend was Helen Gurley Brown's *Cosmopolitan*, a magazine which almost wholly gave itself over to sex—for the single girl.

[13] Mervin Block, "Flapdoodle Writ Large: Astrology in Magazines," *Columbia Journalism Review*, Summer, 1969, pp. 51–54.

[14] Newspapers were in on the astrology boom, too. About 1,200 of them ran astrology columns, according to Block.

[15] Peter T. Chew, "Women's Magazines Dig New Ground," *The National Observer*, June 23, 1969, p. 1.

As the women's magazines flourished and as the general audience magazines began devoting more of their space to women, it was inevitable that magazines edited especially for men would appear. In this category we can place the girlie books and the adventure magazines at one end and *Esquire,* unmatched among men's magazines, at the other.

Started during the Depression years as a fashion magazine with literary pretentions, *Esquire* slipped into something flimsy to titillate World War II servicemen; but in the early 1950s it decided, in the words of Publisher Arnold Gingrich, "to buck the juvenile, high schoolish direction we had been following." At first the magazine lost readers, but it also gained back some of its blue-chip advertisers. Today, with more than one-million circulation, *Esquire* ranks among the best magazines in the world for innovation and quality writing, and, with many women readers, it more properly fits the *quality* rather than the *men's* category.

"One of the beauties of the magazine," Gingrich submits, "is its diversity of style. I adhere to an old adage with a personal alteration: 'He who edits least, edits best.' " This makes for a magazine of some inconsistency, but it also attracts important writers who don't like their work tampered with and who are willing to write for *Esquire* at rates that are considerably below what they would get from other magazines.

Like most of the other slicks, *Esquire* has been highly critical of Spiro Agnew, but in May, 1970 the magazine ran an article by Martin Mayer in admiration of the rhetoric of the Vice President.

The covers are always intriguing, and, like so much of the content, boldly irreverent. The article titles differ from those of any other magazine. The editors follow no rules in writing these titles. And space doesn't bother them. Take this one for an article critical of newspapers (*Esquire* often runs articles on the mass media): "The American Newspaper is Neither Record, Mirror, Journal, Ledger, Bulletin, Telegram, Examiner, Register, Chronicle, Gazette, Observer, Monitor, Transcript Nor Herald of the Day's Events. It's Just Bad News." In a lead article about *Esquire, The Wall Street Journal* (May 8, 1968) remarked: "Sometimes, the articles are as good as the titles."

The Wall Street Journal expresses admiration of *Esquire* because, it says, the magazine is "ideologically uncommitted" and therefore "freer than most magazines to support unpopular people and causes and to knock the unknockables."

Like other magazines, *Esquire* has its mundane service features on fashion, travel, food; but these, along with the reviews, are much better than most. Its gimmick features have struck some readers as a bit much, like the "Establishment Charts" showing who's in and who's out. And there is that feature, "The 100 Best People in the World." But perhaps *Esquire* had its tongue in its cheek.

The magazine, along with *New York* and *Village Voice*, has been identified by John Leo, writing in *Commonweal*, as an organ of the "new journalism," in which fiction merges with nonfiction and the writer becomes as much the advocate as he is the journalist. "The author [it might be Tom Wolfe, Rex Reed, Jimmy Breslin, Norman Mailer, or Gay Talese] orchestrates details and scenes like a novelist, heaping up great piles of carefully selected trivia, brandnames and long quotes, driving toward some cosmic sociological point."[16] But if this describes some of what one finds in *Esquire*, it does not describe it all.

Some people consider *Playboy* in a class with *Esquire*, but that is a little like lumping "Dennis the Menace" with "Peanuts." While it is true that *Playboy* has improved since its peeping-Tom start in 1953, it is still basically a well-designed "skin" magazine. It runs some excellent articles and some fiction by well-known writers, and some of its Q. and A. interviews are notable; but take away the girls, and the magazine's impressive six million circulation would soon melt away.

The name of the magazine alone is enough to keep it forever penned in its hedonism. And how can one give serious consideration to a magazine that runs ads for its own products like the one that urges: "Smoke the Pipe That Hef Smokes" or that runs a feature like "The Playboy Adviser"? Sample question: "I was in Philadelphia on business, and I found myself strongly attracted to a girl I met at a cocktail party. I would like to know of it's acceptable to write her and ask for a date." *Playboy* assured the reader it would be all right. Another feature, "The Playboy Forum," prolonged for years a tedious series on "The Playboy Philosophy,"

---

[16] John Leo, "The Life and Times of Gay Talese," *Commonweal*, October 17, 1969, p. 66.

Hefner Had A Magazine

Hefner had a magazine,
  Which first shocked many folks
With color spreads of half-nude girls
  And sort-of-dirty jokes;

But now we're bombed with raunchy filth
  And pornographic swill,
Which makes poor Hefner's magazine
  Seem more like "Jack and Jill"!

Cartoon by Jack Davis. Poem by Frank Jacobs.
From "Mad's Up-Dated Modern Day Mother Goose."
Copyright 1970, *Mad* Magazine,
E. C. Publications, Inc.

which, judging from the response, many otherwise thoughtful people took seriously.

The reader who calls *Playboy* cerebral should read sometime the legend (yes, there *is* one) that accompanies the "Playmate of the Month." Its bromides and platitudes make the movie fan magazines thoughtful by comparison.

With a special subscription rate, *Playboy* has sold some of the clergy, and it gets much mileage out of this. Perhaps by reading *Playboy* and quoting from it a minister can convince people he is "one of the boys."

Not all the clergy is impressed. Kyle Haselden, late editor of the liberal *Christian Century*, felt that *Playboy* was "more obscene and more threatening to authentic morality than is much of what we call pornography . . . because . . . [it] preaches a fundamentally dishonest doctrine of sex, of womanhood, and of the highest good of life."[17] He quoted Ralph A. Cannon as saying that *Playboy* "panders to juvenile fascination with sexual trivia while calling itself sophisticated."

Criticism of *Playboy* has also come from the far left—from *Ramparts*, with Gene Marine making the case (February 1967):

I'm getting damned tired of all art being campy and all plays being queer and all the clothes being West Fourth Street and the whole bit. . . . Probably the ultimate homosexual force in our society . . . and the one whose evolution best demonstrates the shift from a simply male-dominated society toward one that holds its women in faggoty contempt, is *Playboy*, the mass magazine of airbrushed sex. . . . The black-nylon girly magazines at least appeal to male prurient interest in women; *Playboy* invites its child-male readers to spend thousands of dollars on appurtenances and thousands of hours on techniques, for seducing hairless and apparently brainless little girls.

He adds: "I don't want my daughter to grow up thinking that men want a Playmate. I contemplate with horror a world in which her relationship with men will have to be accompanied by hi-fi rituals, the odor of Piping Rock cologne and three paragraphs of the Playboy Philosophy."

---

[17] Kyle Haselden, *Morality and the Mass Media*, Broadman Press, Nashville, Tenn., 1968, p. 106.

The world of sports

While other general circulation magazines have only recently narrowed their focus, sports magazines have tended always to specialize. Baseball, football, boxing—all the major sports have had their own publications. Several publishers tried covering more than one spectator sport in a single magazine, but none of their publications proved durable until Macfadden Publications brought out *Sport* after World War II. Still published, this monthly magazine treats sports heroes much as the old movie fan magazines used to treat the stars. Theodore Peterson has called *Sport's* coverage "worshipful."

By far the most successful of the general sports magazines is *Sports Illustrated*, brought out by Time, Inc. in 1954. A weekly, it appeals to a well-educated, high-income readership. It covers participator as well as spectator sports, and it relates sports to other aspects of life, like fashion and race relations. By 1969 its circulation had approached the 1,800,000 mark.

At least one of the sports magazines that had been specializing began expanding its coverage. *Sporting News*, which had been a weekly baseball magazine, began running stories on other sports. But other sports magazines stuck to their specialty: *Baseball Digest*, *Ring*, *Pro Football Guide*, and *Pro Football Weekly*.

Quarterback differs from the other football magazines by taking on some of the qualities of *Sports Illustrated*, some of *Playboy*, some of *Mad*.[18]

For sportsmen who like to hunt and fish, there are a number of other magazines, some of them localized. And if the sports-minded reader doesn't find enough material in these magazines, he can turn to the major slicks, which still devote many pages to sports activities and personalities. In Washington, D.C., he can turn to *Sportsweek*, a magazine published by the Washington *Star* as part of its Sunday issue.

The newsmagazines

With the idea that in their day-to-day operations newspapers were not able to put the news into proper perspective and that they were

[18] See Frank Reysen, "Sports Publications–The Rush Is On," *Media-Scope*, January, 1970, pp. 42 ff.

too much wedded to the idea of objectivity, Henry Luce and Briton Hadden in 1923 brought out the first issue of *Time*, the weekly newsmagazine.[19] The first issues carried mostly rewritings from the New York *Times* and the wire services, but a saucy if too-cute style freshened the material. Wolcott Gibbs ridiculed *Time*style later in a *New Yorker* piece: "Backward ran sentences until reeled the mind"; and, because its writers could no longer use the style with a straight face, *Time* gave it up. Still, the magazine remained lively and fact-filled.

Dwight Macdonald feels the magazine has an "obsession with factual trivia." "A huge and expensive research department produces a weekly warehouseful of certified, pasteurized, 100 percent double-checked Facts," he says, "and everything is accurate about any given article except its main points." He adds: "As smoking gives us something to do with our hands when we aren't using them, *Time* gives us something to do with our minds when we aren't thinking."

In recent years, *Time* has made moves to respond to charges raised by critics like Dwight Macdonald. It launched its weekly "Time Essay," a well-researched and well-reasoned discussion of current problems. And where it used to crowd 200 different stories in a single issue, it now runs half as many, but runs them in greater depth.

Although the magazine maintains access to wire-service copy and other publications, most of its material now is staff gathered and written. What comes into the New York offices from the various bureaus is pruned, combined with other material, and rewritten, causing some dissatisfaction among its reporters. *Time* gives few bylines. It practices what is known as "group journalism."

"Group journalism" at *Time* results in a consistency of style and a clearly defined point of view. *Time* is more than a "newsmaga-zine"; but this could be said of *Newsweek* and *U.S. News & World Report* too. *Time*'s place on the political spectrum on most matters, at least until recently, was probably just to the right of center. On the Vietnam war issue, until the end of the Johnson administration, *Time* was pretty far over on the right.

In its international news, *Time* has always rooted for the home team. It's proud of American technical achievements. Sometimes it

[19] See John Kobler, *Luce: His Time, Life and Fortune*, Doubleday & Company, Garden City, N.Y., 1968, and Robert T. Elson, *Time, Inc.: The Intimate History of a Publishing Enterprise, 1923–1941*, Atheneum, New York, 1968.

overreacts. In its enthusiasm in reporting the moon landing in 1969 it reviewed the "particular American genius" of the earlier Manhattan Project which brought us the A-bomb. An amused Milton Mayer in *The Progressive* (September, 1969) observed that *Time* failed to inform its readers that "the particular American genius of that splendid achievement was Einstein's, Franck's, Fermi's, and Szilard's, all of them Europeans."

Much has been written of *Time*'s fairness—or lack of it. Certainly it is clear that, with the exception of the Goldwater candidacy in 1964 when all major media went Democratic, Republicans have fared better than Democrats on its pages. Back in the 1940s one man was "Truman's crony" and the same man in the 1950s was "Ike's golfing companion." In one 1956 issue when Eisenhower and Stevenson were making speeches prior to the election, it was "Ike's Promise" on one page and "Adlai's Pitch" on the other. But Republicans have not always been happy with *Time*, for although it has been hawkish on foreign affairs it has been often progressive— too progressive to suit many Republicans—on domestic matters. And the right wing of both parties, especially on the subject of race, has found much to be irritated about on the pages of *Time*.

Apart from any intended bias, the magazine, in its attempt to be readable, resorts to some rather sweeping generalizations, and this lessens respect for it in some quarters. Roland E. Wolseley in his *Understanding Magazines* cited *Time*'s coverage in 1958 of the merger of International News Service into United Press. *Time* said, ". . . on a coronation story, editors could rely on the Associated Press for dimensions of the cathedral, the United Press for the mood of the ceremony, and the International News Service (sometimes) for an interview with the barmaid across the way." Staffers for the dying INS were furious, naturally, especially when *Time* added to the insult by calling the product of INS "splash and dash journalism." Wolseley himself felt this was a "serious" case of "unproved" generalization. Perhaps. But any newspaperman, familiar with the characteristics of the then three wire services, would tend to agree with the appraisal. INS *was* more interested in human interest and sensational aspects of the news and *could not*, because of a limited budget, cover the news fully.

It is a cliché, but probably true, that the magazine's back-of-the-book section is better than the front; in those special departments

Time is less anxious to impose its—the late Mr. Luce's—point of view on readers. Professional people whose fields are covered consider the departments too popular, too simplistic, but the average reader finds them informative.

One of the most successful promotional ideas for any magazine has been *Time*'s "Man of the Year" cover. To watch the build-up for this in the letters column at the close of each year is to watch PR in its finest hour. How so many people could give so much credence to so trivial an event—what a magazine will put on its first cover of the year—is a mystery perhaps even to *Time* itself. Someone has likened *Time*'s handling of the process to a man contemplating his navel.

In true number-two fashion, *Newsweek* has tried harder in recent years, and for once *Time* feels some competition. Until the Washington *Post* bought *Newsweek* in 1961, the magazine was but a pale imitation of *Time:* bland, predictably conservative. "It has come a long, long way since 1957, when I worked there as a part-time proofreader and found the magazine so dull I never even bothered to take home my free copy," writes Sandy Goodman in the *Columbia Journalism Review* (Summer, 1968). But Goodman disputes the claim, made by *Newsweek*, that it, alone among the newsmagazines, "separates fact from opinion." Goodman has counted any number of loaded words in the magazine, and, although he admits he more often than not agrees with its opinions, he says it offers readers "a wise-guyish treatment of personal conviction." At least *Time*, says Goodman, "has avoided making any self-righteous claims to objectivity."

Newsweek is a little to the left of *Time* on the political spectrum. Certainly it identifies more often with the causes of youth. It won the National Magazine Award from Columbia University's School of Journalism for its Nov. 20, 1967 issue on "The Negro in America: What Must Be Done." The announcement of the award said, "The judges considered the project, clearly labeled as a departure from *Newsweek*'s standard policy, to have been skillfully and responsibly executed. They consider it a useful and important form, when sparingly used, in the news magazine field."

Among newsmagazines *Newsweek* pioneered the use of bylines, first for its columnists, then for its reviewers, later for some of its reporters. Where it offers no bylines, it often uses a device like this

Ordinarily, *Newsweek* is on major newsstands each Monday. To report the outcome of the 1968 presidential election, however, the magazine decided to hold up publication that week until Wednesday, when the returns would be in. The cover had to be planned in advance. Obviously, at least two covers had to be ready: one for Richard Nixon, if he won; one for Hubert Humphrey, if he won. But there were other possibilities. Wallace might win. There might be a deadlock, in which case

in the body of a story: ". . . he told *Newsweek*'s Martin Kasindorf. . . ." In one respect it can be said that *Time* is—or was—an editor's magazine, *Newsweek* a writer's magazine.

In 1969 *Newsweek* still trailed *Time* in circulation (2,400,000 to *Time*'s 4,000,000), but it overtook *Time* in number of pages of advertising. It became not only the "hot book"[20] but also the big book. *Time* attempted to change its "tired" image by liberalizing its editorial stance, by being more generous with bylines and getting away somewhat from "group journalism," and by avoiding cuteness while still staying clever. Readers found it less cocksure than before.

"We used to separate the world into villains and heroes," said the new managing editor, Henry Grunwald. "We've learned things aren't that simple."[21] Nor did *Time* any longer play the hawk on Vietnam.

Vastly different from *Time* and *Newsweek* is *U.S. News and*

[20] See article by Chris Welles, "Newsweek (a Fact) Is the New Hot Book (an Opinion)," *Esquire*, November, 1969, pp. 152ff.

[21] A. Kent MacDougall, "Big Publisher Pledges New Projects Despite a Series of Setbacks," *The Wall Street Journal*, April 15, 1969, p. 23.

the House of Representatives would have
to pick the President. And, finally, the
results might be so inconclusive by the
time *Newsweek* went to press that the
magazine couldn't say who won. Planning for every eventuality is a necessary
part of magazine — and newspaper —
publishing.

World Report, content to serve a rather select clientele: business
leaders, especially, and professional people with conservative and
ultraconservative leanings. Published in Washington, D.C., rather
than New York, *USNWR* is particularly interested in the federal
government and its actions as they affect the economy. It does nothing with the arts, theater, movies, or books.

Despite its devotion to conservatism, the magazine enjoys a reputation for objectivity. The reputation is not altogether deserved. Its
stories are written in straightforward newspaper style, yes. But the
reader soon discovers that the stories played up, the angles covered,
tend to make the point that "liberalism" (the magazine likes to put
it in quote marks) and centralization of government are ruining the
country. Alone among major magazines, *USNWR* has represented
the Southern point of view on the subject of integration and Negro
rights.

Editor David Lawrence best articulates what *USNWR* stands for
in his back-page editorial.

The magazine has shown imagination in its use of charts and

"If I may say so, young man, I hardly pegged you for a U.S. News and World Report reader."

Cartoon by Herbert Goldberg. Copyright 1970 by *Sales Management*.

graphs accompanying its stories and articles. Perhaps its most valuable offering each week is a long middle-of-the-book Q. and A. interview with a figure prominent in the news.

Addicts of weekly summaries of the news can also turn to locally edited weekly reviews found in the Sunday issues of major newspapers. These reviews tend to be less biased but also a little duller than *Time* and *Newsweek*. The best of them still is "The Week in Review," part of the New York *Times*. Another good publication is *The National Observer*, a sprightly weekly newspaper put out by the same organization that puts out *The Wall Street Journal*.

Understanding the editorial process

Magazines carefully plan their issues three to six months or longer in advance, conjuring up ideas for articles, assigning them to staffers or regular contributors. But they still rely on ideas and unsolicited articles from freelancers.

Who are the freelancers? They are newspaper reporters who moonlight, college professors who publish lest they perish, novelists between books, housewives who write as a hobby or to supplement the family income, retired persons with time on their hands—all kinds of people. A few—but very few—freelance full time; they are the professionals. The Magazine Publishers Association estimates the number in this latter category at only about 300.

The smaller general circulation magazines, especially, and the trade journals (or business papers, as they are called) rely heavily on freelancers. A freelancer introduces his idea, usually, with a "query" to the editor; if the editor thinks the idea has merit for his magazine, he encourages the writer to go ahead with it. But the writer works "on speculation"; the editor is not obligated to buy the final product. If the article is acceptable, the author gets anywhere from a penny or two up to a dollar or more per word, depending on the magazine and the number of times he's sold to that magazine. The average article for one of the slicks brings the writer $2,000 or $3,000, and for a small magazine, perhaps not more than $50 or $100. Pay goes to the author when the article is accepted. At one time, most authors were paid only "on publication," which could be months later, or maybe not at all if the editor in the meantime changed his mind about the article. Keeping free-lance writers informed on changing market conditions and advising them on techniques are several trade magazines, the most important of which are *Writer's Digest* and *The Writer*, both monthlies.

Sometimes the writer is a public-relations man affiliated with a company that stands to benefit from the publication of the article, but this does not necessarily bother the magazine. It pays him as would any free-lance writer. The magazine realizes that *every* article tends to help certain people or companies and hurt others, no matter by whom it is written; the test is: is the article of interest to the reader? Magazines—and newspapers too—used to edit out any product or company mention, arguing that such mention was really advertising. Now editors generally take a more liberal position; if a character in the story types on an Olivetti, *let* him. "Olivetti" says more than "typewriter." If the criminal escapes in "a black Ford," let him; "a black car" is not nearly so descriptive.

From the reader's standpoint, one of the most disturbing practices in magazine-article writing today is the putting of quotations into the mouths of the interviewees. It came out during one of the libel cases against *The Saturday Evening Post* during its "sophistricated muckraking" days in the early 1960s that one writer simply *made up* quotations because, as he explained, they were quotes that were typical of what the subject might have said. The practice has grown as magazines encourage writers to appropriate fictional techniques for nonfiction pieces. Quotes in newspaper stories are often inaccurate too, but through sloppy reporting, not usually by design.

Any article accepted for publication goes through an editing process. The major magazines employ staffs of researchers (bright young girls from Eastern liberal arts colleges, in the main) who check carefully each name, fact, and quotation. Usually the writer does not see the edited manuscript unless it takes on a different point of view. Nor does he write the title (or "headline" in newspaper parlance) that appears finally over the article.

The editorial department where all this goes on is one of five main departments of a magazine. The others are advertising, circulation, production, and administration. On a large magazine, according to the Magazine Publishers Association, about 8 percent of the budget goes to the editorial department; on a small magazine, about 17 percent.

The writer is Whatshisname

Pity the writer for the confession magazines. The pay is good. But the poor fellow never makes a name for himself. His articles never get bylines.

One good reason: a few professional writers turn out most of the pieces. Confession magazine editors thus cannot afford bylines. Even readers with only confession-magazine mentality would get suspicious after a while if they saw the same name issue after issue. A fellow couldn't have *that* many love tangles.

The confession writer is not alone.

Even the writer of more worthwhile pieces for more significant magazines remains largely anonymous. Who looks at the bylines on magazine articles? Who can name even a half dozen writers of magazine articles?

Yet, as a serious reader, you should note the author's name before you read any article. And you should know something about him. In most magazines you'll find information in a footnote near the article's beginning or on a separate page near the front of the magazine, as in "Backstage with *Esquire*." As you become familiar with an author and his work you can better judge his facts and evaluate his opinion. When you are *very* familiar with his work, you can probably anticipate him, and, if necessary, avoid him.

When you confront a double byline, with a big name accompanied by an "as told to" or "with" followed by another name, you should realize the big name had little to do with the actual writing of the article. In fact, articles with single bylines by prominent political and entertainment figures are in all likelihood "ghost-written." Rare are the Steve Allens who can write as well as perform.

As a researcher taking information from magazines you should make a distinction between *magazine* comment and *writer* comment. There is a difference. If the material appears in the magazine unsigned—without a byline—you can attribute it, correctly, to the magazine itself. If it is signed, you should attribute it to the writer, giving secondary credit to the magazine in which the work appears.

When you are looking for a specific magazine article you can find it by consulting one of the various indexes available in any library. Some indexes cover technical, trade, and other specialized magazines. Some cover more popular magazines. The index most often consulted is *Readers' Guide to Periodical Literature*, published at frequent intervals during the year by the H. W. Wilson Company, New York. *Readers' Guide* lists by both author and subject matter articles appearing in about 160 magazines: most of the major slicks and some of the minor ones, like *Hot Rod*, *Modern Photography*, *Successful Farming*, and *Travel*. *Esquire* is included, but not *Playboy*. Nor is *True*.

From time to time librarians vote on which magazines to include. Making *Readers' Guide* for a magazine is a little like making All-American for an athlete. Some of the opinion magazines are impressed enough about being among the elect that they make mention of the fact in their mastheads.

CHAPTER ELEVEN

Journalism for an elite

At the end of the Civil War an Irish journalist, E. L. Godkin, in America to write about the South and slavery, founded *The Nation*, an independent weekly for intellectuals. An early issue said the magazine intended to "bring to the discussion of political and social questions a really critical spirit, and to wage war upon the vices of violence, exaggeration, and misrepresentation by which so much of the political writing of this day is marred."[1] In 1881 it merged with the New York *Evening Post*. It became an independent magazine again in 1918, a time when political activists and reformers were launching a number of opinion magazines.

The slicks had discovered at the turn of the century that they could increase their circulations by investigating and reporting corruption in government and business. Called "muckrakers" by Theodore Roosevelt, who was something of a "muckraker" himself, the magazines brought some reform and changed the lives of a few industrialists. But within a few years, fattened on their swollen cir-

[1] Quoted by Theodore Peterson in *Magazines in the Twentieth Century*, 2nd ed., University of Illinois Press, Urbana, 1964, p. 419.

culations and increased advertising linage, they moved to safer ground, leaving a void that a number of new magazines moved in to fill. We know these as *opinion magazines*. *The Nation* was their prototype.

Not that opinion magazines have any corner on opinion in journalism. The editorial page is the heart of most newspapers. And general circulation magazines have always offered some opinion to their readers. *The Saturday Evening Post* up until the end had an editorial page, and once it had its own editorial cartoonist. *Life* runs editorials. *Time* runs essays now. Even the articles in magazines like *Life*, *Look*, *Reader's Digest*, and the women's magazines are filled with opinion. But readers do not buy slick magazines for the opinion they carry. They buy them to relax with.

Readers buy opinion magazines so they can agonize over national and world problems. They buy them to reinforce their already rather firmly held convictions.

Some that died

The Masses has been described as "one of the most remarkable ventures in the history of American journalism."[2] Combining art with radical editorials and articles, it claimed to be a magazine for the working man, but it was far too literary for that. Starkly realistic drawings, displayed on its oversize pages, influenced art in other magazines. Irving Howe remembers the magazine for both its "gaiety" and "innocence." Its antidraft stand brought its editors to court, and though they were not convicted, the magazine died in 1918, to be succeeded by the *Liberator*, which became a Communist Party organ in the 1920s. *The New Masses* succeeded the *Liberator*, and it preached a Stalinist line in the 1930s.[3]

The *American Mercury*, a magazine started by George Jean Nathan and H. L. Mencken in the 1920s, similarly attacked middle-class values, but it had less faith in the common people to solve their problems. Condescending, irascible, and highly readable, the maga-

[2] William L. O'Neill, ed., *Echoes of Revolt: The Masses, 1911–1917*, Quadrangle Books, Chicago, 1966, p. 17.

[3] See Joseph North, ed., *New Masses: An Anthology of the Rebel Thirties*, International Publishers, New York, 1969.

zine became a sort of bible on campuses. In 1926 Walter Lippmann called Mencken "the most powerful personal influence on this whole generation of educated people." The *Mercury*'s skepticism turned to reaction in the 1930s, and the magazine lost its following among intellectuals. Today a magazine bearing the same name caters to the ultraright, little noticed outside its small circle of subscribers.

From the standpoint of circulation, *The Reporter*, founded in 1949, was the most successful of all the opinion magazines. A bi-weekly, it sold well and was slick enough to find space on many newsstands. (Other opinion magazines circulate almost entirely by mail.) *The Reporter* was a liberal but strongly anticommunist bi-weekly. Max Ascoli, its founder-editor, strove to make it "objective but not impartial." His was a magazine widely admired for its reporting in depth. One of the early issues, on the "China lobby," created a sensation in Washington. Later issues took too hawkish a line on the Vietnam war to satisfy many of its liberal readers.

While other liberal magazines in the 1960s moved further to the left, *The Reporter* maintained a more traditional liberal stance, siding with President Lyndon Johnson when it was no longer popular among liberals to do so. The magazine lost increasing sums of money, and Ascoli appeared to lose interest in running it, and so with the June 13, 1968 issue he killed it, even though it had a circulation of 210,000, more than any of the other opinion magazines. *Newsweek* quoted him as saying he might have kept the magazine alive if Johnson had remained in the Presidential race.

Of those opinion magazines that survive, most were founded in this century, several after World War II. All live precariously from issue to issue, their rather high subscription rates barely, if that, taking care of their costs. A small amount of advertising, mostly from book publishers, helps some; family fortunes and donations from believers help more. Subscribers are often asked to kick in some additional money to keep their magazine alive. For instance, William Buckley, editor of *National Review*, once wrote to subscribers asking for donations "because a special emergency has arisen. . . . We define a special emergency as one that interrupts our regular emergency."[4]

---

[4] William F. Buckley, Jr., letter to subscribers, February 26, 1964.

What's in an issue

The typical lineup of features includes editorials; letters to the editor; articles; reviews of books, movies and plays; and a few ads. The typical issue contains 32 pages. Some editors like to mask the thinness of their issues by numbering pages consecutively from the first issue to the last issue of the year.

Much of the content originates outside of the staff. The editors write the editorials, but professors, mostly in the social sciences, write many of the articles. Moonlighting journalists write their share. They find here they can be more outspoken, certainly more subjective, than in their newspaper pieces.

Forward-looking as they are in editorial policy, opinion magazines seem to operate under nineteenth-century ideas of format and design. Martin Fox in *Print* has observed they have "the visual appeal of a flight insurance policy." In the 1960s, though, despite their cheap paper and cost-saving printing procedures, a few put on more attractive dress.

What sets opinion magazines apart

Opinion magazines differ from general circulation magazines in the nature—but not necessarily in the subject matter—of their articles. Where general circulation magazine articles are concrete and anecdotal, opinion magazine articles are philosophical and abstract. In contrast to general circulation magazines, opinion magazines tend to be intense and moralistic. For some readers they are dull and pedantic. They discuss politics, social sciences, and, to a lesser extent, the humanities. In some respects, *Harper's, The Atlantic, The New Yorker, Esquire,* and *Saturday Review* belong with the opinion magazines. But their larger circulations, slicker appearance, and stronger dependence on advertising revenue and newsstand sales put them more properly in the "general circulation magazine" category. Besides, they are not so single-minded.

In some respects, quarterly journals like *Partisan Review* belong with opinion magazines. But they are much more devoted to the humanities than are the opinion magazines. Almost none of the opinion magazines run short stories; few run poetry.

Atlas is another magazine that could be put on the list of opinion magazines. Established in 1960, this monthly reprints articles from periodicals in various parts of the world. It always includes a section on what these periodicals think about the United States. *Atlas* took its name from the Titan who held up the heavens. "Our own more modest purpose," says the magazine's masthead, "is to hold the world up to our readers. We frequently do not agree with the ideas and opinions that appear on these pages. But they reflect what the rest of the world is thinking, and it is vitally important for Americans to know what those thoughts are."

An audience greater than it appears

Most of the opinion magazines exist with circulations under 100,000, some with circulations under 20,000. A small daily newspaper does as well, and its circulation is concentrated in one area.

Then why are the magazines influential?

The answer is: because the reader of an opinion magazine typically is an educator, editor, legislator, or clergyman. He passes along what he reads to much larger audiences.

Robert Sherrill, Washington correspondent for *The Nation*, sees the influence of opinion magazines as "probably far less on the younger generation than it is on that thing called 'mass media,' which watches the opinion magazines closely and imitates them and draws coverage from them in approaching touchy topics. . . . Partly because of the example of opinion magazines, the old stuffy monthlies, *Harper's* and *Atlantic*, are no longer stuffy."[5]

What an opinion magazine publishes often makes news. A newsmagazine, network, or wire service, sensing the article has important implications or that a quotation from it is controversial, may give it additional exposure, crediting the source and elaborating upon the article.

Many of the articles in opinion magazines get additional circulation as reprints. Others appear in anthologies. Some go on to become full-length books, their authors having merely tried out their ideas in the opinion magazines.

[5] Robert Sherrill, "Weeklies and Weaklies," *The Antioch Review*, Spring, 1969, p. 42.

And the pass-along readership of these magazines is high. In the case of *The Nation*, one sixth of the circulation goes to libraries.

How effective are they?

They have always been in the vanguard. Carey McWilliams, editor of *The Nation*, has suggested that the opinion journals function as media for "trial balloon" ideas: "When we print it, and the sky doesn't fall, . . . [the mass media] may do something with the same thing."[6]

Professor John H. Schacht of the University of Illinois College of Journalism and Communication cites a number of articles in opinion magazines that influenced political and social affairs in the United States: "Crossroads for the GOP" by William Rusher in the *National Review* of February, 1963 helped Goldwater get the Republican nomination the next year; "The Catholic as Philistine" by William P. Clancy in *Commonweal*, March 16, 1951, was cited by Justice Frankfurter of the U.S. Supreme Court in his concurring opinion on *The Miracle* case that films could not be banned simply because they were "sacrilegious"; Milovan Djilas, former vice president of Yugoslavia under Tito, was arrested and the world was stirred following the publication of his article, "Storm Over Europe," in *The New Leader*, November 19, 1956 (Djilas said the Hungarian revolution marked the beginning of the end of the Communist system).

But the influence of the opinion magazines is more cumulative than sudden. Issue after issue, the publication chips away at a single social evil; issue after issue it propounds a point of view. Schacht in his assessment entertains the "probability" that "in the long run the journals [of opinion] do exert an influence on public affairs in the United States."[7]

Schacht observes that it is no coincidence that "American social and economic development, foreign relations, even 'life and manners,' have developed during this century along lines held for the most part initially and for the most part consistently by the liberal

[6] Quoted by John H. Schacht, *The Journals of Opinion and Reportage: An Assessment*, Magazine Publishers Association, New York, 1966, p. 61.
[7] *Ibid.*, p. 39.

segment of these journals."[8] He concludes: ". . . No medium of comparable audience has exerted as great an influence for change."[9]

Magazines on the left

In the late 1960s, general circulation magazines became more and more willing to engage in controversy, and most of them—even the Luce publications—moved somewhat to the left. This presented the opinion magazines with a problem. Their area of coverage was being preempted. Some held fast, trying to exist without the visual excitement of the slicks. Others moved further to the left, where to some extent the underground press was already operating. Neither course proved entirely satisfactory. Some observers thought the opinion magazines were losing their earlier influence.

This section will attempt to describe the most important of the left-leaning opinion magazines, but in only a few paragraphs it is impossible to show precisely how one differs from the other. Students will want to become familiar with the magazines and form their own conclusions as to the magazines' character and worth.

We start with the oldest of the opinion magazines.

With more than a hundred years behind it, *The Nation*, a weekly, has given over its pages to some of the greatest names in politics, the arts, and journalism. Its influence extends far beyond its meager circulation, the elegance of its prose far excels its rather shabby appearance. Just recently, in an editorial, the magazine said:

The Nation may be forgiven for taking a certain amount of satisfaction, not unmixed with amusement, at the vast amplification the media are giving themes which our editors and contributors began raising a decade ago and have been hammering at ever since. Bigness surely has its advantages, but in journalism it sometimes seems as if discernment is in inverse proportion to size.[10]

In the mid-1960s a West Coast opinion magazine, *Frontier*, merged with *The Nation*, and in 1968, Harry Golden stopped publishing the *Carolina Israelite* and turned his subscription list over to *The Nation*. Golden became a regular contributor.

[8] *Ibid.*, p. 78.
[9] *Ibid.*, p. 79.
[10] "Real Trouble for the Pentagon," *The Nation*, September 8, 1969, p. 197.

Like other opinion magazines, *The Nation* has devoted full issues to exposing what it considers abuses in the military, FBI, CIA, and other groups. Such exposés often end up in book form.

Any magazine that takes strong stands on controversial matters is bound to have its inter-office squabbles,[11] and *The Nation* has had its share, especially during the 1940s when the magazine seemed to some staffers too sympathetic to Russia.

While *The Nation* is edited in New York, *The New Republic*, a weekly much like it, is edited in Washington, D.C. It has always been a little more sympathetic than *The Nation* to the Establishment. Still it is strongly liberal.

Thanks to sympathetic backers, it has had fewer financial crises. Its circulation is close to 150,000 compared with *The Nation's* 37,000.

Born shortly before World War I, it built a staff out of some of America's most brilliant journalists and thinkers. Walter Lippmann was an early editor. Henry Wallace was editor in the 1940s, prior to his resignation to run for the presidency in 1948.

When it early jumped on the John Kennedy bandwagon it became a sort of house organ for the "New Frontier."

At its 50th anniversary dinner in 1964 Walter Lippmann said: ". . . if the original editors were reading *The New Republic* today . . . they would regard it as the fulfillment of their hopes. For what they hoped for was a journal of unopinionated opinion—one that would be informed, disinterested, compassionate and brave."[12]

One of its best writers is Associate Editor John Osborne, an expert on Richard Nixon. The fact that Osborne sometimes sympathizes with the President prompted *Newsweek* to say that Osborne "sometimes appears to be the house conservative." *The Nixon Watch* (Liveright, New York, 1970) is a collection of his writings. (Liveright Publishing Corporation, one of America's prestige book publishers in the twenties, was recently purchased by *The New Republic*.)

The Progressive, started by Sen. R. M. LaFollette, Sr., in Wis-

---

[11] Read Wilfrid Sheed's novel, *Office Politics*, Farrar, Straus and Giroux, New York, 1966.

[12] "1914–1964: Remarks on the Occasion of this Journal's 50th Year," *The New Republic*, March 21, 1964, p. 14.

consin in 1909, represents a midwestern brand of liberalism. Robert Sherrill calls it "a kind of literate, left-wing *Reader's Digest.*"

One of its frequent contributors is Milton Mayer, a writer whose subtleties of style delight the thoughtful reader. Mayer has written about 600 articles for *The Progressive* and hundreds more for other magazines.[13]

Occasionally *The Progressive* will put out a special issue. All the articles deal with aspects of a single theme, as in "The Crisis of Survival" issue for April, 1970. Or the magazine will consist of one long, well-developed, book-length manuscript. In June 1969 *The Progressive* devoted an issue to "The Power of the Pentagon." It got more notice than any issue since April, 1954, when the magazine examined Sen. Joseph McCarthy. Because of requests for extra copies, the Pentagon issue went to three printings within the month, even though the first printing was for twice the usual number. The Viking Press later brought the issue out in book form.

As a monthly, *The Progressive* cannot keep on top of the news as well as the other opinion journals, and hence operates under a handicap. Its circulation is 36,000.

Another important opinion magazine is *The New Leader* (circulation: 20,000). Started in 1923 as a socialist tabloid, *The New Leader* became a biweekly magazine in 1950. By that time it had severed its ties with the Socialist Party. Today it is closer to the center than *The New Republic* or *The Nation.*

It underwent another change in 1961 to disassociate itself from "stuffy intellectualism." It even changed its looks, becoming what is probably the best-looking but still unpretentious opinion magazine in America. In a March 31, 1968 advertisement in *The New York Review of Books*, it referred to itself as "a magazine that probes serious issues seriously. But it tries to do it with style. With wit. With humor, where appropriate. In short, it communicates, it doesn't obfuscate."

It calls itself "generally liberal," but by that it means that it is open-minded. It prides itself on its "refusal to give knee-jerk response to every doctrinaire liberal shibboleth. . . ."

It claims to have been the first magazine to publish Martin Luther

---

[13] See his *What Can a Man Do?* University of Chicago Press, Chicago, 1964.

King's "Letter from Birmingham City Jail," which powerfully in-
dicted the complacency of white moderates.

After the assassination of Robert Kennedy, one of its writers,
Gus Tyler, criticized the mass guilt complex of many other writers.
"Too much of the breast beating is a public proclamation of self-
righteousness, intended partly to indict others and partly to cop out
of the hard struggle to move ahead with moderation."

The slickest, yet shrillest of the opinion magazines is *Ramparts*,
originally published in San Francisco, now published in Berkeley.
It started in 1964 as an intellectual Catholic quarterly, but, said
founder Edward Keating: "There weren't as many independent
Catholic intellectuals as I had thought."[14] It went secular, became
a monthly, and moved further to the left. "There is nothing in American journalism quite like *Ramparts*," a *National Observer* writer
said in 1967.

One of the editors, Warren Hinckle III, once pointed out that the
magazine tended to be kinder to the right wing than to the liberal
center. "The right wing will at least debate the issues even though
their solutions may be simplistic and primitive. But the liberals
won't even talk about them."

It made its biggest impact when it uncovered CIA activities in
universities and youth organizations in early 1967. The story was
so hot it couldn't wait, and so *Ramparts* took out full-page ads in
the New York *Times* and the Washington *Post* to tell it.

Its editors maintain they do not define their audience and then
go out after it, as the slicks do; they edit the magazine for themselves. Partly through the promotional efforts of the late Howard
Gossage, the magazine was able to build its circulation up to nearly
a quarter of a million copies, but it spent wildly.

Once, when it found copies were not moving fast enough in the
mails, it threatened to launch a campaign to "nationalize" the post
office.

Despite its distaste for the Establishment, it has had to adopt
some of the Establishment's trappings in its fight to stay alive. In
late 1968 it asked its readers for the benefit of advertisers to par-
ticipate in a survey of their backgrounds and tastes. "There comes

---

[14] Keating and the editors fought over money matters. The board of directors in 1967 fired Keating as publisher after he had pumped $860,000 into
the magazine.

a time in the course of every magazine's events when it must ask its readers to travel to the town of their birth and register for a most peculiar census." Obviously, it was doing this reluctantly. It continued: "We have nothing against it in principle, but after we have seen what has happened to magazines totally depending upon it . . . , we will depend on circulation revenues to keep us honest and in business, thank you." It was then a biweekly.

A few months later it made use of the capitalist's tool of bankruptcy, reorganized itself, and went back to a monthly schedule. The staff promised no more missed deadlines, better handling of money. "We're less campy and less smart-ass," said editor Bob Scheer.

Once when it looked as though *Ramparts* would die, *The New Republic* observed that *"Ramparts'* troubles have included internal quarrels, chaotic bookkeeping, and an inability—despite public relations talent—to attract writers with something fresh to say."[15] "What it did," James Ridgeway observed in *The New York Times Magazine* "was to popularize for a wide group . . . trends and currents which the smaller left-liberal political magazines had been talking about for years."[16] He added:

Ramparts was a historical accident. It was begun in San Francisco by liberal Catholics at a time when the revolt in the church was developing. For that reason alone, it drew attention to itself. It also could not help but reflect some of the gusto of San Francisco in recent years. It attacked the Vietnam war in 1965 and 1966 when the antiwar movement was gathering momentum, and when briefly there was a chance of creating a left-liberal coalition. Its money dried up as that coalition disintegrated and politics polarized. . . . The magazine used the culture it attacked to create a mass market and as a result has very nearly been consumed by that culture.[17]

Hinckle left *Ramparts* in 1970 to launch a new magazine in New York: *Scanlan's*, which, after a big splash, found an unenthusiastic reception even among leftists who would be expected to applaud it. Peter Steinfels in *Commonweal* (March 13) called it "an average blend of New Journalism and underground-press styles." It was a

[15] "Two for One," *The New Republic*, February 15, 1969, p. 10.

[16] James Ridgeway, "The Ramparts Story: . . . Um, Very Interesting," *The New York Times Magazine*, April 20, 1969, p. 34.

[17] *Ibid.*, p. 44.

magazine with a sense of humor. In one of its promotion ads it announced it would charge readers for printing letters to the editor, since such letters are "a form of the Vanity Press." The rate was 25 cents per word. "Letters which we find particularly dumb or boring will cost $1.00 per word, and they will only be put into type after the writer's check clears the bank."

Although technically not a magazine, the communist *Daily World*, successor in 1968 to *The Worker*, should be mentioned here. With a circulation of only 12,000, much of it probably made up of FBI agents and other government officials watching it as part of their jobs, the *World* limps along pathetically, not appealing to the conservatives, certainly, and not to the New Left either, which considers the paper irrelevant.

It provides an interesting study of how news can be turned to propaganda. Certainly, it cannot be accused of being objective.

Magazines on the right

Several magazines serve the American right and ultraright. Two are quarterlies: *American Mercury* (circulation: 10,000), now published at Torrance, Calif., which crusades for what it calls "true-blue Americanism" and argues against democracy, calling it "a degenerate form of government"; and *Modern Age* (circulation: 6,000), a far more thoughtful publication with a scholarly and even aristocratic tone.

The largest in circulation is a semiweekly published in New York and sent out free: *Christian Economics* (circulation: 215,000). It combines an interest in Fundamentalist Christianity with concern for the free-enterprise system.

Monthlies include *American Opinion*, the publication of the John Birch Society (circulation: 36,000); *The Freeman*, a "libertarian" publication devoted to private property and capitalism (circulation: 50,000); *The New Guard*, the publication of Young Americans for Freedom (circulation: 25,000); and *The Objectivist*, Ayn Rand's publication (circulation: 21,000).

One of the best-known right-wing publications is *Human Events*, published in Washington, D.C. (circulation: 100,000). On some issues it is moderately conservative, on most it is ultraconservative.

There are a number of right-wing newsletters, like *The Dan*

Smoot Report, but, because of their hysteria, they don't deserve serious reading.

By far the most influential conservative opinion magazine is the *National Review*, founded in 1955 by William F. Buckley, Jr. A biweekly published in New York, it goes to more than 100,000 subscribers and newsstand buyers. It has a bigger newsstand sale than most opinion magazines. It also carries more advertising than other opinion magazines, probably because some company owners believe in its point of view and are willing to support the magazine whether or not the advertising increases sales enough to justify the expenditure.

It uses slick paper stock, original art, and full color on the cover. You'll find a better writing style here than elsewhere, primarily because so much of it is done by Buckley himself, one of the great stylists in journalism. But you have to be pretty well informed to keep up with him.

Probably no other magazine editor is so widely known. In 1967 he made the cover of *Time*. Opinionated and articulate, William Buckley is both writer and public performer.

Unlike most True Believers, he hasn't lost his sense of humor. Once he ran for Mayor of New York. When asked what he would do if he won, he said: "I'd demand a recount." When he sent Norman Mailer a copy of one of his books, he wrote a "Hi!" after Mailer's name in the index.

A letter writer to *Time* called him "a mental muscle-beacher who can't resist rippling his grey matter to dazzle bystanders."

One gets the impression that Buckley does not mean always for his readers to take him literally. He resorts to cleverness sometimes at the expense of understanding. In defense of extremism, he once said: "When a liberal Catholic lies dying, does he receive moderate unction?" He calls Fr. James Groppi, the militant priest from Milwaukee, a "man of gosh."

His magazine carries a sting. When all the editorials and columnists were surveying the effect on the presidential chances of Ted Kennedy after the driving accident in which a young woman, Mary Jo Kopechne, was killed, the magazine started out its "The Week" column (August 12, 1969) with this one-liner: "Equal time for Mary Jo." From another issue of 1969: "Six hundred welfare recipients recently gathered at Wayne State University in Detroit for a meeting. Although some had worked in the past as domestic servants, they would not, they made it clear, willingly accept such work now; they 'would never in this time of technological, economic and human-rights advances, perform such demeaning and low-wage work again.' Instead, they'll stay on welfare."

To add to its subscription lists, the *National Review* has run small ads for many years in the liberal magazines, believing, apparently, that readers of these magazines were liberal enough to want to consider what conservatives were saying. Readers of both the *National Review* and *The New Republic* might be shocked if they knew that in late 1968 the two magazines joined hands to announce to advertisers a special discount rate when they buy space in both publications. The announcement said: "The widely divergent views of the two magazines assure a minimum of reader duplication." *The Atlantic* and *Harper's* had done this some years before, but they were magazines with similar political philosophies.

When it held its 10th anniversary dinner in New York, at least two liberals in good standing, Steve Allen and Theodore White, attended. The *National Review* had run an article by Steve Allen defending the liberal point of view.

Early in 1969, a reader of the *National Review*, Roger Cole of Bethesda, Md., wrote the editor to explain why he would not renew his subscription. After a page and a half of single-spaced arguments against the magazine, he added: "In any case, this letter is becoming too long. It has already taken enough time that it has occurred to me that despite the faults I find, there are aspects of *National Review* I appreciate and cannot obtain a substitute elsewhere—so I'm enclosing both the comments and a check for renewal."

Magazines with religious ties

A number of opinion magazines put politics and social matters in a religious context. They include *The Christian Century* (non-denominational), *Commonweal* (edited by Catholic laymen), *America* (Jesuit), and *Commentary* (Jewish).

Commentary, founded in 1945, is the most intellectual of all the opinion magazines. More than the others, it concerns itself with literature. It has published stories by Bernard Malamud and Saul

Bellow. But it is interested in politics too. It was the first magazine to publish the writings of the New Left, but its editor soon grew disenchanted with the movement.

Dwight Macdonald has called *Commentary* the best magazine for any purpose. Clare Booth Luce has said it is the only literate magazine published in America.

The magazine has added to its usefulness—and stimulated sales— by providing various groups with monthly discussion guides to its articles.

The Christian Century and *Commonweal*, one published in Chicago, the other in New York, are sister publications in the sense that their points of view are almost identical. What criticism the *Century* may have voiced against the Catholic Church all but disappeared on the advent of Pope John XXIII. Perhaps more criticism of the Church comes from *Commonweal* itself. The *Century*'s associate editor, Martin Marty, University of Chicago professor and prolific book writer, often appears on the pages of *Commonweal*. Both magazines are independent of church ties; in political affairs, both are classically liberal. Both are weeklies.

On June 1, 1970, the British fortnightly *New Christian* merged with *The Christian Century*. *New Christian* had earlier incorporated the Catholic journal *Search* with the Anglican journal *Prism*. In announcing the new merger the *Century* observed it was moving "beyond tokenism in a wider ecumenical journalism which obliges Protestants and Catholics to speak directly to each other and, wherever possible, to speak together."[18]

Even the denominational magazines are becoming more liberal. The magazines adjust as the churches adjust, staying slightly ahead of their readers in advocating social changes. But as sponsored magazines, they cannot be as free as religious magazines published independently of the church. *Motive*, the Methodist magazine for college students, in its March-April, 1969 issue dealt with the role of women in society, using four-letter words and dwelling on sex and homosexuality. Church officials stepped in and reorganized the magazine.[19]

[18] "Journalism for Oikoumene," *The Christian Century*, March 18, 1970, p. 316.
[19] Terence Shea, "When Are Church Magazines Obscene?" *The National Observer*, August 11, 1969, pp. 1 ff.

Humor magazines

It would be hard to prove that today's college student does not have the sense of humor his predecessors had, but it is a fact he is not publishing magazines like those that used to send his father and even his grandfather into spasms of uncontrollable laughter. College humor magazines are now largely defunct. Perhaps they were never as good as undergraduates thought they were. "Gawd, These Jokes Were Painful!" Robert Russell muses in an article in *Esquire*.[20]

The first of the college humor magazines was *The Harvard Lampoon* (1876), which seemed willing then to settle for what Russell calls "the faint smile." In recent years the *Lampoon* has put out annual issues parodying other publications. One on *Playboy* had a center spread with a girl tanned only where a bikini would be worn; the rest of her body was untanned. Other magazines appeared in emulation of the *Lampoon*, and in 1923 an off-campus publication, *College Humor*, made its debut to reprint the best from these magazines. It died several times, was revived again, and finally gave up for good in 1943.

After World War II the campus magazines themselves found the going rough. The vets, back from the war, thought them silly; the whole campus scene was changing. Few of the magazines survived.

The success of the *Lampoon* inspired some Democrats in 1877 to launch the wildly funny *Puck*, which passed harsh judgment on Republicans. *Life* (not to be confused with the latter-day magazine of the same name) came along six years later to make people laugh; and by this time the newspapers began running humor columns as regular features.

Humor, some of it with a social conscience, appeared in all the media, but as a full diet in magazine format, it never really caught on. New humor magazines popped up periodically, like *Ballyhoo*, but they never stayed around for more than a few years.

Only a few hold forth today. One is *Mad*. Its success has been remarkable, its contribution to opinion formation largely overlooked by those who should be interested.

[20] December, 1968, pp. 164–169.

Mad started in 1952, the brainchild of Bill Gaines, whose father started the comic book industry in the 1930s. With a circulation now of about 2,000,000 and no advertising, it is, as a theologian has observed, a magazine with an old-fashioned morality.[21] Designed for the 10 to 20 age-group, it systematically satirizes parental hypocrisy, far-left and far-right political thinking, smoking, and especially the press. For the young, it is probably the most effective critic of the press we have.

Who can forget its takeoffs on the *Reader's Digest*, on the Chicago Tribune-New York News Syndicate brand of comic strips, and on the whole field of advertising? With its parodies on current advertisements, it gives readers a healthy skepticism about advertising's claims.

J. M. Flagler of *Look* remembers fondly one of *Mad*'s versions of the typical kids' program: The announcer says: "Let's have some music, Mr. Piano . . . don't bump into Mr. Camera." A kid in the audience says: "I just threw up on Mr. Floor." Its December, 1969 issue took off on gun magazines. A cover for *Passionate Gun Love* features these articles: " 'I Cleaned an Unloaded Gun—and Lived!' The Story of a Once-in-a-Lifetime Miracle"; "A Heart-Warming Memoir: 'The Most Unforgettable Duck I Ever Slaughtered' "; and "106 Exciting Ways to Make Love to Your Gun."

Mad believes in humor first, philosophy second. The politics of the staff and contributors range from far-left to far-right.[22]

Its pages have been collected into innumerable paperback books. In 1969 World Publishing Co. brought out *The Ridiculously Expensive Mad* ($9.95).

Other humor magazines are *Monocle*, containing some highbrow satire, and *The National Lampoon*, started by some former editors of *The Harvard Lampoon*.

The underground press

One more category of publications belongs in our discussion of journalism for the elite. The elite, in this case, consists mostly of alienated youth. Serving these readers as no other publications

---

[21] See Vernard Eller, *The Mad Morality: Or the Ten Commandments Revisited*, Abingdon Press, Nashville, Tenn., 1970.
[22] Bruce Cook, "Yecch! Alfred E. Neuman Is No Idiot," *The National Observer*, October 27, 1969, pp. 1 ff.

can—or will—are several hundred members of what has come to be known as the "underground press."[23]

The phenomenon of publications existing for the sole purpose of chipping away at established institutions is nothing new in America, of course; but the proliferation of them, the tone of their diatribes—that *is* new.

What makes them possible is the sullen mood of a by now rather sizable body of activists and revolutionaries, the permissiveness of the courts, and the availability of an inexpensive printing process, offset lithography, with its ability to utilize crude paste-ups and cheap, cold-type composition. Anyone with a commitment to the cause and a few dollars collected from sympathizers can enter the field. Art Kunkin, publisher of the Los Angeles *Free Press,* largest of the papers with a staff of more than 40, started the publication in the mid-1960s with an investment of $15. By 1970 it was grossing about $700,000 a year.

One of the best known of the underground papers, the *Berkeley Barb,* in 1969, just five years after its founding, enjoyed a circulation of 86,000 and a yearly profit of about $130,000. But that was the year staff members, irritated about their low pay and the penny-pinching ways of owner-founder Max Scherr, rebelled. Scherr let it be known his paper was up for sale. Staff members considered buying Scherr out, but then decided to establish a rival underground paper, the *Tribe.*[24]

From a design standpoint, a few of these publications are remarkably creative, but most resort to what a writer in *Communications Arts* called "seasick graphics." From a writing standpoint, they are lively and provocative, but "taken in large doses, very, very boring."[25]

---

[23] Several anthologies are available: Jerry Hopkins, ed., *The Hippie Papers,* New American Library, New York, 1968; Jesse Kornbluth, ed., *Notes from the New Underground,* The Viking Press, New York, 1968; John Birmingham, ed., *Our Time Is Now: Notes from the High School Underground,* Frederick A. Praeger, New York, 1970; Diane Divoky, ed., *How Old Will You Be in 1984?* Avon-Discus, New York, 1970; Marc Libarle and Tom Seligson, eds., *The High School Revolutionaries,* Random House, New York, 1970. See also: Ethel Grodzins Romm, *The Open Conspiracy: What America's Angry Generation Is Saying,* Stackpole Books, Harrisburg, Pa., 1969.

[24] "The Tribe Is Restless," *Time,* July 18, 1969, p. 46.

[25] See David Sanford, "The Seedier Media," *The New Republic,* December 2, 1967, pp. 7, 8.

The underground Los Angeles *Oracle* justifies the underground press this way:

Almost without exception, most established newspapers and maga- zines . . . tend to reflect the prejudices of their sponsors; they are short-sighted, slow-moving, usually defensive of the status quo. The underground press is more concerned with conveying truth than earn- ing money. . . . It fulfills the need for independent information about the turbulent currents of our rapidly changing way of life.[26]

But *Esquire* observes: "Despite its refreshing vitality, the under- ground press is too noisy. This is not to denigrate its objectives or its considerable achievements; rather, because its methods are so deliberately crude—full of illiteracies and self-righteousness, and devoid of wit—a dispassionate reader is tempted to turn off."[27]

Their main targets are the military, the straight press, the police, and narcotics agents. A measure of their impact was felt in 1969 when the Los Angeles *Free Press* published a stolen list of names, addresses, and telephone numbers of narcotics agents in California and, in effect, invited readers to harass them. Many of the papers promote the legalization and use of marijuana.

They are anything but objective. They argue that true objectivity is a myth, anyway. To them, news is a four-letter word.

And they are by now anything but "underground." The news- papers are hawked from the street corners of major cities and uni- versity towns and available even at newsstands. Much of their circulation comes from tittering businessmen attending conventions and office workers on their lunch hours buying papers out of curi- osity, especially to read the "want ads" in which deviate attempts to make connection with deviate.

Although part of this is put-on, it was inevitable that publications would arise to devote themselves fully to the one enduring attrac- tion of the underground press: its blatant pornography. So now the new underground sex papers: *Pleasure, Kiss, Screw, Rat,* and *The New York Review of Sex.*

The two publications said to have started it all are *The Realist,* a magazine founded by Paul Krassner in 1958, and *The Village*

[26] Quoted by John Gruen, "The Ear-Splitting Underground Press," *Vogue,* Feburary 15, 1968, p. 44.
[27] "Editor's Notes," *Esquire,* October, 1969, p. 12.

Voice, a weekly paper in Greenwich Village that first appeared in 1955.

Krassner first worked with *Mad*. Calling his new magazine "the fire hydrant of the underdog," Krassner filled it with outrageous interviews, articles, and literary miscellany, sprinkled with obscenities, but with an offsetting lift of humor. By 1968, he had built his more-or-less monthly publication, edited from incredibly poorly ordered offices, to a circulation of 100,000, more than most of the serious opinion magazines.

Krassner once stated his philosophy: ". . . Existence has no meaning, and I love every minute of it."[28] *Life* calls him the dean of the underground press, but Krassner's magazine is clearly above the level of the papers started in the shadow of *The Realist*.

The Village Voice stood well to the left of regular New York newspapers and paid particular attention to the arts. It introduced the work of Jules Feiffer, among others. By 1963, the paper was operating in the black. Once in the vanguard, the *Voice* now finds itself written off by much of the underground press as hopelessly square. A writer in *Evergreen Review* calls it a "middle-age matron in [a] miniskirt."[29]

Publications that start out on the fringes often become more respectable as they pick up circulation. This happened, for instance, to the *National Enquirer*, which until 1968 dwelt on torture and bizarre sex. Typical of its articles was one saying "I'm sorry I killed my mother, but I'm glad I killed my father." Now, moving from newsstand to supermarket sales, the *Enquirer* has fashioned itself into a near family-type publication, although its reporters still find that when they tell a prospective interviewee "I'm from the *Enquirer*," they get the door slammed in their faces. The underground press will change too. It already has. And some of the papers may find themselves quoted favorably one day among members of the Establishment.

According to *Playboy* (September, 1969), two of the papers, the *East Village Other* and *Rat*, have hired the capitalistic Dun & Bradstreet Collection Division to hound nonpaying subscribers.

---

[28] "Easygoing Advocate of the Outrageous," *Life*, October 4, 1968, p. 46.
[29] J. Kirk Sale, "The Village Voice (You've Come a Long Way, Baby, But You Got Stuck There)," *Evergreen Review*, December, 1969, pp. 25 ff.

And according to William Murray in *Esquire* (June, 1970), employees at the Los Angeles *Free Press* now punch a time clock.

In 1966 five papers, including the *Free Press*, banded together to form the Underground Press Syndicate to exchange cartoons and other features and to solicit advertising. By early 1968 the syndicate had 40 members in the United States, Canada, and England. And then in 1968 came another underground press agency: Liberation News Service, selling its news stories, reviews, and essays to subscribers for $180 a year. Members can get LNS service via teletype. Raymond Mungo describes his "life and hard times with Liberation News Service" in *Famous Long Ago* (Beacon Press, Boston, 1970).

In some cases, an underground newspaper contracts with a straight newspaper to do its printing. A Port Washington, Wis., publisher of a chain of three weeklies found this can be a dangerous business practice. When he took on *Kaleidoscope*, a Milwaukee underground paper, local stores in his area cancelled their advertising contracts with his own newspapers. In a year's time, it could have meant the loss of $200,000 in advertising revenue. One writer observed: "Ironically, many of the businessmen trying to roast . . . [the publisher] at the financial stake probably look upon boycotts as vicious weapons when working men use them in pursuit of decent wages."[30]

Editors of underground newspapers have found themselves in demand as panelists at journalism conventions, and there, with obvious delight, they castigate their more conservative colleagues.

The underground press clearly has had some influence on the straight press. For example, the Detroit *News*, frankly imitating the format and to some extent the content of underground newspapers, in 1969 launched "The Other Section," an every-Thursday part of the regular paper that attempts to bridge the gap between young and old. Among other features, the section runs articles critical of the Establishment press. "There's only one policy," said Robert E. Lubeck, who is responsible for the section. "No four-letter words. They were used by the underground press for shock value. Now that's worn off and there's nothing to be served by their use."[31]

---

[30] Sig Gissler, "Witch Hunt," *The Progressive*, September, 1969, p. 31.
[31] Don Ball, "Detroit News Opens 14-Page Section to Under-35 Blasts," *Editor & Publisher*, September 20, 1969, p. 9.

The art and graphics of the underground press have inspired both advertising and publications designers. Its angry, scatological prose has furthered the "new journalism" found in some of our magazines. One observer has concluded that youthful readers, when they graduate to the straight press, won't be content with the dullness there.[32]

The alternative press

Standing to the right of the underground press but to the left of the Establishment press are a few publications press scholars now refer to as the "alternative press": militant papers that buck the journalistic tide and do it responsibly. The best example is the San Francisco *Bay Guardian*. Started in 1966, the more-or-less-monthly tabloid has launched attacks on Pacific Gas and Electric Company, real estate developers, and others. In 1970 it fought the Newspaper Preservation Act by filing a lawsuit charging that the Act violates the First Amendment. (The Act excuses newspapers in certain cities, including San Francisco, from provisions in federal anti-trust legislation.) Bruce B. Brugmann, *Guardian* publisher, says the Act encourages monopoly by allowing big papers to pool profits and fix advertising rates. "If anything in this city is a failing newspaper," he says, "it is the *Guardian*, not the *Chronicle* or the *Examiner*. What we find in San Francisco are not failing newspapers, but a couple of crybaby millionaire publishers."[33]

[32] Jack A. Nelson, "The Underground Press," *Freedom of Information Center Report No. 226*, School of Jornalism, University of Missouri, Columbia, August, 1969. See also Robert J. Glessing, *The Underground Press in America*, Indiana University Press, Bloomington, Ind., 1970.

[33] Peter Barnes, "Farewell, Free Enterprise," *The New Republic*, Oct. 17, 1970, p. 16.

CHAPTER TWELVE

Must reading

"I've given up reading books," said Oscar Levant. "I find it takes my mind off myself." Someone else said: "Why should I buy a book? I already have one." But there are enough people buying them and reading them these days to keep more than a thousand publishers in America producing some 30,000 different titles a year.[1]

True, some of the titles don't sell more than 400 or 500 copies. But some go into sales of hundreds of thousands. The estimate of total copies of books printed each year runs to two billion.

When the publisher sees that sales of a given book are brisk enough, he orders it back on the press for a new *printing*. A book may go through several printings. If after four or five years the publisher sees a new audience developing for the book, and if he feels some of the material in the book is outdated, he asks the author to revise the book; then he brings it out in a new *edition*.

Nearly 200,000 titles are "in print" as of this writing. This figure includes the most recent books published plus books from

---

[1] This figure includes about 8,000 new editions of books previously published.

publishers' back lists still offered for sale. When an edition of a book is sold out and when the publisher decides not to bring out a new printing or edition, the book is no longer "in print." But buyers wanting an out-of-print book can find it through one of the many dealers in second-hand books.

Categories of books

Publishers divide books into two broad categories: (1) textbooks and reference books and (2) trade books. The first category includes all books published specifically for classroom use plus books meant to be reference sources, like dictionaries and encyclopedias. The second category includes all other books, fiction as well as non-fiction.

Increasingly, professors are adopting trade books—especially paperbacks—as textbooks, so the two categories become blurred, but publishers continue to regard them separately because their marketing programs differ. For one thing, trade books generally have a shorter sales life than text and reference books.

Publishers find textbooks rather consistent if unspectacular money-makers. They find trade books much more exciting—and frustrating. A few trade books make unbelievable profits. Most fail. Roughly 60 percent of trade books end up in the red, 36 percent break even, and 4 percent make a good profit. The trade books that really take off are almost always works of nonfiction: controversial or inspirational or practical or gossipy. A few novels do almost as well, but most do miserably. Not many publishers handle novels.

The GPO

The preceding figures do not include the books published by America's largest publisher: the U.S. Government Printing Office, Washington, D.C. Established in 1895 to meet librarians' needs for systematic distribution of government-sponsored publications, the GPO now acts as publisher and book-seller for all government agencies. With "editorial offices" scattered throughout the federal government, it can say it has 27,000 titles—all non-fiction—"in print."

Its most popular publication is *Infant Care*, first published in

1914, now a 108-page paperback. Some 14,000,000 copies have been sold.

Other "best sellers" are the *Surgeon General's Report on Smoking and Health*, the *Warren Commission Report*, and *Your Federal Income Tax*. The office sells some 70,000,000 copies of its publications every year, but some of them are mere leaflets selling for as little as five cents. GPO publications are reset and repackaged by private publishers and sold at fancy prices. Private publishers can do this because what the government publishes cannot—and should not—be copyrighted.

Unique among government agencies, the GPO actually makes a profit: a little more than a million dollars a year.[2]

A little history

In world history, books antedate printing itself. The first books were "published" by scribes, making word-for-word copies of original manuscripts. The printing press, and especially movable type, revolutionized book publishing. Still, it took centuries before publishers really brought out books for the masses.

In the colonies, the first press, set up at Cambridge, produced its first piece of printing in 1639: a book of psalms which preceded by half a century the first newspaper. With the coming of each new medium—first the newspaper, then the magazine, then radio, finally TV—the book industry thought its days were about done; but by reassessing its audience and broadening its base, it has managed to survive. By the late 1960s, largely because of governmental emphasis on education, book publishers in America seemed healthier than they ever had been.

In his *Book Publishing in America* (McGraw-Hill Book Company, New York, 1966) Charles A. Madison divides the history of the industry into four eras: from the colonies' beginnings to 1865—emergence of book publishing from local ventures to nationwide enterprise; 1865–1900—the parallel growth of genteel publishers and "gilded age" merchandisers; 1900–1945—the commercialization of book publishing with its hospitality to "men of literary

[2] James L. Harte, "America's Busiest Bookstore," *Minutes*, February, 1969, p. 12.

discernment as well as to gross bookmongers"; and 1945–present—postwar concentration on textbooks, paperbacks, mergers, and public financing, with "the persistence of publishing as a cultural activity."

How books get published

Technically, a writer can reach his audience without bothering to go through a publisher. But what writer has the money to gamble on a book, the self-confidence to edit it, the technical knowledge to work with typesetters and printers, the design sense to put the book together, the promotional instinct to get the book noticed, the staff to distribute it?

The book publisher is essentially a middle man between the writer and his audience. Presumably, he knows book audiences better than the author does, and he has the facilities to reach them.

He does not, in most cases, do his own printing. He hires that out. If he publishes 500 or 600 titles a year, obviously he uses many different printers. He may use more than one printer to produce a single book—one for the illustrations, another for the text, another for the dust jacket.

In most cases it is the author who comes up with the book idea and sells it to the publisher. But sometimes the publisher conceives of a book, then hunts for an author to do it. *The Guns of August* was suggested to the author by the publisher.

Some houses have been known to survey the market *first* to see if a book will sell, then assign it to an author. At least one publisher, who sells books by mail, is said to send out his impressive brochures selling a book, and if enough orders come in, *then* he'll have it written and published. If the promotion doesn't draw enough response, he'll refund the money.

Publishers take at least six weeks to decide on a submitted manuscript. Nine times out of ten the decision is "Sorry." When a manuscript is accepted, the publisher sends the author a contract setting forth the terms of acceptance. On nonfiction books a publisher may offer a contract after seeing only an outline and a few sample chapters. In such cases, the publisher agrees to give the author an "advance"—a sum of money ranging from a few hundred dollars to several thousand dollars. The publisher deducts the advance from the first royalty payment due the author after the book begins to sell.

Under most contracts, the author earns 10 percent of the retail price of books sold. The percentage (the "royalty") goes up slightly when the sales level reaches a certain point. Royalties are generally lower on paperback books and juveniles.

At the turn of the century some book writers began employing agents to place their manuscripts and to dicker with publishers over royalties. Naturally, publishers preferred to deal directly with their authors. They found agents a little hard-headed when it came to money. Cass Canfield of Harper & Row tells the story of a London publisher who asked one of his writers, A. G. Gardiner, how he was coming with his life of Christ. Gardiner said the first part was in the hands of his agent. The publisher looked hurt. "To think, Mr. Gardiner, that you should have dealt with an agent, particularly in a case involving the life of Our Saviour, is really more than I can bear."[3] Today nearly every serious free-lance writer has an agent. Publishers now prefer to work with agents—for one reason, because agents weed out incompetent writers. It is as hard for a writer to find a good agent to represent him as it is for him to sell his manuscript directly to a publisher.

The "vanity press"

No wonder some writers turn to subsidy publishers—the "vanity press," as it is known in the industry. Not willing to accept the "Sorry" verdicts of agents and regular book publishers, they succumb to advertising in the writers' magazines, where a line-up of publishers—we use the term loosely here—each month hints at easy money and quick fame. Perhaps these writers know better, but the urge to get into print is too strong. They send their manuscripts in and, sure enough, they get encouraging letters in return. "This manuscript is indicative of your talent."[4] That line, honest enough when you consider it, sends a writer scurrying to the bank, and soon he's got a book to his credit, but at a cost of several thousand dollars. For under a subsidy publisher's contract, the

---

[3] Cass Canfield, *The Publishing Experience*, University of Pennsylvania Press, Philadelphia, 1968, p. 58.

[4] See "The Vanity Press," *Newsweek*, December 23, 1968, pp. 83–85.

writer himself has to pay the costs of publication. The book does not sell, because it is an abomination to begin with, and the publisher's facilities to promote and distribute it are limited, if they exist at all.

Most "vanity press" authors come from the ranks of the elderly and the poorly educated. But some of the writers are well educated. Some of the presses advertise in opinion magazines and academic journals. Here is a quotation from an ad sponsored by Exposition Press in *Trans-action*, a journal for social scientists (June 1970): "Book publication is one of the foundation stones of a scholar's career in gaining recognition and advancement. . . . Your inquiries and manuscripts are invited (all subjects welcomed). An editorial report is furnished without obligation."

The head of Exposition Press, Ed Uhlan, is surprisingly frank about his operations in *The Rogue of Publishers' Row*, a book the firm circulates to prospective authors. Despite the admissions, the clients keep coming. Once the Federal Trade Commission conducted some hearings into subsidy publishing, and Uhlan's firm suffered— or so it thought—from the publicity. But with the papers carrying full accounts of the hearings, in came an old gentleman who said: "I saw your ad [!] in the paper this morning. I didn't understand all that part about that there FTC, but I read enough to know you're the fellow I want to publish my book. It's about my mother's childhood in Idaho."[5]

One of the subsidy publishers, Vantage Press, alone publishes 350 books a year. Even regular book publishers do some subsidy publishing, especially in the area of company histories. *Newsweek* estimated in 1968 that one out of every 30 books published is wholly or partially subsidized.[6]

Most of the Who's Who books are vanity books in that they sell mainly to the persons listed. Even the most prestigious of them, *Who's Who in America*, relies heavily on sales to biographees: about a third of the yearly press run of 60,000 copies.[7]

---

[5] Told by Eleanor Morehead in "How to Pay for Writing," *Esquire*, February, 1961, p. 96.

[6] For a detailed account of the come-ons writers encounter, see Robert Byrne, *Writing Rackets*, Lyle Stuart, New York, 1969.

[7] See Gilbert Cranberg, "The Business of Selling Vanity," *Saturday Review*, May 9, 1970, pp. 65 ff.

Copyright

The federal law on copyright, applicable to all journalistic media, prevents a writer or his publisher from plagiarizing the work of another, selling it, and thus depriving the original author of the revenue he might otherwise earn. The law does not keep an author from taking *part* of what someone else has written, however, and republishing it. But the original author should be credited, and only a limited portion of what he wrote may be used.

How much can an author safely take from another without violating the copyright law? The law does not say specifically. Generally speaking, an author can take a paragraph or two and feel confident he will not be slapped with a violation of copyright suit. If he is willing to quote *indirectly* from the original source, or rephrase the information, he can take as much as he wishes. After all, it is the *way* of telling something that can be copyrighted; information and ideas are in the public domain and can't be copyrighted.

To be on the safe side, most writers, if they borrow more than a few lines and quote them directly, write first to the original writer or his publisher and obtain permission to do so. Permission is usually readily granted.

As this book was written, Congress was thinking about tightening the copyright law, partly because of the growing use of copying machines to reproduce sections of books for educational purposes. One contemplated change would give an author longer protection with his copyright. As the law now stands, a book (or any printed piece) can be copyrighted for only 28 years. The author or publisher may apply for a 28-year extension; and that's it. After 56 years, any book or any magazine falls into the public domain and anybody may republish it, without credit, without payment to the original source. This explains the popularity of the classics with some publishers; publishers need pay no royalties on them.

The vicissitudes of book publishing

All publishing—and book publishing especially—is a gamble. Cass Canfield of Harper & Row estimates that "The element of chance in trade publishing is less than in poker and about the same as in baseball."[8]

Sometimes an author fails to get his manuscript in on time, and the publisher has to revamp his schedule and announce a new publication date to the trade. Or a manuscript, when it does come in, fails to live up to expectations, and the publisher must write off a sum of money already invested in the project.

And sometimes, for reasons still inexplicable to publishers, a natural—a book with all the ingredients of a big seller, one beautifully written, carefully edited, and fully promoted—falls flat.

What makes a book sell

The real money in trade-book publishing is to be found in book club rights, movie rights, foreign rights, syndication, magazine placement, and even in phonograph records. Publisher and author often split these revenues 50–50.

But before a book can earn these revenues, it has to make some dent as a regular book, selling in the stores.

Books present a unique selling problem. Each new one—and some publishers produce as many as two a day—requires its own well-thought-out marketing program. The publisher, in his advertising program, for instance, can't very well use as his theme: "Buy a new book today." He has to play up the special appeal of each new book on his list.

What makes a book sell? Nobody really knows. But all of these factors contribute:

1. *The subject.* Sometimes the subject alone will do it. In the past, books about Lincoln have done well; so have books about doctors, and dogs—causing one observer to suggest the ideal book title: *Lincoln's Doctor's Dog.* In our time, anything about the Kennedys has done well.

With the growing militancy of blacks and with America's increased attention to civil rights in the last few years, books by and about blacks have done well too. One of the best selling paperbacks in the late 1960s was *The Report of the National Advisory Committee on Civil Rights.* The Negro Book Club in 1969 listed

[8] Cass Canfield, *op cit.,* p. 45.

5,000 "African-American" titles available. Textbook divisions of major publishers were trying to meet the needs of the many black studies courses on campuses. One writer observed, "Every major publisher now has a black history or culture series of one kind or another."[9] Small, black-oriented publishing houses were forming in major cities. And Johnson Publications, Chicago, better known for its magazines, like *Ebony*, had gotten into the book publishing business.

2. *Advertising.* Occasionally a book does much better than the publisher expects. These are the "sleepers." *Games People Play* was one. So was *The Peter Principle.* But when a book like *Games People Play* catches on, its publisher, even at that date, goes into an extensive advertising campaign to capitalize on the book's rising tide.

Publishers do some advertising for every book they publish. Often they make use of advertising agencies which specialize in book accounts.

By other companies' standards, book publishers' advertising budgets are low: no more than a couple of thousand dollars per book, usually. But a promotion-minded publisher, like Bernard Geis and Associates, will spend up to $50,000 or more. Geis spent $130,000 to advertise *Valley of the Dolls.*

Book publishers use all the media of advertising, of course, but a favorite is direct-mail advertising, because so much of the business—perhaps 25 percent—comes from mail order sales. People buy books by mail because book stores are not always nearby, because they still get a kick out of opening packages that come in the mail, and sometimes because they may be embarrassed about the nature of the books they buy. Many of the sex technique books, for instance, rely heavily on mail order sales.

Publishers of specialized books find that they can reach their selective audience easier by mail—by renting a mailing list—than by any other way. A book publisher who specializes in mail order sales can operate with a very small staff and on a very small budget.

Many think of book publishing as a business with high ethical standards, but examples of chicanery are easy to find in this area as in all others. In the area of book advertising, for example,

[9] Mel Watkins, "The Black Revolution in Books," *The New York Times Book Review*, August 10, 1969, p. 8.

one sees much to criticize. Some readers have been hard-pressed to find much similarity between a book and the dust jacket description of it. And look what paperback publishers can do with their covers. How exactly does the nude on the cover relate to the story inside? Art Buchwald has shown that an enterprising publisher could even do a job on so innocent a book as *Snow White and the Seven Dwarfs*. Buchwald's blurb reads: "The story of a ravishing blonde virgin who was held captive by seven deformed men, all with different lusts." And on *Alice in Wonderland:* "A young girl's search for happiness in a weird, depraved world of animal desires. Can she ever return to a normal, happy life after falling so far?"

3. *Promotion.* One way Stein & Day promoted the book *The Arrangement* by Elia Kazan was to offer free copies to every head of a household in Mount Pleasant, Iowa. It was a stunt to capitalize on an announcement by the library board there that the book was "too obscene to have in our library." The board had returned the book to the publisher. In a press release, the publisher said it was making the offer "so that citizens can decide themselves whether Mr. Kazan's book is 'obscene' as their library alleges, or whether the Library Board is practicing censorship inconsistent with American traditions." This got the book considerable additional nationwide attention.

One of the most highly publicized books of recent times was William Manchester's *The Death of a President*, published by Harper & Row. The book got mixed reviews: some said it was beautifully written and significant; some found inaccuracies in it and quarreled with the author for doing it as an "authorized" book. As an "authorized" book it was subject to review by the Kennedys, and Mrs. John Kennedy, because of some passages she considered embarrassing, insisted that revisions be made prior to publication. Manchester balked. *Look* magazine became involved because it was serializing the book. (Someone at the time suggested the magazine be renamed *The Manchester Guardian.*) The fight that resulted was so widely publicized that another author, John Corry, wrote a book just about that: *The Manchester Affair* (Putnam, 1967). There was some speculation in the book publishers' trade press that in this case the publicity resulting from the fight was too intense; sales of the book itself were actually less than expected. Reading the book apparently would have been an anticlimax.

Perhaps nothing sells a book better than television exposure. Alexander King was practically unknown among middlebrows until he appeared on the *Jack Paar Show*. Dr. Haim G. Ginott's *Between Parent and Child* was going nowhere until he got a guest spot on the *Today Show*. Doubleday's PR department arranged 15 radio and TV interviews in New York alone for Arthur Hailey when that firm published his *Hotel*.[10]

4. *Serialization.* Book publishers once felt that running part of a forthcoming book in a magazine interfered with sales. If people read it in a magazine, then they wouldn't buy the book. DeWitt Wallace faced this kind of response when he asked Harper & Brothers for permission to condense and reprint 50 pages from Alexis Carrel's *Man the Unknown* in 1936. So Wallace made this offer: if sales didn't pick up after the *Digest* reprinting (the book was already published) he'd pay Harper & Brothers $5,000 instead of the normal $1,000 fee for reprint rights. Sales quadrupled.[11]

If a book is good enough, excerpts of it run in a magazine should have the effect of whetting the reader's appetite. He goes out then to buy the book either to get the complete story or just to have it in bound form for his library. He may not ever actually read the book version, but he feels good knowing it is there on the shelf.

Someone ought to conduct a study to find what percentage of books purchased are actually *read* by the purchaser. Publishers are aware that book buyers are not necessarily book readers. Books do have value as shelf fillers and status symbols. A whole range of overpriced "coffee table" books comes out before Christmas each year to catch people when they are in a buying mood.

"Best sellers"

The sports world is plagued with its All-American lists, the book world with its "best sellers."

What is a "best seller"? Well, it's almost anything you want to make of it. Any book that sells more than 20,000, 30,000 or 40,000 copies can be a "best seller." But the industry generally puts the

[10] Bruce Cook, "How A 'Best Seller' Gets That Way," *The National Observer*, February 3, 1969, p. 22.

[11] James Playsted Wood, *Of Lasting Interest*, rev. ed., Doubleday & Company, New York, 1967, p. 56.

minimum figure at 75,000 hardback copies for novels and 100,000 for non-fiction titles.

Whose list do you want to believe? None of them is scientifically compiled. Someone calls around to selected bookstores and asks, "What's selling?" and the bookseller looks around and guesses. Maybe he's got a display up front of an overpriced book he wants to get rid of. Well, it *could* be a best seller.

It's just possible that an eager-beaver publisher, knowing which stores the *New York Times Book Review* calls to compile its list, could hire people to make a run on a given book at those stores. Once a book gets included on one of the "best seller" lists, it gets the attention it needs and it becomes, quite literally, a "best seller."

Of course, some of the books that make this list are junk books, there because they pander to mass tastes. The Chicago *Tribune,* to counter this, runs not a "best seller" list but a list it calls: "Among the Best Sellers." Then the paper can be a little choosy. Other papers run a supplemental list of books that *should* be on the "best seller" list: like "Recommended Books" or "New and Recommended."

The all-time best selling book is the Bible. And for some 60 years after it was published in 1887, its closest rival in America was Charles Sheldon's *In His Steps,* a religious novel with estimated sales of eight million. More recent big sellers include Dr. Benjamin Spock's baby book (20 million copies), the *Better Homes and Gardens Cook Book, Hammond's Pocket Atlas,* and the novel *Peyton Place.*[12]

Remainders

Although publishers, for most of their books, order initial press runs of no more than a few thousand, their press runs may still be too high. Not all copies sell. Something has to be done to clear them out.

Even a book that goes into additional printings and sells well for a while eventually reaches the point when further efforts to sell it don't pay off. For most books, two years is long enough. Again, something has to be done with the remaining copies.

The books lie there in the publisher's warehouse, no one having ordered them. Some have been returned by stores. The publisher

[12] See Alice Payne Hackett, *Seventy Years of Best Sellers,* R. R. Bowker Co., New York, 1968.

declares the book "out of print," and he "remainders" the leftover copies.

This involves selling copies at a sacrifice to houses that specialize in marketing books at bargain prices. Marboro, which advertises in the *Saturday Review* and the New York *Times,* is one of the biggest. Some books in their new "remainder" state find their way back to book stores, where they are used in sales promotions.

The person buying a remainder may get a book that is a few years old but, unlike some book club editions, it is the book in its original state and at a fraction of its original cost.

Book clubs

In 1926 the book-club idea took hold with the Book-of-the-Month Club and the Literary Guild. Booksellers wrung their hands at first, but they found that the clubs not only did not cut into retail sales of books but actually made book-buyers out of people who previously did not buy them.

Book clubs—there are 80 of them now—decide on a book usually before the book is published, while it is in a galley-proof stage (before the type has been arranged in pages). Some clubs publish their own editions, smaller in page size than the original editions, but, as their advertising suggests, "not a single word is cut." Sometimes the book club rents the printing plates from the original publisher.

Book clubs must advertise extensively to replace members who drop out after the first year. About half of the members do leave after the first year, but some come back later.

Book-club profit revolves around man's laziness and disorder. The club asks the member to go out of his way to fill out a card saying "No" to the current selection; if he fails to do that, he has ordered the book. When it comes, he finds it too much trouble to wrap and mail back.

Book publishers work very closely with the book clubs. One publisher, Doubleday, itself owns about 30 clubs and programs, including the Literary Guild and the Dollar Book Club.

The paperback "revolution"

The paperback "revolution," starting with Pocket Books in 1939, was not so much a revolution as a renaissance. Paperback books had been popular in the nineteenth century and died out then only because the publishers killed each other off in price wars.

In making their comeback, paperbacks at first offered readers only reprints and low-quality original material. Gradually the paperback publishers improved their offerings. Eventually, major publishers themselves got into the paperback business.

Today, hardbound books and paperbacks complement each other. Sometimes a publisher brings out hardbound and paperback editions of a given book simultaneously.

Paperback books go through the regular publication steps, but publishers can, when the occasion demands it, bring out a paperback in a matter of a few weeks or even a few days. (The regular paperback or hardbound book takes nine months to a year to publish once the manuscript is received.) "Instant paperbacks," as they are called, are usually written by journalists used to the rigors of newspaper or wire-service deadlines; the books capitalize on the death of a famous person or some momentous news event, such as a moon landing. Some publishers find it profitable to issue instant paperback versions of reports issued by emergency federal commissions. A publisher has to be sure of the potential of such books, because when it publishes an instant paperback it pays high production costs plus air freight charges and puts up with disruptions in its regular publishing program while all staff members concentrate on the one book that has to get through.[13]

In 1968, paperbacks, both quality and mass, accounted for 7,241 of the 30,387 books published.[14]

Anything goes

Of all the media of communication, books have been freest of censorship. The reason is clear: books are read primarily by an educated elite, a group least likely to sit still for censorship. Of course, some books destined for high school readers have had rough going. The John Birch Society, the American Legion, and

[13] See Alfred Balk, "The News Between Covers," *The New York Times Book Review*, February 15, 1970, pp. 4 ff.
[14] "1968: Subject Analysis of American Book Title Output," *Publishers' Weekly*, March 10, 1969, p. 23.

similar organizations have applied pressure on school boards.[15] In our past, we have witnessed book burnings. But these occasions grow rarer. And with the new freedom to say what one wants to say in magazines and even in newspapers, books are not alone in the freedom they enjoy.

That books, leading the way, went so far as they did resulted in some pretty gamy reading. Goodman Ace was moved to rename the "best seller" list "The Topless Ten."

One publisher that has specialized in "snickering sex," as someone has called it, is Bernard Geis and Associates, a firm set up originally to publish merely cheap, corny "non-books." But in September, 1967, five prominent partners pulled out of the Geis firm, and Random House said it would no longer distribute Geis books. Dissent had been brewing since the firm's *Sex and the Single Girl*.

Geis and Associates had latched onto an intriguing idea: to publish novels with heroes based on real people. You couldn't miss the identities. But they were off just enough to keep the publisher from getting into libel suits. *The Carpetbaggers*, for instance, was not about Howard Hughes. *The King* was not about Ronald Reagan and Frank Sinatra. *The Exhibitionist* was not about Jane Fonda. *The Voyeur* was not about Hugh Hefner.

As a protest against the novels of Jacqueline Susann and Harold Robbins (Geis authors)[16] 25 writers for *Newsday*, a Long Island, N.Y., newspaper, wrote chapters for a potboiler called *Naked Came the Stranger* (Lyle Stuart, New York, 1969), and saw it rise to the best-seller lists. It was the idea of Mike McGrady, columnist on the newspaper; he outlined the plot and assigned the chapters. He told his writers: "Good writing will be blue-pencilled into oblivion, and there will be an unremitting emphasis on sex." None of the writers knew what the others were doing. McGrady did some editing in fitting chapters together and chose the name Penelope Ashe as the "author" of the book. Within a few days after publication it had sold 25,000 copies, and a paperback contract and movie rights had been negotiated. After the hoax was revealed sales went much

15 For recent information on book censorship see the book edited by Eric Moon: *Book Selection and Censorship in the Sixties*, R. R. Bowker Company, New York, 1969.

16 But Miss Susann's recent *The Love Machine* was published by Simon and Schuster.

higher. One of the writers, John Cummings, who spent four and a half hours on his chapter, said the book is "just a collection of clichés and sexual aberrations."[17]

What one book writer can accomplish

Journalists—especially those who write books—can profoundly affect the course of events. Consider the case of Ralph Nader.

When as a student at Harvard Law School he drove across country and witnessed several accidents, he saw how easily the cars apparently had crumbled upon impact and began to ask questions. He found that in a law suit growing out of an accident, the driver, not the car manufacturer, carried the burden of proof. It seemed to this young man that the design of the car and the way it responded should be considered too.

As he probed further, he discovered the public generally was apathetic, the car makers not very cooperative. And so he began writing, first magazine articles, then a book. He called it *Unsafe at Any Speed.*

One Chevrolet model, the Corvair, literally bowed out as a result of the author's revelations. His book brought about an admission from the car makers that they should indeed share some of the blame for accidents. Congress got interested. New laws were passed and highway safety, at least insofar as car design is involved, was somewhat improved. Now even after cars are sold they are called back by manufacturers to correct defects. All because Ralph Nader wrote a book.

Nader went on to investigate the safety of gas pipelines and later the meat packing and other industries. He eventually set up offices in Washington, D.C., to act as a sort of unofficial consumer's ombudsman. He broadened his base to work for justice for the American Indian, union reform, and other causes. An article in *Life* in 1969 concluded: "Naderism is becoming an important social force."[18]

---

[17] Mike McGrady has written a book on the hoax, *Stranger than Naked, or How to Write Dirty Books for Fun and Profit: A Manual*, Peter H. Wyden, New York, 1970.

[18] Jack Newfield, "Nader's Raiders: The Lone Ranger Gets a Posse," *Life*, October 3, 1969, p. 56a.

You knew Nader had arrived when the cartoonists and the magazines took off on his book (which earned him $60,000). A *New Yorker* cartoon showed a sports car that had crashed through a fence, its driver defending himself to the police. "I was waiting for *Unsafe at Any Speed* to come out in paperback." *Grump* ran an "exposé" on furniture manufacturers and called it *"Unsafe at Any Sitting."* The article called for padded head rests on rocking chairs to prevent "chair lash" when rocking. In late 1969 *Time* put Nader on its cover.

Nor was this the first time a book-journalist had affected a nation.[19] Rachel Carson did it with *Silent Spring*. Jessica Mitford did it with *The American Way of Death*. And years earlier, Upton Sinclair did it with *The Jungle*, a book that brought about the 1906 Meat Inspection Act.

What the imprint tells you

Before he decides to give his time to a work of nonfiction, the wise reader finds out something about the author and his qualifications. Perhaps he knows the author through his earlier works. Perhaps the dust jacket biography convinces the reader the author is an authority on his subject.

To a lesser extent, the publisher's imprint says something about the nature of the book. Generally speaking, well-known houses like Harper & Row, Random House, McGraw-Hill, Doubleday, and Little, Brown put out a more reliable—or at least a better edited—product than the smaller houses. But quality, even among the big houses, varies considerably. Random House in late 1969 put its Vintage imprint on *The Woodstock Nation: A Talk-Rock Album*. It took five days to write. Author Abbie Hoffman reported: "Lying on the floor in an office of the publisher, I'm flying high on adrenalin, excitement, no sleep, rock music and pot. Using what I can find lying around, I write out every word by hand."[20]

The big houses have catholic tastes. We expect books of popular appeal from them; so we are surprised when a house like Viking

[19] See Robert B. Downs, *Books That Changed America*, Macmillan, New York, 1970.
[20] "Random House Rushes 'The Woodstock Nation,'" *Publishers' Weekly*, September 29, 1969, p. 46.

Press announces, as it did in 1966, the publication of *European and American Snuff Boxes: 1730–1830*. (You can have it for only $30.)

Certainly the top editors of major publishing firms would not agree with the theses of all the books they publish. It would be hard to imagine anyone at Houghton Mifflin, for instance, applauding what Hitler said in *Mein Kampf;* yet the firm published that book in the 1930s because it felt, rightly, that it should have the attention of American readers.

Occasionally a big house will bring out a book of high literary or social significance that appeals only to a limited audience, knowing full well the book will lose money. The house does this to add to its prestige. Perhaps it will succeed in getting librarians, at least, to notice other books on its list. On the other hand, to add to its profits for the year, it may bring out a book of confession-magazine quality; but for this book, to protect its image, the publisher slaps on a subsidiary imprint.

It is easier to come to a decision about the worth of a book when the imprint is that of a smaller house—one that produces fewer, say, than 50 books a year. These houses tend to specialize. Their product is predictable.

Some small imprints have become rather familiar. Who does not know by now the specialty of Grove Press? A cartoonist has shown a nude at a switchboard. She's saying into the receiver: "Grove Press." This was the firm taken over temporarily in April, 1970 by the Women's Liberation Movement with its demands related to "crimes against women." The Movement's leaders charged that the firm had "earned millions off the basic theme of humiliating, degrading, and dehumanizing women through sado-masochistic literature, pornographic films, and oppressive and exploitive practices against its own female employees."[21]

Lesser known to the ordinary reader are imprints belonging to

[21] "Grove Fires Union Activists; Women's Lib Seizes Offices," *Publishers' Weekly*, April 20, 1970, p. 38. But Grove Press, which first came into prominence with the publication of the unexpurgated version of *Lady Chatterley's Lover* and later the books of Henry Miller, is now much more than a publisher of scatological works. It published *Games People Play* and Malcolm X's *Autobiography*. Some of its works in sociology are notable and are widely adopted as textbooks in colleges. (See "*Evergreen* in the Underground," Chapter 10 of Martin Mayer, *All You Know Is Facts*, Harper & Row, New York, 1969.)

Franklin Watts, which specializes in juveniles; Watson-Guptill Publications in art books; R. R. Bowker Co. in books about books; Frederick Fell in self-help books; Wm. C. Brown Co. in textbooks; Stackpole Books in books about guns and the outdoors; Charles E. Tuttle Co. in books about Japan.

The 1960s saw the beginnings of a number of lively, small houses that found it possible to publish books without the usual staff and facilities. One of these was Chelsea House, so named because its founders lived at the Chelsea Hotel (the firm has since moved to its own quarters). The hotel switchboard operator used to answer the phone: "Chelsea"; and callers naturally assumed she was an employee of the publisher.

Chelsea has specialized in publishing works in the public domain. It was the first to bring out a reprint of an old Sears, Roebuck catalogue. Other Chelsea books include a collection of inaugural addresses of the Presidents and a collection of State of the Union addresses. These do not make very good reading, but they represent the kind of books libraries cannot resist buying. Chelsea House's books are distributed through an arrangement with Random House.[22]

Most book publishers, large and small, are located in New York, the nation's mass media capital, but Boston has a few book publishers, and so do other large cities. A number of religious publishers have clustered at Grand Rapids, Mich., in Dutch Reformed Church country. Almost every state has its small regional publisher specializing in local history and lore. One of these, Caxton Printers Ltd., Caldwell, Idaho, has branched off into political works of an ultraconservative stripe.

In a category by themselves are the university presses, set up originally to publish books of remote scholarly interest. Every major university now has one. As conceived, these houses did not intend to make money. They simply meant to make possible an exchange of findings and observations among educators. A few engaged in subsidy publishing as they took on not very readable dissertations. But now many have ventured into more lucrative lines: even into textbooks. And most of them compete with commer-

[22] See Charles Sopkin, "The Chelsea Boys and How They Grew," *New York*, March 2, 1970, pp. 46–50.

cial publishers. They pay royalties and advertise in magazines like *The New York Times Book Review* and the *Saturday Review*.

Why read reviews?

"Nature, when she invented, manufactured, and patented her authors, contrived to make critics out of the chips that were left over," said Oliver Wendell Holmes. Nevertheless, every author must subject his work to the critics, and critics can make the difference as to whether or not a book sells. Nothing pleases an author more than to find expressions like "must reading" and "a long-needed book" in a review of his work. But the review doesn't have to be admiring. Just getting the book *noticed* by reviewers is enough to spur sales. And the promotion department of a book publisher can find *something* in even the most scathing review, pull it out of context, and play it up in the ads. "The book is both original and interesting—but the parts that are original are not interesting and the parts that are interesting are not original. . . . ," a review might read. The publisher in his advertising might quote only this from the review: "original and interesting." Or, here's a typical dismissal of a book by Dorothy Parker: "This is not a novel to be tossed aside lightly. It should be thrown with great force." What's to prevent the book promoter from using just the first sentence?

Book publishers generally regard attention by *The New York Times Book Review*, even if it's unfavorable, as vital to a book's promotion if it is a trade book. Only about 2,200 books make it each year. Also important to the success of a book is notice by the general circulation magazines, which have only lately gone in for reviewing; *Book World*, a publication of the Washington *Post* and the Chicago *Tribune*; *The New York Review of Books*; and the *Saturday Review*. Notice by the quality and opinion magazines is important, too, although their reviews more often pronounce final verdicts on the worth of books than influence sales.

Notice by *Library Journal* and *Publishers' Weekly* is important in reaching librarians and book dealers.

For specialized books, publishers try to get their books reviewed in appropriate specialized magazines.

Book-review editors of publications receive free copies of books prior to the time they're released to the general public, pick those they think readers would be most interested in, decide on who the reviewers should be, and send the books out for review.

The New York Times Book Review pays $100 and up for reviews, but many other publications expect the reviewer to be content with the book itself as payment. *The Christian Century* sends along a second book as a token payment to its reviewers. Book reviewers are perhaps the most underpaid of all journalists. Their real income comes from the satisfaction of passing judgment.

What's in it for the reader? Why should he read book reviews?

1. *For news about books.* Obviously, the reader can't possibly see each of the 30,000 new books issued every year. Turning to the reviews, he can take note at least of the books deemed important by book-review editors. He can expect to find descriptions there less biased than jacket copy, because reviewers, theoretically, are not trying to sell books.

Theoretically. Unfortunately, there is a lot of back-scratching among reviewers, some of whom write books themselves. Their attitude seems to be: You say nice things about my book and I'll say nice things about yours. Furthermore, reviewers tend to write to impress their colleagues with their erudition rather than to serve the reader.

2. *For evaluation of books.* If the reader is thinking about buying a book, he will want to know something about it first. Will it be worth his money? Should he put a reserve notice in for it at the library? A reviewer can help him make his decision.

But some reviews sound as if the reviewer didn't even read the book, much less study it. Perhaps he made his notes from information on the jacket, taking literally Sydney Smith's remark: "I never read a book before reviewing it. It prejudices one so!"

Certainly the reader has a right to expect to be told *why* a critic likes or dislikes a book. Barbara George, responding to Granville Hicks's review of *In Cold Blood* in the *Saturday Review,* said in a letter-to-the-editor that she didn't like Hicks's final sentence, which was: "I will point out, however, that although this is a very, very good book *Crime and Punishment* is a great one." Barbara George wanted to know why Hicks felt this way. ". . . He indicates in his closing sentence that he has judged the book by some higher standards and found it wanting. I will point out, however, that, until Mr. Hicks will tell us what these standards are, he will remain a very, very good critic, but not a great one."

The review reader should pay particular attention to the reviewer's credentials. Is he qualified to comment on the book? A man who is himself an expert in the field covered by the book can better evaluate the book than some peripatetic reviewer who sees himself as kingmaker.

If possible, the reader should read more than one review of a given book. He may be surprised at how intelligent men with good intentions can differ.

However, the reader should not read reviews and feel he's read the book. A review is, after all, second hand. If the review interests the reader, chances are the subject in its original state of discussion will interest him more.

Stan Hunt in a 1961 *New Yorker* cartoon ridiculed the reliance of some readers on reviewers when he showed a library patron stopping at shelves marked, respectively, "Fiction, Well Received," "Fiction, Mixed Reviews," and "Fiction, Poorly Reviewed."

3. *For tangential benefits.* Some reviewers are not content to stay with the book under discussion. They use the book as an excuse for writing an essay. Reviewers in *The New York Review of Books* are guilty of this. While this practice may annoy the books' writers and publishers, it may well reward the reader. Some of these "book reviews" can stand by themselves in the information they impart and the ideas they bring out.

And if the reader gets nothing else out of reviews, he learns something about the fine art of putting someone down. "The covers of this book are too far apart."—Ambrose Bierce. "Mr. Henry James writes fiction as if it were a painful duty."—Oscar Wilde. "A redeeming feature of the work is that no talent was wasted in the writing of it."—*The New Yorker.*

For that matter, why read books?

In no other medium does an author have so much room to maneuver as in a book. He has room to explain all the subtle turns of his subject. He has room to cite all his sources and identify them. He can list other books on the same subject. And in the back of his book, he can run an index to all the information in the book, making it easy for the reader later to find exactly what he needs.[23]

A book has its unique value to readers.

But putting a piece of journalism into a book does not in itself make it any worthier than journalism found in less permanent form. Quality varies in book publishing just as it varies in newspaper and magazine publishing. As readers sharpen their critical facilities, they will conclude that a majority of the books published, quite apart from the fact that they deal with areas the reader is not interested in, are not worth their time. Too many publishers think H. L. Mencken wasn't kidding when he said that no one ever went broke underestimating the intelligence of the American public. Charles A. Madison observes: "Good books have always been the exception rather than the rule. . . ."[24]

Time magazine and other observers have described one group of books—those put together with scissors or tape recorder to cash in on a ready market—as "non-books." Ghostwritten autobiographies, "as told to" books, books of photographs with cute captions, some inspirational books (like the completely serious book, *The Power of Prayer on Plants*), and many self-help books (like *The Secrets of Long Life*)[25] would certainly fall into the nonbook category.

Yet when all of this has been said, the fact remains that the minority of genuinely good books among any year's crop of newly published titles represents the peak of achievement in journalism and the arts.

The format of the book offers a writer the best chance he will ever have to utilize his creative skills fully and to explore his topic in searching depth. Moreover, of all the various forms of journalism and writing, the book involves the most relaxed set of publication deadlines and thus affords the opportunity for the kind of

[23] To get more out of books, see Mortimer J. Adler, *How to Read a Book: The Art of Getting a Liberal Education*, Simon and Schuster, New York, 1940.

[24] Charles A. Madison, *Book Publishing in America*, McGraw-Hill Book Company, New York, 1966, p. 403.

[25] This book, by Dr. George Gallup and Evan Hill, published by Bernard Geis and Associates, got this reception from *Time*: "Longevity statistics that a newspaper could summarize in half a column, padded to book length by some extraordinarily foolish anecdotes and a questionnaire in which the reader can test his chances of living long enough to see publishing get even worse."

careful editing and polishing that may not be possible in most magazine and newspaper writing. When a piece of writing in book-length format is good, it is very, very good indeed.

As the educational level of Americans rises and their leisure time increases, the book continues to thrive, despite competition from other media. More visually oriented media have their newly-won place, of course, but they cannot do the whole job of communication.

Perhaps writer David Dempsey has the best response for those who, like Marshall McLuhan, preach the demise of the book: "Has anyone ever said, 'How well I remember the slide transparency that changed my life'?"[26]

[26] David Dempsey, "Humanist Wedges to Learning," *Saturday Review,* July 12, 1969, p. 28.

CHAPTER THIRTEEN

News under license

The third and fifth decades of the twentieth century saw the addition of dramatic dimensions to the picture of the world made available to the public by the media of mass communication. First radio in the 1920s, and then television in the years following World War II, emerged as distinctive new channels for the dissemination of news and opinion.

Much of the discussion in this book's earlier chapters about the problems involved in gathering, writing, and presenting information to the public is applicable to radio and television as well as newspapers and magazines. But some aspects of the two electronic media are unique; they demand separate consideration of their nature and of their effects.

One point that must be noted at the outset has to do with the primary function of the broadcast media.

The chief and original purpose of newspapers was to transmit information and opinion to a wide audience; the carrying of commercial messages and the entertainment of the readers, though important, were secondary functions.

'Don't cut THAT nude . . . she's in the commercial!'

Cartoon by Tom Darcy. Reprinted with permission from Newsday, Inc.

But radio and television, through much of their relatively short lives, have assigned first priority to the entertainment of their audiences. Also, while the print media have had two bases of financial support—advertising and subscriptions—the broadcast media have been wholly dependent on revenue from the sale of time to advertisers.

These facts of life have helped to determine the nature of the products that radio and television have put before the public. Advertisers and their agents have had a more direct role in controlling the nonadvertising content of the two broadcast media than has been the case with newspapers and magazines.

The control exerted by advertisers over radio and television programming has been evident chiefly in the entertainment content of the broadcasters' offerings. Advertisers wanted to reach as large an audience as possible with their sales message, and entertainment programs seemed to represent the best means of attracting listeners and viewers in great numbers. For a measurement of the drawing power of such programs, the advertisers depended on audience-rating figures compiled by agencies that regularly polled samples of the viewing audience to find out how many sets were tuned to which offerings. Such polling is far from a science, yet the ratings of program popularity came to have life-or-death power over programs and performers.

The influence of the ratings on the advertisers who paid the bills led to a homogenization of much of the broadcasting content offered during prime time (the evening hours, when audiences are largest). Proven, crowd-getting patterns (bland situation comedy, violence-ridden drama) were favored,[1] and the unusual or the innovative got little encouragement. Material likely to be offensive to a principal sponsor was rejected or toned down. The over-all scene was described by Newton Minow, at that time chairman of the Federal Communications Commission, as a "vast wasteland."[2]

---

[1] Al Kaufman shows why in a cartoon in *TV Guide*. A man and woman are watching TV. The man says, "This program is thought-provoking, original and significant. See what else is on."

[2] In the eyes of at least some observers, the situation had not improved much by the end of the 1960s. A book-length report, *The Alfred I. DuPont-Columbia University Survey of Broadcast Journalism, 1968–69*, published by Grosset & Dunlap, included the following judgment by the director and five distinguished jurors who compiled the report:

But Minow and other critics exempted many of the news shows from the "wasteland" indictment. The news programs, particularly at the network level, were superior in quality to most of the entertainment material that had surrounded them on the broadcast schedule. Moreover, they had grown up as stepchildren through much of the history of broadcasting; sponsors and advertisers, preoccupied with the audience-attracting possibilities of the entertainment programs, paid little attention to the news shows and made no serious effort to control their content. By the time the newscasts had established themselves and had come to be recognized as drawing cards in their own right, it was too late for sponsor influence to move in on them as had been the case with the entertainment programs. The radio and television newsmen had declared themselves in the journalistic traditions of the longer-established print media of information; in that spirit, most broadcasters stoutly resisted sponsor influence over news shows, sometimes even more stoutly than had their counterparts in the print media. TV newsman Walter Cronkite observed in his 1969 William Allen White address at the University of Kansas: "I can testify that the executives of my network are far less meddlesome in the news process than the publishers for whom I've worked."

The broadcast journalists did not, however, escape criticism altogether. They were spared the accusation of sponsor-domination, but they came under fire on several other counts. Their critics had a field day in 1969 after the Vice President of the United States, apparently with White House approval and backing, launched a direct frontal attack on the practices of the major network newscasters.

Vice President Spiro Agnew, in an address carried by all three TV networks, castigated what he called "the tiny and closed fraternity of privileged men" who prepared, packaged, and interpreted the "news that 40 million Americans receive each night."

The television set is on in the average American home for over six hours every day. The radio accounts for another two to five hours, depending on the age and sex of the listener. Into this vacuum television broadcasters for the most part have chosen to pour a torrent of situation comedies, adventure-detective-westerns, soap operas, ball games, variety, audience participation and talk-talk-talk shows. These, along with radio's endlessly repeated headlines and pop tunes, are punctuated in staccato clusters by messages lovingly fashioned to recommend the unnecessary to the unwitting, the superfluous to the superficial. Across vast distances, at enormous expense, and with enormous ingenuity, shallow calls to shallow, morning, noon, and night.

He charged that the news executives and on-camera commentators filtered the news through their own liberal political biases; that television news gave undue emphasis to gore and violence; that the TV camera had been used to build obscure agitators into nationally known celebrities; and that the "instant analysis and querulous criticism" engaged in by the news program anchormen and commentators had poisoned the public's mind against the actions of the incumbent administration.

Leaders of the broadcasting networks responded angrily and defensively. Columbia Broadcasting System president Frank Stanton called the speech "an unprecedented attempt by the Vice President . . . to intimidate a news medium. . . ." National Broadcasting Company news president Reuven Frank said that it was "just another case of the messenger being blamed for the message. If we hurt them with our coverage they say we say too much. If we hurt them by not covering, they say we say too little."

Yet an outpouring of telephone calls, wires, and letters from throughout the country indicated that the Vice President had touched responsive chords in many viewers and listeners. Although his attack had at least some political motives, Agnew had given voice to several concerns shared by a substantial number of Americans who had come to sense the fact that broadcast journalism had special characteristics that affected the nature of the news report. These characteristics are for the most part inherent in the nature of the broadcast media. Some of them affect the quality and accuracy of the flow of the news; some of them can be compensated for without damage to the news report; and some of them are more imagined than real, bogeymen created by Agnew and other critics who do not fully understand how the broadcast media function. Let's take a look at some of the characteristics of broadcast journalism and at the ways in which they affect the performance of these information media.

What can they do in 14 minutes?

One difference between the newspaper report and the newscast is quantitative. All of the media are limited in terms of the amount of news they can offer the consumer in a given day's package. But the limitations pinch hardest of all for the broadcaster. The number of pages in a newspaper can vary from day to day, and when the news flow is heavy a bigger than usual issue can be published. But there are only so many minutes and hours in the broadcast day, and most of them are preempted by the entertainment content that brings in the advertiser's dollar.

The producer of one half-hour network news show estimates that by the time he has allowed for the commercials, sports, and the weather report, he has approximately 14 minutes left in which to present the "hard news" of the nation and the world. The local station news director has a similar tight fit for local and regional news.

The distillation that goes on in the processing of news for the newspaper must be carried even further in the case of broadcast news. A 25-second film clip, with the announcer's voice in the background, may have to convey the significance of a development reported in a full column of newspaper copy. And many kinds of news for which the newspaper can regularly find room simply never show up at all in the broadcast report.

Cronkite, long the star newsman of CBS, once observed: "We do such a slick job that we have deluded the public into thinking that they get all they need to know from us. And the people, if they are to exercise their franchise intelligently, need a flow of bulk information. We can't give it to them."

Cronkite and other leaders of the broadcast industry had been concerned, long before the Agnew outburst, about the way in which the broadcast news report is received by the listening and watching public. Surveys have demonstrated that increasing numbers of Americans are relying on television as their primary source of news; yet the broadcasters themselves admit that TV doesn't—and can't— give the whole news picture. The viewer who turns away from the set feeling that he has been brought up to date on the world is probably no better off than if he had skimmed through a half dozen newspaper headlines and lead paragraphs.

"You see it happening"

The broadcast news report often has a stronger impact than that of the newspaper report because the electronic media convey an impression of greater recency; additionally, in the case of television, the visual dimension puts the news on a "see it now" basis and invests it with authenticity.

The impression of recency gained by the listener or viewer may indeed be legitimate much of the time, but not always. Some television shows are put on video tape or film hours ahead of the broadcast deadline and the news they contain may be a good deal more stale than the version in the evening paper that arrived on the doorstep an hour earlier. Often television and radio news broadcasters do not adequately identify those portions of their report that have been prerecorded.

The additional, "you see it happening" impression conveyed by television can also be misleading, simply because the viewer very likely does not realize how the "reality" on the screen may have been processed and modified before he has had a chance to see it.

When a reader goes through a newspaper account he is aware that he is reading a reporter's condensed version of the event. The same reader watching a television newscast may not be as aware of the judgmental and editing factors that were involved in boiling down that same event to the few screened glimpses he now is watching. He typically regards the TV version as more believable and trustworthy than the newspaper story.

As we have noted, there are numerous ways in which distortion can enter into a printed news report. Similar distortions can just as easily occur in television news coverage; two cameramen, filming the same riot, by their selection of the segments on which to focus, can come up with dramatically different versions. Yet each of these versions, when it comes on the television screen, will give the viewer the mistaken impression that he is "seeing it all happen."

Another, related kind of distortion in television news arises out of the understandable preference of the TV newsman for a story with a strong visual dimension.

Television news directors try their best to avoid keeping the camera very long on the static scene of an announcer at a desk, reading from wire-service copy. They want film clips or at the least still photographs to use as backdrop, perhaps with the announcer's voice on the sound track. So if there is a choice to be made between a trivial story that has some accompanying film footage, and a more consequential item that has none, the nod often goes to the illustrated trivia. (This is much more true of local newscasts than of the network shows, of course, since film of local news events is expensive in terms of the typical small station's budget.)

Television newsmen will contend that this criticism is overstated, and to some extent misguided. As one network correspondent put it, "We aren't supplying an inferior sort of newspaper coverage—we're supplying television coverage. . . . Being condescending toward us for our reliance on pictures is like knocking a newspaper article for not being a book, or a movie for not being a novel. Our coverage just gives another aspect of the news."[3]

"Made-to-order" news

Vice President Agnew, as had others before him, complained that the TV version of the news constitutes a misrepresentation of reality for yet another reason. They charged that TV newsmen sometimes *manufacture* the news as well as cover it. They contended that the presence of the cameras could cause or accelerate a news development, particularly one involving some kind of disorganized group activity.

---

[3] The critics' rejoinder to this is that much television news coverage must be classified as both different and inferior. Sir William Haley, Director General of the British Broadcasting Corporation and former editor of the London *Times*, made a study of American television in 1969 for Columbia University and the Alfred I. DuPont Foundation. In his report he characterized television news coverage as "occasionally brilliant" but all too often "meretricious, superficial, and spotty."

This is more markedly so [Sir William continued] on individual stations than on the networks. On many of these stations entertainment values do reign. The approach is: "Who is new in town? How can we fill the time while we show his face on the screen?" I have been asked to appear on television in a city I was visiting—in a news program—and to be introduced, expound on Britain's economic problems, General de Gaulle, Lord Thomson's newspaper empire, and England's attitude to the presidential election campaign, all in two minutes. Even on the networks, the constant urge to parade faces before the camera, strings of people, some hardy regulars, others with little or no relevance, each uttering one or two sentences of hardly any value, is another example of the subordination of news to entertainment. The editors of the programs are not concerned to be constructively informing and explaining, they are desperately trying to hold their jobs by holding their ratings. Brightness is all. The subordination of real news values to visual news values is not peculiar to American television. It is as bad in Britain. (Quoted in *The Alfred I. DuPont-Columbia University Survey of Broadcast Journalism, 1968–69*, ed. by Marvin Barrett, Grosset & Dunlap, New York, 1969, pp. 61–62.)

As William A. Wood, author of a textbook on broadcast journalism, describes it:

> One example is the involvement of television correspondents and crews in protest marches or demonstrations. The pro or anti civil rights group, the pro or anti Vietnam groups, create the news by making their protest in a public place; when television goes out with its cameras to cover this news, it can rarely keep from having an effect on the news. . . . It is a common experience of stations to receive telephone calls from demonstrators alerting them to what's coming, and in case after case the demonstration begins when the cameras are ready to roll—on cue, as it were.[4]

It is of course true that any news reporter, for whatever medium, can have some effect upon the way in which a news situation develops. Newspaper or wire-service reporters stationed at the statehouse, the city hall, or the national capitol sometimes become involved as movers and shakers as well as recorders of events, simply because they are in constant contact with the powers that be and often on close and friendly terms with them.[5]

Yet the mere appearance of a pad-and-pencil reporter on the scene of a news development is rarely enough to change the nature of that event; he is usually unobtrusive and unrecognized. Not so the TV reporter, with his lights, cameras, trucks, and numerous assistants. His advent can constitute a catalyst to action for those participants in the news whose objective is public notice.

The result, as depicted in the following story by Chancellor William P. Tolley of Syracuse University, can be spectacular.

---

[4] *Electronic Journalism,* Columbia University Press, New York, 1967.

[5] In a discussion of the role played by Washington correspondents, a *Wall Street Journal* reporter wrote that:

> . . . The fact is that the influential Washington press corps' powers extend considerably beyond reporting and interpreting the news unfolding in the capital. Unknown to their readers, newsmen here, and particularly investigative reporters, sometimes are the prime promoters or offstage prompters on the Congressional hearings, legislative battles and other events they are chronicling, theoretically with detachment. This practice of "not only getting it from the horse's mouth but being inside his mouth" is "almost a way of life for many columnists and some reporters here," says Laurence Stern, an assistant managing editor of the Washington *Post.* (From a news story, "Capital Newsmen Often Play a Role in Creating the Events They Cover," *The Wall Street Journal,* September 11, 1968, p. 1.)

When reporters and television cameras outnumber the campus demonstrators, something is wrong with our mass media. And, unhappily, after endless TV exposure of dissent and rebellion, faculty and students accept the distortion as true and begin to clamor for a piece of the action. Is it unfair to suggest that the mass media have encouraged the contagion of student and faculty discord? From my experience the evidence is overwhelming. Nor am I alone in feeling that the mass media no longer limit their role to reporting the news. They create it.[6]

The responsible television newsman or film editor does what he can to avoid such unfortunate results. Wood notes that a Miami film crew arrived at the scene of a reported disturbance and found the demonstrators sitting on a curb awaiting the newsmen's arrival before going into their act. "The station aired the film but told their audience what the situation was *before* the film was shot."

The decision makers

Another of Agnew's criticisms of television news was the charge that a "small and unelected elite" group of producers and anchor men decide what the American public will know about the news, and that their decisions are dictated by their liberal political views.

The Vice President was probably fairly close to the truth about the size of the group of decision-makers. *Time* magazine, commenting on the Agnew speech, identified a group of a dozen men—on-camera commentators, news executives, and producers—who among them had a controlling influence on the content of news programs on the three major networks.[7]

The rest of Agnew's charge—that these few were all liberals and that they allowed their ideology to influence their news judgment —was more difficult to validate.

Probably most of the men at the top managerial and ownership levels of the broadcasting industry are as conservative in political viewpoint as most of their counterparts in the print media. It may also be true—again, as in the print media—that a majority of the working newsmen in the broadcasting field would be found in the liberal camp, if an ideological saliva test were applied. This point

[6] Quoted in *Syracuse Alumni News*, May, 1969.
[7] *Time*, November 21, 1969, p. 20.

was indirectly acknowledged by one CBS Washington commentator who said at the time of the Vice President's speech: "My feeling is that the White House is out to get all of us, all the liberals in all the media."[8]

But even if this much could be established, it would not necessarily follow that the liberal newsmen in the broadcast media deliberately slanted their news coverage. A great many radio and television reporters and commentators started out in the newspaper business, and brought with them into broadcasting the traditions of objectivity that are respected in the newspapers and wire services. As Avram R. Westin, executive producer of the American Broadcasting Company's evening news programs, observed at the time of the Agnew speech:

My politics are more conservative than Vice President Agnew would have people believe, but that doesn't matter. My job is to keep my politics and those of others off the air. You can't always be objective because you bring your experiences to things—so you try to be fair. We are on guard. We're not infallible. We try.[9]

On occasion, matchless power

Whatever complaints may be made about television news—internally or externally—all of its critics are obliged to acknowledge its vast impact and influence.

There is no doubt, for example, that the national movement against the continuation of the Vietnam war was able to grow from a handful of campus dissenters to a large-scale expression of popular will largely because of the kind of coverage that television was giving to the war.

The battlefront films that came into the living rooms of America each evening on the TV newscast constituted a kind of intrusion of the face of war that differed from the coverage given to previous conflicts in which this nation had been involved. The viewer was projected directly into the front lines, forced to view the ugliness of battle close-up, and—most important of all—on a see-it-now basis. The result was a build-up of national revulsion that was utilized by

[8] Quoted in *Newsweek*, November 24, 1969, p. 90.
[9] *Time, op. cit.*, p. 21.

the antiwar protesters to help bring down a President and alter a national policy.

In the judgment of at least some observers, it was television coverage that magnified the impact of the civil-rights drive of 1963 so that it resulted in the passage of significant national legislation.

And when the full resources of the medium are focused on a situation, its influence can be matchless. During the days of dread and shock that followed the assassination of President John Kennedy it was television—together with other elements of the press—that kept the nation from giving way to panic. Round-the-clock coverage of the events of that tragic weekend served both to unite the public in an unprecedented sharing of grief and to provide reassurance that the governmental processes were continuing despite the loss of the head of state.

Other cases in which the network resources were mustered to provide rapid, in-depth coverage in the aftermath of major news developments indicated the potentialities of television as a reporting medium. Such crisis efforts are extremely costly, however, both in resources and in preempted commercial time. Day-by-day coverage must be on the much more limited basis of the 15- or 30-minute news roundup program.

But even on that basis, and setting aside the specials and spectaculars, the influence of television news is impressive. A medium that has nightly access to 40,000,000 viewers has vast leverage by anyone's yardstick.

Stars were born

Some of that enormous leverage exerted by the major network shows derives from the special standing of the newscasters involved. The star system is characteristic of national network newscasts, and the chief commentators (anchor men) rank with movie celebrities, both in fame and salary. (Such luminaries as David Brinkley for NBC and Walter Cronkite for CBS reportedly earn from $200,000 to $400,000 annually. When they go out to cover news situations they—rather than the news personality they are covering—become the focus of the crowds.)

The major national news commentators, simply because they are widely known celebrities with substantial personal followings, can shape the audience reaction to a given news item simply by a slight change in voice inflection, or by the lift of a skeptical eyebrow at precisely the right moment.

The NBC team of Huntley and Brinkley, who during the years they were together were the most successful combination in the history of television newscasting, provided an interesting case study of the newsman-celebrity and his influence on the flow of the news. The pair first teamed up to cover the 1956 political conventions and clicked so well together that they were moved into the lead role for the NBC news organization later that same year. Through the decade and a half that followed they became as much a fixture of the American scene as the politicos, astronauts, and Mafia members whose activities they reported in their nightly commentary.

Behind them there grew up an awesome assemblage of supporting newscasters, engineers, producers, directors, and technicians. A breakdown of the manpower involved in a single Huntley-Brinkley newscast—including everyone from writers to motorcycle couriers who rushed film to the studio—showed that a total of 330 persons helped to get the show on the air. Of the total, seven, including the two stars, actually appeared on camera.

A *New Yorker* magazine author, William Whitworth, wrote a profile of the team, noting that "their sheer famousness, impressive by show-business standards, is downright unreal by the standards of journalism, electronic or otherwise." Whitworth pointed out that the two men, and particularly Brinkley, had profoundly affected the development of the TV news industry.

. . . Brinkley . . . has altered to a considerable extent the tone of American news broadcasting. Until he rose to stardom, the dominant style was a grave one, formed in the crisis years before and during the Second World War and best exemplified by [Edward R.] Murrow's work. Brinkley brought to the industry an understated wit, an irreverence that seemed to be based on a coherent viewpoint rather than on a pose. . . .[10]

Brinkley, Whitworth reported, was a reporter and writer as well as newscaster. He insisted on writing his own copy, and in the judg-

[10] "An Accident of Casting," *The New Yorker*, August 3, 1968, pp. 34-60.

ment of many, including the heads of NBC, he was the best writer in the business. He also covered some of the stories that he reported, or at the least was able to bring some personal expertise to the writing of them because his contacts with news sources were kept fresh and active. But, according to Whitworth, the Huntley approach was quite different:

> Huntley and Brinkley have very dissimilar jobs. Brinkley's gives him a chance to write and report, but Huntley's seldom does, for a number of reasons. Huntley's beat, in a sense, is the whole world minus Washington. The best stories on his portion of the program tend to be photographic—wars, natural disasters, riots, and the like—and so are covered by camera crews and correspondents, whose reports need little from Huntley beyond a few words of introduction. As for the non-visual stories—the ones that Huntley simply reads on the air, with perhaps a map or a drawing in the background—these are based, for the most part, on wire service reports, which must be verified, condensed, and rewritten to meet the program's style and time requirements. . . . Occasionally there will be an item of particular interest to Huntley, perhaps concerning foreign affairs or race relations, and then he can express himself by writing what amounts to a little editorial. . . .

Conscious of the kind of leverage their every word or gesture conveys, such network stars as Cronkite try conscientiously to avoid the "little editorials" as much as possible. They make a consistent effort to report the news rather than color it; but their effort to that end is far more difficult than that of the reporter for the print media, who has to worry only about the distortion reflected in the words he writes.

Meanwhile, back at the ranch . . .

It is a long span, in several respects, from the mighty television stars to the small-town newscaster. The variation in quality is often as marked as the distance in geographic or size-of-audience terms. Broadcast news at the small-market radio or TV station can be very sketchy, based on a "rip and read" use of the wire-service file and a hasty rewrite of the local newspaper's report.

On the small station, the newscaster is primarily a reader of copy; in radio, particularly, he also typically has several other roles to carry out, including that of commercial announcer, disc jockey, and perhaps even part-time engineer. He has little opportunity to write news, and almost none to go out to cover it live.

The hard-pressed small-station newsman does have some help from the wire services. They furnish a special broadcast wire report, with news copy written to the special needs of the radio and television newsmen. The style is characterized by short sentences, simplified phrasing, a conversational tone, and the repetition of central news facts. Numbers are rounded off, and proper names are usually held back until the person involved has first been otherwise identified, by occupation or by his involvement in the news event. All of these devices are designed to make the news account understandable at first hearing, since that is all it will have.

On the staffs of larger stations there are local news teams, whose work supplements the copy supplied by the wire-service broadcast file. Some of the very large TV and radio stations have as many as 40 or 50 full-time newsmen covering the local and regional scene, which compares with the staffing given to that same news sector by a metropolitan newspaper.

On the cable

Some expansion of both news and other kinds of programming at the local level may result from the spread of the cable TV systems.

Cable systems had for years brought programming from all three networks to towns isolated from metropolitan areas and served inadequately, if at all, by local TV. By the end of the 1960s cable TV systems were concentrating on the big city markets as well. Laying cable was much more expensive in the cities than in the small towns, but the customer potential was also much greater.

Business Week said that the cable TV industry expected to serve up to half of all homes in the United States by 1975. And a 1969 ruling by the FCC gave the cable operators the go-ahead to originate their own programs and to sell time to advertisers, which opened up new possibilities of service. To quote *Business Week*, cable TV was "changing the entire face of American Communications."[11]

11 "Cable TV Leaps into the Big Time," *Business Week*, November 22, 1969, pp. 100–108. See also the special issue of *The Nation*, May 18, 1970: "The Wired Nation," by Ralph Lee Smith.

"Our guest today . . ."

One aspect of broadcast news coverage deserves special attention —the interview show.

The exact counterpart of the TV interview show is not to be found in the newspapers, although some magazines (notably *U.S. News and World Report*) have developed something like it.

Some of the interview shows scheduled in the late evening hours are purely entertainment. But others, particularly the array of Sunday spectaculars, constitute a significant component of the overall news scene.

The Sunday shows such as "Meet the Press," "Face the Nation," and "Issues and Answers," are all alike in format. A guest who is someone currently involved in the news is interviewed by a panel of newsmen who poke and prod at him mercilessly in an effort to generate some kind of news break. Often they succeed, sometimes because the news source has chosen to make the program a springboard for an announcement or a trial balloon.

The interview shows provide a significant kind of public service in that they put before the public some of the nation's leaders or would-be leaders in a setting not under their control, and without benefit of the usual public relations screen. In responding to the searching, sometimes waspish questioning of the panelists, the guests reveal themselves and their philosophies as perhaps never before. Although they know they are in for punishment, the dignitaries accept invitations to the panel shows anyway; they don't want to miss an opportunity for a showcase appearance before a national television audience.

Of course, the watching audience may not always be fully aware of the news significance of the unfolding drama of the interview confrontation. As Reuven Frank, president of NBC News, put it once in a memo to his staff:

. . . The Sunday afternoon interviews of the famous and frightening are much more useful to the Washington bureaus of the wire services and the New York *Times* than they are to the television audience. They still make news, if what appears on front pages is the criterion for news. But unless he is waiting for a lead sentence to be spoken, even a professional is likely as he listens to miss the one big news story of the program. Certainly the audience is not sure what it heard until it reads the Monday morning newspapers.

Nevertheless, the audience does come away with a new perspective on the news celebrity who occupied the griddle that particular Sunday, and that constitutes a useful, if not unique, complement to the general flow of the news.

And now, a word from the boss . . .

In addition to news and interviews, the information content of the electronic media also includes a certain amount of opinion, as is the case with their print counterparts.

The expression of opinion over radio and television may crop up in the news report itself, often inadvertently but sometimes deliberately (Chet Huntley was not the only newscaster who tucked "little editorials" in at the end of his report of the day's events). Or opinion may be worked into the format of the full-dress 60- or 90-minute network documentaries or "specials," most of which are artful blends of investigative reporting and aggressive case-making.

And, finally, at the local level, opinion may also be presented in the form of conventional editorials, very similar to those in the newspaper. Such editorials are offered as expressions of the station's institutional viewpoint and are usually read on the air by the station manager or his representative.

These various forms of editorializing have not always been a part of the broadcasting scene. For many years the Federal Communications Commission frowned on expressions of opinion by broadcasters, and that frown was enough to make the station owners and their newscasters steer well away from anything that involved taking sides.

In recent years the FCC has progressively altered its stand, finally coming around to the point of encouraging broadcasters to venture into the realm of opinion. Gingerly at first, but with increasing enthusiasm, the broadcasters have responded. According to a 1966 survey made by the National Association of Broadcasters, more than 50 percent of all radio and television stations engage in at least some editorializing. Station WMCA in New York City became the first radio outlet to schedule regular editorials, beginning in 1954, and WTVJ of Miami, Fla., claims to have been the first television channel to institute similar programming beginning in 1957.[12]

Some stations resort to editorials only infrequently, when a topic particularly interests management. Others, such as KCMO of Kansas City, present brief editorial comments daily. Typically, the formal editorial represents a far smaller proportion of the broadcaster's over-all news and information package than is the case with the newspaper or magazine. The broadcast editorial can carry a potent wallop, however, particularly if it is delivered by a newscaster with a large personal following.

The use of a regular news broadcaster to deliver the station's editorial expressions tends to blur the line between news and opinion. A similar blurring takes place, of course, when a newscaster is also expected to deliver the sponsor's commercial—a routine doubling-up on most local stations and even on some network news shows. (The superstars such as Walter Cronkite usually refuse to handle commercials, however.)

Expressions of opinion from sources other than the broadcasters also find their way into the programming of radio and television in the form of the talk shows and in the segments of program time purchased by private individuals or groups as a means of getting their views put before the public. The talk shows, typically featuring a provocative moderator who fields telephone calls from listeners or viewers, have come on the scene only in recent years and have been largely confined to radio. But they have proven popular with audiences, and consequently with sponsors.

In one sense the call-in shows provide an electronic equivalent of the letters-to-the-editor section of the newspaper or magazine. In radio, however, the callers are usually anonymous, whereas letters to a newspaper almost always are signed.

Author and critic Jessica Mitford, among others, thinks the call-in shows serve a useful function:

It would be easy to dismiss them as so much vacuous drivel beamed to idle minds. Yet that is not the whole story. They do offer a lively change from the bland output of much of the mass media. Newspapers

[12] *Electronic Journalism, op. cit.,* p. 62.

across the country are becoming more and more uniform as they substitute the canned syndicated column for original writing. Television,
cowering further and further away from controversial or disturbing
issues, has retreated into its own wishy-washy fantasy land. In contrast, the talk shows thrive on nonconformist ideas. They at least offer
the potential of uninhibited discussion and rough-and-tumble debate.
Perhaps, in an overtranquilized land, this is the key to their success.[13]

Outside opinion also appears on the broadcasting schedule in the
form of purchased advertising time.

Opinion or idea advertising (designed to sell or promote a doctrine or a viewpoint rather than a product) has long been a feature
of the print media. It can take the form of corporate advertising,
designed to improve the image of a company, or it can be a vehicle
for an expression of opinion by an interest-group, as when a number of academic and business leaders took a full-page ad in the
New York *Times* to plead for an improved civil rights law.

On radio and television—particularly radio—opinion advertising
has most frequently been packaged in the format of current-affairs
commentary prepared and presented by religious groups or nonprofit foundations. In most instances, the viewpoints advocated in
such programs are from the conservative end of the ideological
spectrum, although there also have been programs espousing liberal
philosophies and presented under the sponsorship of trade unions.

The magazine *TV Guide* reported in 1967 that spokesmen of the
radical Right were being heard on more than 10,000 radio and
television broadcasts each week in the 50 states. The magazine
observed that:

For the last decade, groups of self-appointed "super-patriots" have
energetically been purchasing TV and radio time at an accelerated
pace until, at this writing, whole sections of the nation are awash with
a brand of vitriol which is neither rational political dissent nor the
constructive goading of responsible reformers.

For a number of obvious reasons, radicals of the Left have no voice
on American TV and radio similar to that of their Rightist opponents.
An avowed Communist has no access to tax-free foundation money, nor
to the contributions required for the purchase of air time. He cannot
easily invoke religious fundamentalism nor patriotism as a cloak for

---

[13] Quoted in *Harper's*, May 1966, p. 53.

his activities and is precluded by the force of public opinion from openly advocating the tenets of communism.[14]

TV Guide quoted an Anti-Defamation League estimate that almost $20,000,000 a year was being spent for such programming by rightist groups, backed by "an impressive but comparatively small number of tax-exempt foundations, business corporations and wealthy individuals, plus the one- to five-dollar contributions of hundreds of thousands of average citizens who have been frightened by this propaganda barrage and who, to an alarming extent, have succumbed to it."

In theory, so decided an imbalance in program content should not occur on the broadcast media, since they are under the regulation of a government agency (the FCC) that has established policies intended to ensure balanced treatment of controversial matters. But these policies, as will be seen below, are not very consistently enforced.

The licensed media

The existence of the Federal Communications Commission symbolizes a significant difference between the role occupied by the electronic media in our society, and that occupied by their longer-established counterparts, the newspapers and magazines. Radio and television stations are licensed by an arm of the federal government; every three years they must seek renewal of those licenses on terms laid down by the FCC; a station owner who for any reason is denied renewal of his license is at that point out of business. The print media, of course, are subject to no such controls. The First Amendment shields them effectively.

Why are the broadcast media thus controlled when newspapers are not?

Because the only means by which the broadcasters can reach their audience is through use of a finite number of carrier waves—radio frequencies or television channels.[15] To prevent chaos in the

14 *TV Guide*, April 15, 1967.
15 There are 105 different broadcast positions on the AM radio broadcast band, and only 12 channels on the equivalent band of television carrier waves in the VHF (very high frequency) range that most TV sets are equipped to receive. There are approximately 70 more TV channel spaces open in the UHF

use of the airwaves, with overlapping signals blotting each other out and filling the ether with an unintelligible babble, some agency has to parcel out the right to use a given radio frequency or television channel in each broadcasting region. In the early days of radio the broadcasters themselves requested the federal government to take on this assignment, and in the Radio Act of 1927, later replaced by the Federal Communications Act of 1934, the government accepted the charge. The Federal Communications Commission was established to do the job and instructed to make sure that the public airwaves were being utilized by the licensees in "the public interest, convenience, and necessity." The act also directed that the commission refrain from censorship of the content of broadcasts.

The 1968 FCC report listed 7,351 licensed broadcasters in the United States, 840 of them TV stations and the rest either AM or FM radio. Obviously, with that many license renewals to be evaluated during a three-year period, the commissioners could not possibly spend much time on very many of them. This fact has effectively diluted the role of the FCC with respect to the broadcasters theoretically under its supervision.

From the standpoint of the broadcasters, the role of the FCC should be to act primarily as a traffic policeman to keep people from bumping into each other on the frequencies. But the commission has at least tried, with varying degrees of persistence through the years, to fulfill more completely than that its responsibilities as set out in the Communications Act.

There have been four ways in which the FCC has attempted to affect the nature of the broadcasting industry by the exercise of its regulatory power.

1. It has sought to ensure that ownership of the licensed radio and television stations would not be unduly concentrated. The FCC will permit a single individual or corporation to own a maximum of seven AM radio stations, seven FM radio stations, and seven televi-

---

(ultra high frequency) range, but for various technical reasons these have not come into wide use. Within a given broadcast pattern (the distance over which a signal can be received clearly) only so many operators can be licensed, or their broadcasts would overrun each other. No comparable limitation of physical channels exists with respect to the print media, of course. The effective limits in those fields are economic rather than physical.

sion stations—and only five of the TV stations may be in the VHF (very high frequency) band, which is the commercial range currently being utilized. This restriction has prevented the growth of large chains.

2. It has required that a prospective licensee, or a license holder seeking renewal, provide assurance that his station will devote a "reasonable" amount of its broadcast time to public service broadcasting—that is, news, public affairs, educational offerings, religious programs, and various categories of "sustaining" (not commercially sponsored) material.

This sounds better on paper than it works out in practice. Only a tiny handful of license renewal applications have ever been denied by the FCC, and these involved flagrant violations of standards. In the average renewal case, a minimal showing of "public interest" effort usually suffices to earn another three-year franchise. As one television producer put it,

. . . The FCC does list "news, public affairs and all other programs exclusive of entertainment and sports" in its forms for those who seek licenses or their renewal. And the commission does ask how much time broadcasters propose to devote, in what time blocks, what staff and facilities will be employed, the source (network, recorded or local) and how much local or regional coverage is planned. Yet the FCC neither establishes nor enforces any standards. Stations whose logs are totally deficient in programming under those rubrics regularly win licenses and renewals. . . . Instead of compelling stations to prove that they serve the public interest, the FCC renews their license unless somebody else proves the contrary. The commission's own staff hasn't the resources. The public rarely intervenes because it doesn't know that it can. . . .[16]

Any member of the public, however, does have the right to offer evidence to the commission at the time of a local license renewal if he feels that the licensee is not fulfilling his responsibilities. The renewal hearings are publicized locally, and are held within the region in which the station operates, though not often in the home community itself.

One such citizen intervention that finally achieved some result was begun in 1964 in Jackson, Miss. A local group, aided by Dr.

[16] Arthur Alpert, "Your Time Is Their Time," *The New Republic*, October 18, 1969, pp. 17–21.

Everett Parker of the Office of Communications of the United
Church of Christ, complained to the FCC that WLBT-TV in Jackson
was discriminating against the black population of the community
by blanking out civil rights news, failing to provide coverage of the
black community, and making use of pejorative references to blacks.
The FCC at first dismissed the complaints, holding that such a group
had no standing before the commission. An appeal to the United
States Court of Appeals won a verdict for the complainants' right to
press their case, and they thereupon re-entered their action with
the FCC in 1965. Once more the FCC dismissed the complaint, on
the ground that the alleged discrimination by the station had not
been adequately documented.

The determined band of citizens once again turned to the court,
and in his final decision before leaving the Court of Appeals to become Chief Justice of the United States, Judge Warren Burger held
again for the complainant group, rebuked the FCC for failing to give
the complainants a "hospitable reception," vacated the license of
station WLBT-TV, and invited new applicants to seek the franchise.[17]

In the aftermath of this case, and perhaps also inspired by several
other challenges to franchise holders in other parts of the country,
Senator John O. Pastore of Rhode Island introduced in 1969 a piece
of legislation widely assumed to be aimed at protecting the interests
of broadcasters in their valuable licenses.

Pastore's bill would have the effect of making it extremely difficult to dislodge a broadcaster once he had been awarded a franchise.
It would bar a competing applicant from challenging a radio or television license unless the established broadcaster had *already* had
his license revoked by FCC action. An opponent of the measure,
Senator Philip A. Hart of Michigan, observed that this was roughly
equivalent to forbidding anyone to run for public office unless the
incumbent had already been impeached and removed. If the Pastore
legislation were to become law, the incidence of license revocation
in the broadcast industry—already rare—would be likely to vanish
altogether.[18]

3. The FCC has promulgated a "fairness doctrine," which spec-
ifies that any broadcast license holder must grant free time to reply
to any individual or organization that has been attacked on the air.

[17] Barrett, *op. cit.*, pp. 31–32.
[18] *Ibid.*, p. 30.

Its purpose is to ensure that all sides of a controversy will have equal access to the public airwaves.

4. Finally, the commission administers the "equal time" provision embodied in Section 315 of the Federal Communications Act. In effect, this provision requires that if a broadcaster sells time to one political candidate during a campaign, he must be ready to sell an equal amount of time to the candidate's opponent or opponents; if the broadcaster makes free time available to a candidate, he must make equal segments of time available without charge to the other candidates in that race.

As might be expected, the equal-time provision is more often invoked successfully than is the fairness doctrine. In the case of both provisions, the initiative typically comes from the aggrieved party, and candidates are more likely to be aware of their rights than is the average citizen.[19] Moreover, the fairness doctrine is difficult to pin down in practical terms; unless a given program has been monitored or taped the question of its fairness is almost impossible to determine, and the commission does not have the resources to maintain constant watch on all the broadcast output of 7,300 stations.

Even when there is a permanent record, the FCC may be reluctant to take action in a fairness case. In 1969, for example, the commission announced that it would no longer accept complaints about individual newscasters slanting the news because it was not "the national arbiter of the truth" and could not enter the "quagmire" of investigating every complaint about news presentation. The statement came in a ruling on a charge that CBS had slanted the news in its 1968 documentary, "Hunger in America." The commissioners decided that the issue in the case really wasn't fairness, but whether

[19] The equal-time provision was given a new interpretation during the summer of 1970, when the Democratic National Committee and some individual antiwar senators asserted that members of the opposition party should be entitled to free air time to respond to Presidential messages to the people, whether in a campaign year or not. Three questions were raised by the assertions: 1. Is the political party out of power at the White House entitled to "equal time" on television to reply to messages by the President of the United States to the American people? 2. If free time is granted, who is the appropriate spokesman to make the response for the opposition party? 3. Are various factions in Congress entitled to time on television, to solicit funds and public support for partisan causes, in noncampaign periods? One network executive complained of "endless proposals to commandeer television time." And an FCC official observed: "The situation is worse than I have ever seen it before." (From *U.S. News & World Report,* July 27, 1970, p. 56.)

CBS had deliberately attempted to slant the presentation. Since it had concluded that the alleged slanting was not deliberate, the FCC said, "no further action is warranted."

Even though the various forms of FCC control have not been unduly restrictive for most broadcasters, the potentiality for a tighter clampdown always exists, and will so long as the licensing agency remains in being. Whether firm control really could be brought to bear on the far-flung broadcasting industry either for good ends (improving the quality of programming) or for bad (stifling the journalistic voice of the electronic media, as Vice President Agnew seemed to be trying to do in 1969 when he invoked the name of the FCC in his celebrated attack on the TV newsmen) has not yet been tested in any significant fashion.

As the presentation of news comes to be a more and more important aspect of the over-all broadcasting mission, such a test may very well come, and in its outcome every citizen will have a stake.[20]

[20] A comprehensive discussion of how the American viewer feels about television and the uses he makes of it is to be found in Gary A. Steiner, *The People Look at Television; A Study of Audience Attitudes*, Alfred A. Knopf, New York, 1963. For a brief, informal appraisal of TV, see Robert Montgomery, *Open Letter from a Television Viewer*, James H. Heineman, New York, 1968. See also Nicholas Johnson, *How to Talk Back to Your Television Set*, Little, Brown and Co., Boston, 1970 (Johnson is an FCC Commissioner outspokenly critical of the industry); Charles Sopkin, *Seven Glorious Days, Seven Fun-Filled Nights*, Simon and Schuster, New York, 1968 ("My frank opinion now is that there is *no* way to make television better. It is what it is"); William Small, *To Kill a Messenger: Television News and the Real World*, Hastings House, New York, 1970 (the title is based on the fact that ancient Persian generals ordered messengers killed when they brought bad news); Barry Cole, ed., *Television*, The Free Press, New York, 1970 (articles from *TV Guide*); and Edward W. Chester, *Radio, Television and American Politics*, Sheed and Ward, New York, 1969. See also the novel about TV news reporting, Ned Calmer, *The Anchorman*, Doubleday & Co., New York, 1970.

CHAPTER FOURTEEN

Where Madison Avenue
crosses Main

Wolcott Gibbs in *The New Yorker* wrote it off as "a remarkably silly book," but *The Hucksters*, Frederic Wakeman's 1946 novel exposing big-time advertising, provided the impetus for a number of novels in which ad men played lead roles.[1] A selection of the Book-of-the-Month Club, *The Hucksters* later became a movie starring Clark Gable. The villain in the story bore remarkable resemblance to the blustery George Washington Hill of the American Tobacco Company, and the agency depicted sounded a lot like Foote, Cone & Belding, for whom Wakeman once wrote copy. Many years later, Fairfax M. Cone, a principal in the agency, wrote: "With the filming of the story and its repeated showing [on the late, late show] over a period of almost twenty years, it has undoubtedly had more influence on public opinion than either Upton Sinclair's exposé of the unsavory meat packing industry in *The Jungle* or Ida M. Tar-

---

[1] Among them: Herman Wouk's *Aurora Dawn* (1947), John G. Schneider's *The Golden Kazoo* (1956), Shepherd Mead's *The Admen* (1958), Edward Hannibal's *Chocolate Days, Popsicle Weeks* (1970). Sloan Wilson's *The Man in the Gray Flannel Suit* (1955) was in a similar vein, but the hero was a PR man.

bell's *History of the Standard Oil Company,* which focused the country's attention on the evils of monopoly forty years before." He added: "It is doubtful whether Vance Packard's *The Hidden Persuaders* could have achieved anything like the acceptance it did without the lurid setting of the scene by Fred Wakeman."[2]

In the world of make-believe the advertising man is as often ruthless and conniving as the whore is loving and generous. Tom Gavin of the Denver *Post* tells of a couple of admen meeting on the street. One says to the other: "You hear that Joe Parsnip died?" "No, what did he have?" "A few small industrial accounts."[3]

Some advertising men no doubt are like that: insensitive, cynical about what they do, merciless in achieving their goals. But others —surely most others—have the same standards, the same goals, the same concerns as other men who hold down white collar jobs. Some of their work, especially if they are associated with advertising agencies, is invigorating, even glamorous; much of it is routine and dull.

To keep our discussion in this chapter to a manageable length, we shall speak mostly of advertising by business firms to sell products and services. But business firms—like nonprofit organizations—use advertising to sell ideas too. Idea advertising—sometimes called "institutional advertising" (see next chapter)—often involves the promotion of a cause only remotely related to the products or services of the ad's sponsor.[4]

For a more complete discussion of the broad aspects of advertising see Martin Mayer's *Madison Avenue, U.S.A.* (Harper & Row, 1959), probably the fairest and most discerning popular appraisal ever written but now a bit dated; David Ogilvy's *Confessions of an Advertising Man* (Atheneum, 1963), opinionated and highly readable; Rosser Reeves's *Reality in Advertising* (Knopf, 1961), committed to "hard sell" techniques; Joseph Seldin's *The Golden Fleece* (Macmillan, 1963), suspicious that the consumer is being taken; Samm Baker's *The Permissible Lie* (World, 1968), awed by adver-

---

[2] Fairfax M. Cone, *With All Its Faults: A Candid Account of Forty Years in Advertising,* Little, Brown and Co., Boston, 1969, pp. 164, 165.

[3] Retold by Cleveland Amory, "Trade Winds," *Saturday Review,* August 9, 1969, p. 10.

[4] Idea advertising can also be used by individuals who have something to say but who can't afford to establish their own publications. For a few dollars they can rent space—or time—and reach an audience, if only on a one-time basis.

tising's evils; Jerry Della Femina's *From Those Wonderful Folks Who Brought You Pearl Harbor* (Simon and Schuster, 1970), spirited but distorted; and Fairfax Cone's *With All Its Faults* (Little, Brown, 1969), quietly defensive.

The levels of advertising

The advertising business is organized at four different levels.

1. *Advertising departments of advertisers.* Almost every large company has an advertising department. The department coordinates the company's advertising activities and may produce some of the advertising, especially some of the pieces that are distributed by mail. It represents the company in its dealings with its advertising agency. If the company does not have an advertising agency, the advertising department handles all the jobs an agency would be expected to handle.

2. *Advertising departments of the media.* The media have advertising staffs too. A newspaper, for instance, has one group of admen handling national or brand-name advertising, another handling classified advertising, still another handling local—or retail—advertising. The retail advertising staff—often called the local display advertising department—is the largest. Men in that department solicit advertising from local retailers and then, because most of these advertisers don't have their own ad departments or agencies, write the copy, lay out the ads, and see that they're set in type.

Some media employ *representatives* (or *reps*, as they're called)—organizations whose function it is to solicit advertising from the agencies located in distant advertising centers.

3. *Advertising agencies.* An advertising agency plans, produces, and places advertising for advertisers. Advertisers represented by agencies are called *clients* or *accounts*.

Clients include nonprofit organizations, like the American Cancer Society or the Peace Corps, as well as business firms. For nonprofit clients the media sometimes—but not always—donate time and space while agency men volunteer creative services.

4. *Specialty shops.* Advertising, like other businesses, has developed specialties, and some organizations have grown up to handle these specialties. For instance, most advertising agencies buy their

illustrations from *art studios*. They have their type set by *type houses*. Some of them engage *research organizations* to test the market and the effectiveness of the ad in reaching the market. Newspapers make use of national *mat service organizations*, which supply ready-made art in mat form (no engravings necessary) for local advertisers.

Kinds of advertising

Advertisers make use of six different kinds of advertising:

1. *National advertising.* Sometimes called "brand name" advertising, this advertising has as its purpose the selling of products to people who will themselves use them. Most of the advertising that goes into general circulation magazines and on broadcast networks is national advertising.

2. *Retail advertising.* Its purpose is to get people, some of whom may be presold on particular brands of merchandise, into the stores. Price is almost always prominently displayed. Most newspaper and local radio station advertising falls into this category. Sometimes retail advertisers and national advertisers get together to share the costs of the advertising, in which case it is called *cooperative advertising* or *co-op*.

3. *Mail order advertising.* This kind of advertising often combines elements of national and retail advertising. The retailer, in this case, is a company far removed from where the purchaser lives, so transactions are conducted by mail. Mail order advertising makes use of existing media, but it also depends to a great extent on its own publications (leaflets, catalogues, and other direct mail pieces).

4. *Trade advertising.* The retailer, the wholesaler, and the broker are also "customers," in that they buy products and in turn sell them to others. Manufacturers realize they have to do a selling job on middle men, too; and so they advertise to them. But here, instead of stressing the benefits of using the product, the advertisers stress the profits that can be realized from stocking and selling their products. Manufacturers reach the trade largely through trade magazines or direct mail.

5. *Industrial advertising.* Manufacturers are customers, too, when they buy raw materials and machines to use in their manufacturing

processes. The people who supply the raw material and machinery reach their customers through ads in business magazines and direct-mail pieces.

6. *Professional advertising.* Physicians prescribe drugs. Architects recommend building materials. The manufacturers of these products, through ads in professional journals and direct mail, sell doctors, architects, and other professional people on the merits of these products. Some of the best written and designed ads fall into this category, but the average person never sees them, just as he never sees trade and industrial advertising. When he thinks of advertising, he thinks only of national or retail advertising.

Yet advertisers in all these areas—national, retail, mail order, trade, industrial, and professional—depend to a great extent on the mass media to reach buyers. All of the advertisers help keep the media alive with their space and time purchases.

Advertising as a public service

Partly because they were concerned about the country's welfare and partly because they wanted to build their image, advertising men representing the advertisers, the media, and the agencies set up the War Advertising Council in the 1940s. The council helped the government sell bonds, build morale, and do some of the other propaganda jobs necessary during wartime. So successful was this volunteer organization that, after the war, it continued as the Advertising Council, creating ads for a number of worthy causes, among them forest-fire prevention, church attendance, and aid to higher education. The media provided free space and time.

On an individual basis agencies and ad men devote time to a number of other causes. Campbell-Ewald, Detroit, helped the police department there with a recruitment campaign, tripling applications within a month. In a similar campaign the Cleveland Advertising Club brought in 1,400 applicants for 500 police jobs there, "the largest group of applicants since the depression years," said Mayor Carl Stokes. Rock Bergthold & Wright, San Jose, signed an ad in *Time* telling "what it's like to be a cop today."

North Advertising Incorporated in Chicago, following the shooting of Robert F. Kennedy, produced and sponsored a series of ads calling for gun legislation. Although the agency's clients had no connection with the campaign, a group of gun lovers and assorted rightwingers organized in an attempt to get the clients to drop their agency or face a boycott of their products.

The client as king

An agency doing an ad for its own signature, either in the area of public service or to recruit new clients, is free to do what it likes. The ad has only to win the approval of members of the creative team which puts the ad together. But an ad drawn up for a client must be approved not only by agency staff members but also by the client and his advertising staff. The original idea may be subjected to a series of compromises, and the ad, as it finally appears in print or over the air, often is not as good as when it started out.

Not many agencies can operate with Doyle Dane Bernbach's attitude: if the client doesn't like the ad as presented, he can find a new agency.

Once in a while an agency resigns an account. But most of the time agencies seem to be trying hard to hold on to their clients. What makes agency life so hectic—and that was one of the points made by *The Hucksters*—is that clients are fickle. Revlon, with so many agency changes that ad men have lost count, is a prime example.[5] Past accomplishments by the agency count for little. Doyle Dane Bernbach lost the Avis account, even though the agency had taken Avis from nowhere to a spot just behind Hertz with the slogan "We try harder." On the other hand, some agency-client relationships are remarkably long-lived. Chesebrough-Pond's, the cosmetics company, has been with J. Walter Thompson for more than 80 years.

To prevent jealousies from developing among clients, no agency accepts a new account that is directly competitive with an account it already has. But sometimes an agency resigns an existing account to take on a similar one that is bigger and more profitable.

The role of agencies

Advertisers in the United States now spend close to 20 billion dollars a year to reach their audiences. Much of this spending is

[5] Sometimes Revlon quits its agency; sometimes its agency quits Revlon.

directed by the several hundred large advertising agencies headquartered mainly in New York City, many of them on or near Madison Avenue.

Although agencies are currently arguing the merits and even the ethics of their system of compensation, they still earn most of their money through rebates from the media. The system works like this: the media of advertising—newspapers, magazines, and broadcast stations and networks—sell their space or time to agencies at a price 15 percent below the stated price. The agencies in turn bill their clients the stated price. The difference represents the agencies' fee for creative services rendered. "The actual ads are produced almost as a sideline, as if the artist charged for the frame and threw in the painting as a bonus," grumbles Dugald Stermer of *Ramparts*.[6]

The media are content with the arrangement because the agencies supply the ads ready to run. The media do not have to write copy, do layouts, or produce the commercials.

The arrangement dates to the last century, when agencies were nothing more than space brokers. Media were scattered then, records hard to keep, circulation figures misleading; and it took an expert not only to decide which media to advertise in but even to figure out where they were. Advertisers went to agencies primarily to get their advertising placed. It was natural for these agencies to offer copywriting and design help, and gradually the idea of full-service agencies took hold.

When agencies buy artwork, typesetting, and other services from the outside, they pass these costs on to the clients with a handling fee. For advertising that is not commissionable—not eligible for the 15 percent rebate from the media—a special fee is charged. Agencies seem to be moving in the direction of charging on a fee rather than a kickback basis for all advertising.

An agency measures its size by the amount of each year's "billings." Billings include the cost, before the 15 percent discount, of the space and time an agency buys for all its clients.

Agencies have personalities just as newspapers and magazines have. A person in advertising can take one look at an ad and tell which agency did it, not because he knows that the company is a client of that agency but because he recognizes a style or approach

---

[6] Dugald Stermer, "Advertising Is No Business for a Grown Man," *Ramparts*, September, 1969, p. 21.

that is peculiar to the agency. But it was with some pride that the president of J. Walter Thompson, world's largest advertising agency, declared once that "there is no such thing as a J. Walter Thompson ad."

Agencies tend to fall into one of two categories: (1) those that rely more on research than intuition in putting together a campaign and (2) those that believe that creativity is king. But perhaps the distinction is too harsh; most agencies believe in both research and creativity. It's a matter of which one is stressed.

The pendulum swings one way in advertising, and then swings back. In the 1950s and early 1960s admen were research-oriented. If figures couldn't be brought to show a campaign would work, it wouldn't be tried. In the late 1960s creativity made gains. A number of smaller "hot shops" or "boutiques" sprang up to take advantage of the trend. Their selling point was that they were unencumbered by the past. Their principals were young, their ideas wild. Some of the well-established agencies argued that these new shops were less interested in selling than in "doing their thing."[7]

The new shops took their cue from the spectacular rise of Doyle Dane Bernbach, which had built the Volkswagen and Avis accounts, among others; Ogilvy & Mather, which created the man with the eye patch for Hathaway shirts; and Jack Tinker & Partners, which cured Alka-Seltzer's upset stomach.[8] Perhaps the most celebrated of the new shops—in a couple of years it became a giant itself—was the shop set up in 1966 by Mary Wells who left an $80,000-a-year job with Jack Tinker & Partners. Some of the clients went with her.

The quarterback in an agency situation is the *account executive* or *account supervisor*. Representing the agency, he works directly with the client's advertising manager. The account executive draws on the talents of the agency's *copywriters* and *art directors*. The details of getting the ad in print are handled by a *production manager*. A *media buyer* decides where the ad should appear.

As far as the media are concerned, the media buyer is the key figure in an agency. Perhaps you've noticed advertisements in *Ad-*

---

[7] It is interesting to note that as the "boutiques" become successful they tend to adopt the more thorough, more businesslike approach of the larger, sounder agencies.

[8] But in 1969 Alka-Seltzer moved to Doyle Dane Bernbach, and Jack Tinker & Partners folded and then started up again.

vertising Age and *Editor & Publisher* and even in *The New Yorker* telling of the virtues of a given publication. These ads are not there to pick up subscribers; they are there to sell media buyers or their clients on the merits of the publication as an advertising medium. When media buyers lose confidence in a publication, the publication falters, as we saw in Chapter Ten. The number of subscribers is not nearly so important to a publication as the number of advertisers, although the number of subscribers determines, to some extent, an advertiser's interest in the publication.

At one time advertisers had no choice but to accept a publication's claim as to the number of subscribers it had. Later the media, agencies, and advertisers got together to form the Audit Bureau of Circulations, which verifies for newspapers and magazines that circulations are as claimed. Trade journals have a similar organization. Radio and TV audiences are not so easily measured, but several organizations attempt to do a job for these media too.

Advertisers have some rather inflexible ideas on where their ads should be located in a publication for best results. In spite of research conducted by the media to prove them wrong, most advertisers continue to believe that up-front placement is better than back-of-the-book placement and that a right-hand page gets better readership than a left-hand page. They often request such placement and complain when they don't get it. They are willing to pay premium prices for cover or centerfold position.

All advertisers want their ads next to regular editorial matter. They don't want to be buried in a sea of ads. This is why newspapers, with their many ads per page, attempt to arrange them in half-pyramids: they are able that way to get at least part of each ad next to a news story.

A desire to go with the medium that offers the most responsive audience for the product logically should motivate the media buyer. Sometimes other considerations intrude. A number of companies, through their agencies, have purchased space in media simply because company management likes the editorial policy. The Schick razor people, long associated with ultraconservative causes, often buy space in the *National Review,* even though, for a consumer product, that magazine may not be the best channel through which to reach potential customers. Knott's Berry Farm advertises in right-wing journals because its owner believes in right-wing causes. Dr.

Ross dog food used to do the same thing. Schick and the Kemper Insurance Company dropped ABC from their advertising schedules once because Howard K. Smith gave Alger Hiss a hearing on a program not even sponsored by them.

When the Arkansas *Gazette* in the 1950s editorialized for compliance with the Supreme Court decision on integration of schools, some local advertisers boycotted the paper. But many others continued to advertise, despite pressure from their customers. Leo Burnett Company, Inc., a Chicago-based advertising agency, advised media buyers to work that paper into their schedules whenever possible.

An ad in the New York *Times* in early 1968 provides an interesting example of product advertising and politics coming together. General de Gaulle, then president of France, had been much in the news. Konner's Chevrolet, Levittown, N.Y., ran this headline in a three-column by seven-inch ad costing approximately $1,300: "NOT WANTED. IF YOU OWN A FRENCH AUTOMOBILE, DON'T BRING IT TO US IN TRADE! WE DON'T WANT IT!" The copy opened with criticism of France's showing against the Germans in World War II and then launched into an attack on de Gaulle's actions to keep Britain out of the Common Market, his statements on U.S. involvement in Vietnam, and his pulling out of "the stabilizing gold pool" in an attempt to "undermine" the U.S. dollar and "hurt our economy." "So, if you're got a French car, why don't you send it back to France and try to get some American Dollars back?" the ad said. It was signed by the general manager, who added a P.S.: "My wife dumped her French perfume down the drain this morning."

The media's underpinnings

Roughly two-thirds of a newspaper's or magazine's revenue and just about all of a radio or TV station's revenue comes from advertising. Advertisers do not normally buy space in print media or time on electronic media to provide support for those media. They buy space and time to do a selling job. That the media are kept alive by such purchases is incidental to the advertising process. But how important those purchases are to the free flow of information in our society!

Consider the alternatives.

1. *Government-sponsored media.* While a case could be made for government news and opinion media to use as a yardstick by which existing media can be measured, no serious student of the press advocates public-supported media *in place of* privately owned media. Under such a circumstance news and opinion would surely evolve into propaganda. Who, then, would be in a position to criticize?

2. *Owner-subsidized media.* What we are talking about here is the underwriting of news and opinion media by men with wealth. Readers would either get the publications free, or at cost. Some media already are financed this way. But surely this is not the ideal way to finance the nation's newspapers. The wealthy tend to have similar political affiliations, similar social values. The editorial policy of papers would be more monotonously conservative than it is today.

You can argue that the press *now* is subsidized—by the advertisers who pay most of the costs of publishing and who provide most of the profits. But the control one advertiser exercises over media content is small compared to the control that could be exercised by an ideologue absorbing all the costs and answerable to no one, including the readers. In the electronic media, try to imagine the diatribes that would be carried continuously over a whole string of advertising-free stations owned by one of the "super-patriots" mentioned in Chapter Thirteen.

3. *Reader-financed media.* Among the media as they now exist, only books, a few quality magazines, Pacifica Foundation radio in several cities, and films (if you want to consider them as news and opinion media) are paid for completely by the people who use them. The typical hardbound book costs from five to ten dollars. If a daily newspaper were to drop all advertising and if it had no financial angel to make up the difference, you'd have to pay from 25 to 50 cents to get your copy. For a magazine, two dollars or more. Obviously, few readers could afford such publications.

Are you a medium?

The media of advertising include not only the basic media of communication—the news and opinion media—but also media created solely to carry advertising. These include billboards, point-of-purchase displays, and direct-mail advertising. Direct-mail advertising (leaflets, booklets, and similar printed matter) as a medium ranks right up with TV in dollars spent by advertisers—and just below newspapers, still the number one advertising medium.

There is one other medium.

The work pants you buy have a label ingeniously sewn into the back-pocket seam so that it can't be torn away without ripping the pocket. Your swim suit has a diving girl on the front, instantly identifying the maker. The department store puts your purchase in a bag—handsome enough—that says exactly where the purchase was made. The car you drive not only has its name affixed in a metal script in front and on the trunk; it has a license plate framed in an advertisement to tell others exactly where you bought the car. If you drive a pickup truck, you are used even more blatantly: the name of the truck is stamped in the tailgate itself in letters a foot high.

You drive in to one of the tourist traps along the highway, and upon return to your car find your bumper has become a miniature billboard to tell the world you were there. Behind the wheel, you catch yourself singing a catchy commercial jingle.

When you get back home you take the car back to where you got it for a tuneup and you accept a ride in a courtesy car with a sign on the side that tells your neighbors where you've been.

If you are called upon to speak at a convention, you endure the explosion of a flash bulb in the middle of a sentence and then see yourself in the paper the next day with the name of the hotel etched boldly in the front of the lectern from which you spoke.

We are, each of us, unwittingly walking and driving advertisements.[9]

Policing the ads

While the federal government, particularly through the Federal Trade Commission, the Food and Drug Administration, and the Federal Communications Commission, has some jurisdiction over advertising, its policing powers are limited. What protection the consumer enjoys comes largely from the media themselves.

Except in the electronic media, where federally supervised "equal time" provisions dictate to some extent what a station must run, the media can refuse to accept any advertising, so long as they do not

[9] In addition we voluntarily pass along to friends information about products that please us.

violate restraint of trade laws. A publication, for instance, can say "No" to an advertiser for a good reason (the product may be inferior or the ad itself may be misleading) or for the flimsiest of reasons (the publisher may not like the design of the ad). The advertiser may be asked to change the ad before it is accepted. *Seventeen* used to insist that swimsuit manufacturers airbrush out the navels on their models.

Every newspaper and every magazine has a list of products or appeals it will not tolerate. *The Saturday Evening Post* in the 1930s refused to accept liquor advertising (but when the magazine world became more competitive later it decided liquor wasn't so bad after all). A number of magazines, including *The New Yorker* and the *Saturday Review,* following the Surgeon General's report on smoking, refused to accept cigarette advertising. In January, 1970, the New York *Times* adopted the policy of refusing cigarette advertising unless the copy carried a health warning and a statement as to the cigarette's tar and nicotine content. And, by mutual agreement, the broadcast industry and the tobacco industry have parted company.

Magazines like *Good Housekeeping* and *Parents' Magazine* have worked out seals of approval that guarantee readers that the products are as advertised. Readers of some magazines have found that when a product proves to be faulty, they can get a refund by writing to the advertising department of the magazine in which the ad appeared.

A number of newspapers, among them the Arizona *Republic,* the Phoenix *Gazette,* and the Copley papers in San Diego, no longer accept any ads, no matter how tasteful, for X-rated movies. But newspapers fight a losing battle with the ingenious admen. Insist that breasts be covered with a bra, and the advertiser will comply, but he'll paint it on so crudely that readers will quickly get the idea that it was put there just to get the ad into the paper. Loren Osborn, ad manager of the Concord, N.H., *Monitor,* says papers should not be restrictive with movie ads. "I will allow just about anything. . . . If the movie might offend anyone, let's show it like it is in the ad so they can find out beforehand and not be rudely surprised once they've taken a seat in the theater."[10]

What bothers one newspaper does not necessarily bother another.

[10] "Laundering the Sheets," *Time,* May 30, 1969, p. 54.

A Washington, D.C. bookshop discovered this in 1967 when it advertised hippie buttons in the three dailies there. All accepted the ad, but all wanted changes in the copy. The Washington *Post* and the *Daily News* both insisted that a "Chaste Makes Waste" button be omitted from the ad. A "J. Edgar Hoover Sleeps with a Night Light" button didn't bother the *Post,* but it did the *Daily News.* The *Post* also turned down "Snoopy Sniffs Airplane Glue."[11]

A publication's policy on what it will accept in advertising is not always based on truth and good taste. It is sometimes based on provincialism. Some newspapers, for instance, will not accept advertising from retail establishments in other cities. They bow to the pressure from local retailers—local advertisers—who cry that local dollars will go out of town.

The language of advertising

Some of the best art and typography in the media today comes from advertising artists and designers. It would not be hard to make a case to show that the excellence of design in magazines was largely inspired by innovative advertising art directors.

The text matter in advertising—the "copy" as it is called—has not kept pace. While a few memorable passages can be cited, like those in Volkswagen advertisements, the bulk of what one reads in the ads—especially in retail ads—is not as well reasoned, not as well phrased as what one reads in the editorial columns of the publications in which the ads appear.

Perhaps that is the nature of advertising. For one thing, the advertising copywriter does not seem to stand much in awe of the language. One finds few purists in the ranks of advertising copywriters. They know well enough that "Winstons taste good like a cigarette should" and "Us Tareyton smokers would rather fight than switch" are indefensible from a grammatical standpoint. But they argue: "That's the way people talk." They know that people should not "Shop Macy's"; people should "Shop *at* Macy's," but the shorter version moves faster, and that's important to a copywriter. He makes verbs out of words meant to be nouns. He uses phony transitions

[11] Letter to the editor of *The New Republic* from John Whiteley, July 1, 1967, p. 34.

to tie his paragraphs together. Above all he makes his tone conversational.

Once in a while, objections to the copywriter's mannerisms come from within the ranks. Dan Jenkins of Rogers, Cowan & Brenner, Beverly Hills, has written: "I'm getting awfully tired of the truncated copywriting everybody is doing these days. Short sentences. Followed by no sentences. Like this. It doesn't sell. It just irritates. Me."[12] But the practices continue.

From the customer's standpoint, how the copywriter says it is less important than what the copywriter says. Protected by anonymity (maybe ad copy should be bylined) the copywriter settles for phrasing not likely to impress the thoughtful reader or listener.[13] Examples like the following are still too easy to find:

"Hurry! The supply is limited." One suspects the very opposite is true: the hapless store is overstocked. If the supply *is* limited, and if the product *is* as good as the ad says, why didn't the store buy more in the first place? And if the supply is limited, why does the store create a desire for the product only to disappoint late arriving customers?

"Open evenings and after Church on Sunday." Here, the reader is supposed to think, is a used car dealer who probably goes to church himself; that's why he can't open until Sunday afternoon. As a religious man, he'll surely treat his customers right.

"Prescribed by four out of five physicians." Can that be possible? Certainly. All the advertiser has to do is get groups of doctors together to find out what they advise—for headaches, for hemorroids, or whatever—and if most of the physicians in each group pick some product other than the advertiser's, never mind. Eventually he gets one group together in which his product comes out best, and that's the "survey" he talks about in his advertising. You can do anything with statistics. As someone once observed: "Ever since they put those Smokey the Bear ads in the New York subways, there hasn't been a single forest fire in Manhattan."

"Half-price sale." Buy the first tire at the regular price and get a second tire at half price. That might be a half-price sale to the

---

[12] Letter to the editor of *Advertising Age*, August 4, 1969, p. 35.

[13] Retail advertisers are the most frequent offenders. The big national advertisers are more careful in making claims. Some of them even get informal opinions from the FTC before running their ads.

copywriter, but to the man actually doing the buying, if he stops to think about it, it is nothing more than a three-quarter price sale.

"No sales to dealers." The reader is supposed to conclude that somehow the prices are even lower than wholesale. Here's a chance for the ordinary citizen to buy better than even a dealer can buy! But don't bet anybody will be at the door checking ID cards. A variation of the "No sales to dealers" line is: "Dealers welcome."

"The tars and nicotine trapped in the filter never reach your lungs." Not if they're trapped. But what about the ones that aren't?

"Lasts 25 percent longer." Longer than what? The copywriter doesn't say. If you as a reader are obliging enough to complete the sentence by putting in the name of a competing product, the advertiser will appreciate it. He didn't say it; you did. Or if you want to assume that the new product lasts longer than an earlier version of it lasted, that's all right too. It's a sort of do-it-yourself advertisement.

A San Francisco brewery some years ago made clever use of the incomplete comparative when it called its beer "one of America's two great beers." The ads never mentioned what the other "great" beer was. It was whatever one the reader thought it was.

Copywriters have been such spendthrifts in their use of superlatives, real or implied, that the old ones have deflated in value, and there aren't many unused ones left. In the public mind now a miracle product is one that merely works. The deluxe line is only ordinary. King size is the smallest size available. When a company comes out with a genuine improvement in its product, there are no words left to describe it, or no words that a conditioned public won't yawn over.

Advertising as whipping boy

Of all the products of journalism, advertising is the most ubiquitous. We see ads wherever we look, we hear them wherever we go. The typical American family in the course of a day is said to encounter more than fifteen hundred of them.[14]

Constantly clamoring for attention, some ads are as likely to build resentment as win converts. By their very nature their excesses and

[14] John S. Wright and Daniel S. Warner, *Advertising*, 2nd. ed., McGraw-Hill Book Company, New York, 1966, p. 3.

their mistakes lie exposed, waiting for the criticism that is bound to come.

Advertising has always had its critics. Criticism of advertising grew intense during the Depression of the 1930s when its cost became difficult to justify. Economists led the attack. In the 1940s, as we have seen, novelists took over. In the 1950s, sociologists—and their follow-up man, Vance Packard—stepped in. In the 1960s the critics allied themselves with the politicians.

People don't like advertising if for no other reason than that they don't like to admit that they are vulnerable to it.

To Arnold Toynbee, advertising is an evil. To J. Kenneth Galbraith, it is wasteful. To Arthur Schlesinger, Jr., it is awful.[15]

In his spiritual autobiography, Malcolm Muggeridge writes:

> . . . If you happen to cast an eye through the advertisements in your color supplements, you will see displayed there a credulity which would be the envy of every witch doctor in Africa. . . . I never met a man made happy by money or worldly success or sensual indulgence, still less by the stupefaction of drugs or alcohol. Yet we all, in one way or another, pursue these ends, as the advertiser well knows. He offers them in Technicolor and stereo sound, and there are many takers.[16]

The syndicated cartoon panel *Graffiti* by Leary shows this message scrawled on a wall: "Abominable Snowmen Dwell on Madison Avenue."

The critics build an impressive case. This chapter has already presented some of it. The case boils down to six basic charges:

1. Advertising makes people buy things they don't need or can't afford.

2. Advertising confuses customers by stressing trivial differences between brands.

3. Advertising makes things more expensive because manufacturers pass the costs of advertising along to their customers.

4. Advertising encourages monopoly. Only big companies can afford to advertise.

5. Advertising is vulgar, tasteless, and misleading. Winston asks

[15] See Victor S. Navasky's article, "Advertising Is a Science? An Art? A Business?" *The New York Times Magazine*, November 20, 1966, pp. 52 ff.

[16] Malcolm Muggeridge, *Jesus Rediscovered*, Doubleday & Co., New York, 1969, pp. 53, 57, 58.

its critics, "What do you want, good grammar or good taste?" as though the two were incompatible.

6. Advertising is not necessary. If a product is good enough, word of mouth will do the job. Look at Hershey and its candy bars.

But the proponents of advertising have some answers.

Advertising does not force people to buy. It merely announces, suggests, persuades. Nor can admen know exactly how a campaign is going to work. "Advertising is not a science with laws, rules, and prescriptions which if followed precisely lead to predictable results each time they are applied," John Crawford writes in his textbook for advertising students. "It can accelerate the downfall of a poor product as quickly as it can promote the rise of a good one."[17]

Advertising is largely news about products, and readers generally treat it as such.

Indeed, some of the best-received features in a publication are the advertisements. The housewife, especially, would find her daily newspaper a disappointment without the ads from retail establishments. One of the troubles with the short-lived West Coast edition of the New York *Times* was the fact that it omitted the ads of the stores in Manhattan. People on the West Coast may not have been able to respond to such advertising, but they enjoyed seeing it nevertheless. Many New York *Times* readers, especially those who read the Sunday paper, preferred to wait the four days for the mail delivery of the more complete New York edition.

Advertising in some product categories may stress trivial differences, but in other categories, the differences are considerable. This is especially true of appliances, cars, and other high-ticket items.

At least one authority defends advertising on economic grounds. Dr. Jules Backman, research professor of economics at New York University, found in a 1967 study that advertising is *not* anticompetitive, it does *not* lead to monopoly power, it does *not* generate excessive profit, it does *not* set up a barrier against new companies entering an industry, it does *not* contribute to consumer price increases.[18]

Dr. Backman shows, for instance, that the most intensively adver-

---

[17] John W. Crawford, *Advertising*, 2nd. ed., Allyn and Bacon, Boston, 1965, p. 2.

[18] See his *Advertising and Competition*, New York University Press, New York, 1967.

tised products have characteristically increased in price by a smaller amount than have the poorly advertised products. He concludes that expenditures for advertising do not represent a net cost to the economy. If ad costs were eliminated, he points out, other marketing costs would go up, possibly making the selling job more costly overall than it is *with* advertising. Of course, the cost of advertising is built in to the price of the product, but advertising makes possible greater sales which means lower production costs and hence lower prices.

Admen have two defenses against the criticism that only big companies can afford to advertise. One is this: a wide variety of media are available, in every price range, with every kind of audience. The other defense is this: with (among other things) the right kind of advertising, a small company can itself become big. Examples: Polaroid, Xerox, Sony.

As for the charge that advertising is vulgar, tasteless, and misleading: admen have to admit that some of it is. But such advertising is usually confined to products facing excessive competition, or, on the local level, stores catering to nondiscriminating buyers. And the vulgarity and tastelessness is not dissimilar to that found in some of the news and editorial content of the media carrying the advertising.

Admen are less willing to admit that advertising misleads. At least they will argue that ads are more truthful today than they have been in the past. For one thing, the federal government, especially through the Federal Trade Commission, exercises some policing power. Business itself has organized Better Business Bureaus in metropolitan centers to, among other things, put pressure on advertisers to stick to the truth. Consumers themselves have organized several product testing organizations, including Consumers Union, which publishes *Consumer Reports,* and Consumers' Research, which publishes *Consumer Bulletin.*[19] And the news and opinion media have set rather strict standards of what ads they will and will not accept.

Finally, admen argue that word-of-mouth communication will no

[19] But when a product gets a good rating, the manufacturer is not allowed to mention it in his advertising. Consumers Union has brought to court several manufacturers who did, arguing that the manufacturers had hurt CU's reputation for impartiality.

longer do the job in today's complex society. Even Hershey Chocolate Corporation admits it. When in the late 1960s Mars candy bars began outselling Hersheys, what was then the one big holdout against consumer advertising went looking for an agency.[20]

In his lectures on advertising to students at the University of Oregon, Dr. Willis L. Winter with this list summarizes what he considers to be the contributions of advertising to "our socio-economic welfare":

1. Advertising creates mass markets for products, thus raising our standard of living and expanding the job market.

2. Advertising serves as a buyers' guide for consumers, providing information on a wide range of products, both new and established. In the words of Turner Catledge, then managing editor of the New York *Times*, "Advertising is news."[21]

3. Advertising supports the mass media, contributing two-thirds of the revenues of most newspapers and magazines and virtually all the revenues of radio and television stations.

4. Advertising adds value to products by pointing out previously unrecognized attributes either physically or psychologically inherent in the products.

5. Advertising fosters better products through sharpened competition. It engenders better quality control through clear brand identification and manufacturer accountability.

6. Advertising lowers selling costs by making the salesman's job easier or by replacing him entirely, as in the case of mail order houses, supermarkets, and discount stores.

Arguments over advertising's worth, pro and con, are not conclusive. The trouble with many critics is that they lump the various categories of advertising together, and they fail to consider the various functions that advertising performs. Much of their criticism is really directed to the competitive free-enterprise system, for which advertising is only a means of communication. Fairfax Cone has said: "Most of the viewers who fear advertising as an evil force give it too much credit."[22]

The trouble with advertising proponents—and they mostly include

---

[20] See "Hershey Names Ogilvy for $10,000,000 Effort," *Advertising Age*, February 17, 1969, pp. 1 ff.

[21] Turner Catledge, Gideon Seymour Lecture, University of Minnesota, 1958.

[22] Fairfax M. Cone, *op. cit.*, p. 8.

advertising men themselves—is that they fail to admit, even to themselves, the true nature of their work: they are not philanthropists or advance men for a better social or economic system; they are nothing more, nothing less than salesmen. Selling is—or can be—a useful occupation. Those in it should not try to make it appear to be something other than what it is. Nor should their critics.

CHAPTER FIFTEEN

For immediate release

Like the adman, the public-relations man makes use of the news and opinion media to reach an audience and influence it. Unlike the adman, the PR man does not pay for the time and space he gets. How successful he is depends upon his ability to supply a publication or broadcast facility with material comparable to that supplied by the medium's own writers and photographers. In effect, the PR man becomes an unpaid member of the staff.

Public relations: what it is

Public relations is both a *condition* and an *activity*. As a condition, public relations is what people think of a company, organization, or public figure—the client. It is the client's "image."

As an activity, public relations includes everything from publicizing events to manipulating people. It involves public-opinion measuring, advice to management, news-release writing, publications work of all kinds, broadcasting, speechwriting and making, film-making, corporate design, money raising, personnel work, lobbying, tours, meetings, committee work, advertising, training programs, selling, promotion, entertaining—the list goes on.

The public-relations man develops his programs and materials for a number of different audiences. These break down into two basic publics: an internal public and an external public. The internal public consists of employees, people in management positions, and stockholders. The external public consists of customers, potential customers, dealers, suppliers, citizens in the community where the plants are located, civil officials, lawmakers, and others, depending upon who the client is.

People have a tendency to confuse public relations with both advertising and publicity. Public relations is a broad term, broad enough to include both advertising and publicity.

It differs from advertising in that it is essentially institution-oriented whereas advertising is essentially product-oriented. On the surface, at least, public relations is more interested in reputation than in sales.

A major difference between PR and advertising is that in advertising the client is always identified. The print media insist that the client identify himself somewhere in the ad so that the reader will know it is an advertisement he's reading, not news or editorial matter. If the advertiser has designed his ad to simulate news or editorial matter, the medium puts a sort of warning at the top: "An Advertisement." Even though the medium offers the advertiser help with the wording of the ad and, in some cases, insists that changes be made in order to make the ad conform with certain standards, the space is the advertiser's to use as he wishes.

On the other hand what the PR man submits to the medium goes directly into the news and editorial hopper, along with material submitted by the medium's own staff members, to become an integral part of the publication or broadcast. The PR man exercises no control over how his material is used or *if* it is used. He takes his chances.

If the material is used, the reader or listener may not know that a PR man originated it. Not that the PR man minds. He knows that the credibility of the information about his client is enhanced if the reader believes that a working journalist rather than a propagandist originated the story and wrote it. It is better to have a friend tell others how good you are than for you to do it yourself.

The various front organizations set up by trade associations and other organizations are an extension of the PR man's acceptance of the idea of anonymity. Give the front an impressive name to mask its true identity, and it will have an easier time with its propaganda. The Tobacco Industry Research Committee with its stubborn denials of the link between cigarettes and disease operated more effectively under that name than it could have with a more descriptive name, like, say, the Tobacco Industry Defense Council Against the Surgeon General's Report.[1]

Public relations differs from publicity in that publicity represents only the telling of a story. Public relations includes the telling but also all the activity that made a story possible.

In *The Commerce Journal* of Canada some years ago Roy A. Abrahamson described the difference between public relations and publicity this way: A woman wearing clothes a size too small is using publicity; a woman wearing a subtle perfume is using public relations.

Any number can play

Because public relations involves so many different activities, it appeals to a variety of persons as a means of earning a living. Not all are really qualified, and this embarrasses the professionally oriented men and women in the field, but there is little they can do to run the others out. PR has an organization, the Public Relations Society of America, which sets standards, but any policing the organization can do does not affect nonmembers. In 1969, five years after PRSA had started a program to "accredit" PR men, only 15 percent of the organization's 4,536 members had taken and passed the necessary exams. Under a "grandfather" clause another 20 percent had been accredited when the program started, but without taking the tests. A survey taken by Jack O'Dwyer and reported in his PR newsletter showed that most PR men, in and out of PRSA, didn't approve of the accrediting program.[2]

---

[1] "Research" in recent years has become a virtue word with PR men. The reader is wise to question the word when he sees it used by an organization set up by profit-making companies to influence public opinion.

[2] *Jack O'Dwyer's Newsletter: The Inside News of Public Relations,* New York, October 29, 1969.

In their frequent conventions, PR men make speeches to each other about their professional status. Is public relations a profession—or merely a craft or business? If *profession* is strictly defined, of course, public relations does not qualify. There is no licensing. There is no body of knowledge that each PR man must master before he is allowed to practice. Anyone can rent an office, hire a secretary, get some letterheads printed—and he's in business.

The former chairman of Avis Rent-a-Car, Robert Townsend, shook up the PR fraternity in 1970 with some advice, offered somewhat facetiously, in an article in *Harper's*: organizations should fire their PR departments. "Most businesses," he wrote,

have a normal P.R. operation: press releases, clipping services, attempts to get interviewed; all being handled, as usual, by people who are embarrassingly uninformed about the company's plans and objectives. . . . We eliminated the P.R. staff [at Avis]. And we called in the top ten or so people in the company and the telephone operators and told them they were the P.R. department. The telephone operators were given the home phones of the ten people and asked to find one of them if any of the working press called with a question.[3]

No matter what you call him

While the public-relations man builds and polishes an image for his client, he worries about his own. Not that he steps out from behind the scenes for any public recognition; no public-relations man worthy of hire does that. But he wonders sometimes what his neighbors and especially what his colleagues in business think about him. (Would you want your daughter to marry a public-relations man?)

He has never known exactly what to call himself. When he became a force in American journalism in the nineteenth century, offering, as was customary then, a bottle of whiskey to a city editor in return for some favorable mention of his client, he called himself a "press agent." Later, eschewing bribery, he became a "publicist." Still later, a "director of information." As he expanded his activities, listening as well as talking, making of his work, in the

[3] Robert Townsend, "Up the Organization," *Harper's*, March, 1970, p. 84. From the book published by Alfred A. Knopf.

phrasing of Edward L. Bernays, a "two-way street," he became a "public relations man" or "public relations counsel."[4]

But to many newsmen he is still a "flack" or, more insulting, a "tub-thumper."

"The engineering of consent"

Bernays calls public relations "the engineering of consent."[5] The term is pretentious, but it does illustrate the broad scope of PR. As an activity, it represents now much more than the "press agentry" of the nineteenth century.

PR men see their work as falling into three categories:

1. *Publicizing the client.* This they do by mailing or delivering news releases to the various media, by arranging events so the media will assign their own writers to the story, and by publishing their own media.

Publicizing the client is a tough job—and it's getting tougher. With an increasing number of clients clamoring for attention, getting notice for any one of them is almost impossible. Add to this the growing numbness of readers to the constant barrage of propaganda and publicity. The reader just doesn't care. And why should he?

Furthermore, the attention a publicist can engender may do more harm than good. A classic case involves the attempt in Cincinnati in 1947 to make the city "United Nations-conscious." After a six-month crusade with all the gimmicks and a constantly repeated slogan, "Peace begins with the United Nations—the United Nations begins with you," a poll showed only half as many people as before considered the UN as a means of preventing war, and fewer people than before thought the U.S. should join an international force to keep peace. Apparently all the noise had only served to arouse suspicion.

2. *Sizing up various publics.* The PR man wants to find what the client's image is and how it can be improved. Here the public-

---

[4] Edward L. Bernays, whose PR career spans half a century, wrote a number of books, including his memoirs: *Biography of an Idea*, Simon and Schuster, New York, 1965.

[5] Edward L. Bernays, ed., *The Engineering of Consent*, University of Oklahoma Press, Norman, Okla., 1955.

relations man utilizes the tools the social sciences have developed.

In a speech to the Public Relations Society of America in 1961, Howard P. Hudson of Ruder and Finn, New York public-relations organization, said, "Public relations consists of the practical application of social science principles to specific problems." No PR program of any consequence is likely to develop until first a survey of public opinion is undertaken.

But the PR man's knowledge of the social sciences is often superficial. The true social scientist is likely to regard the PR man's polling sample as unrepresentative of the audience he's measuring. Nor does the PR man always interpret his findings accurately. Furthermore, the tools of the social scientists, even in expert hands, are not as exacting as some PR men want to believe.

3. *Helping the client make management decisions.* In this role the public-relations man acts as the company conscience. He operates under the assumption that before his company can enjoy good public relations (used here as a noun) it must first *deserve* good public relations. The PR man can't tell a story unless there's a story to tell.

Society doubtless has benefited to some extent from industry's preoccupation with public relations. Industry has begun to believe its own public relations and is acting accordingly. Edward L. Bernays calls this "enlightened self interest," and notes its surge since the end of World War II.

Who needs it?

Public relations should be thought of as an activity not only for profit-making organizations but also for nonprofit organizations. Government itself engages in public-relations activities.[6] One is hard-pressed to think of *any* organization that doesn't make use of the services of a PR man. The media themselves, often critical of the activities of PR men, have their own PR departments.

Some organizations put their public-relations activities in the hands of one of their own employees, someone who may have a vice president's title. Other companies hire outside public-relations firms. Such firms operate much as advertising agencies operate.

[6] See Delmer D. Dunn, *Public Officials and the Press,* Addison-Wesley Publishing Company, Reading, Mass., 1970.

Two of the largest are Hill and Knowlton and Carl Byoir and Associates.

PR and the politician

No one is more public-relations conscious than the politician.[7]

Perhaps you have gone to a meeting to hear a political candidate, noticed the sparse attendance, and wondered how, under the circumstances, the candidate could seem so unruffled about it, why he would go ahead and make his speech after all. He gave his speech, and perhaps gladly, because he knew it was being reported in the press. It didn't make any difference that a mere handful showed up to hear him. Thousands would read what he said on the front pages. That's enough of an audience to play to.

Theodore Roosevelt used to make his significant announcements on Sunday afternoon because he knew that Monday morning papers were hard-pressed for news. There would be less competition for headline space. Politicians knew how to use the press. It was a large part of their job.

In the nineteenth and early twentieth centuries the politician acted as his own PR man. But with the proliferation of media and the increasing apathy of readers to their "messages," politicians, bewildered by the enormity of the job, have in recent years turned their press relations, sometimes even their administrative chores, over to journalists. The PR man is firmly established now as an aide to the politician. As Stanley Kelley, Jr. pointed out in the mid-1950s in *Professional Public Relations and Political Power*,[8] the politician has an almost naive faith in the magic of public relations.

Kelley views the emergence of PR men in politics with some equanimity. It has, he points out, done away with the "boss" system. The machine, the party, the precinct organization—these now are not so important. Now the *media* are what's important; and so far as the political candidate is concerned, it takes a PR man to know how to use them.

[7] See Edwin O'Connor's novel, *The Last Hurrah*, Little, Brown and Company, Boston, 1956. See also Dan Nimmo, ed., *The Political Persuaders: The Techniques of Modern Political Campaigns*, Prentice-Hall Spectrum Books, Englewood Cliffs, N.J., 1970.

[8] Stanley Kelley, Jr., *Professional Public Relations and Political Power*, The Johns Hopkins Press, Baltimore, 1956.

What are other likely results of increased involvement of PR men in politics?

Kelley sees a bigger percentage of people voting, an erosion of local control, an injection of issues into campaigns, and an acceleration of the "star" system, with big publicity build-ups prior to the nomination. Theodore White's three *Making of the President* books substantiate Kelley's predictions and so does Joe McGinniss's book on Nixon, *The Selling of the President, 1968.*

The "institutional ad"

Industry's concern about its image is a twentieth-century phenomenon. In the nineteenth century, "The public be damned," William Vanderbilt's classic response to a reporter's question about the decline of services on the New York Central, more accurately reflected its attitude. But after some 20 antibusiness novels late in that century and after the muckrakers had had their day at the turn of the century, industry became concerned.

The Pennsylvania Railroad, among the first to take action, hired ex-newspaperman Ivy Lee to polish its image. Lee came up with a revolutionary idea: instead of hiding facts about accidents and keeping reporters away, the line should make it easy for the press. Take reporters to the scene. Volunteer information. Lee figured that by cooperating with the press, the railroad would come out looking better when the stories were written.

Industry in general enjoyed a good press in the 1920s, thanks largely to the new profession of public relations, but with the Depression of the 1930s, the pendulum swung back. Perhaps PR had done its job too well. If industry could be credited for good times, it could also be blamed for bad times. World War II gave industry a chance to redeem itself as the nation united in a common cause, but reaction set in again after the war as the economy made its adjustments.

PR men developed the "institutional ad" in the 1930s to fight growing antipathy. Such an ad read a lot like a newspaper editorial and often occupied a full page in a newspaper. Its job was to sell the free-enterprise system, which was being threatened, many in industry believed, by Franklin Roosevelt's New Deal.

Examining industry's free-enterprise campaign after the war,

He took the apple.

And tossed the core.

That did it. Eden just wasn't
the same old Eden.

Today there are billions of Adam's children
walking the Earth.

They litter the Land.

Pollute the Air.

They worry themselves sick about it.
And blame the other guy. Or they single out
some industry. This one or that one,
the bigger the better.

Okay.

Except for one thing: since 1959, industry-caused
pollutants are down 28.3% in the Bay Area.

And getting smaller. Even though there's
more industry!

(Actually, only 11% of today's
polluted air is the result of industry.)

The point is that today, like yesterday,
industry's goal is still to give you
all the things you want.
Not only in goods and services,
but clean air as well.

Did it all start with Adam?

William H. Whyte, Jr., concluded it was "an insult to the intelligence and, as many businessmen themselves suspected, a prodigious waste of time and money to boot."[9] But if institutional advertising failed in its initial assignment it failed because it was badly used. As a tool currently available to the PR man it enjoys widespread use for all kinds of clients and for every conceivable cause.

Manufacturing news

Go through each story in a newspaper for a given day and see if you can figure out how the story originated. Was it a story the reporter stumbled onto in the course of covering his beat? Was it a story the city editor uncovered and then assigned? Or was it a story dreamed up by a public-relations man in an attempt to draw attention to his client?

Surveys of the origin of news content have found that one-quarter of the stories in a newspaper started with a public-relations man. Perhaps the PR man sensed a story about his organization that was just waiting to be told. Perhaps he planned some event that could not be ignored by the news media. Either way, the public-relations man wrote the story (or made it possible for a newspaper reporter to write the story), and his client enjoyed the resultant publicity.

Much of what the PR man turns out is junk: obvious puffery, with no real value to readers. "Artificial dissemination," someone has called it. But some of the releases interest editors. Why?

In the first place, no paper can completely cover the whole news scene. No staff is big enough. So a paper's stories and features are for every issue supplemented by material submitted by outsiders.

In the second place, the newspaper is not particularly concerned that some organization or some person (PR activity goes on in behalf of individuals, too) will benefit from a story's being published. The test for a news release must be: is it news? Is it of interest to the readers—a sizeable segment of the readers—of this newspaper?

Everyone with an axe to grind quickly learns what is reportable and conducts himself accordingly. In the words of one observer,

[9] William H. Whyte, Jr., and the editors of *Fortune, Is Anybody Listening?* Simon and Schuster, New York, 1952, p. vii.

"From the demonstrator on the street to the President of the United States the behavior of the actors in the news is affected by journalism. All the subjects of news tend to conform to journalism's standards of what is reportable."[10]

News releases

Nothing would please the PR man more than to have the newspaper cover his story with its own staff. In most cases, the story isn't that compelling. So the PR man writes it up himself. He usually duplicates his release and either mails or delivers copies to the various papers. Some papers run the release as is; the better papers do some checking, edit the copy, perhaps combine it with some other story. If the story is important enough, the PR man may send it in before the news has actually taken place and indicate to the editor when the story should be published. If the story is only routine, the PR man marks it "For Immediate Release," meaning the paper is free to run it right away. Since they are under no obligation to the PR men, not all editors honor release dates anyway. They regard the elaborate planning of PR men with amused tolerance.

If he's adept, the PR man tailors his release not only for a particular paper or group of papers, but also for a particular department within the paper. All departments are fair game. What the sports department will run will not necessarily be what the regular news side will run. Sometimes the women's page editor is the editor to appeal to. Or the church page editor.

The PR industry has its own system of syndication. If an organization doesn't want to—or isn't set up to—distribute its own releases, it can work through an organization that, for a fee, will do the job. Such an organization—there are several—puts a number of releases together in a printed publication and sends copies out to all editors with an invitation to use what material they wish. If PR men want to reach financial pages—where releases are especially welcome—there is a PR wire service available.

The National Association of Manufacturers, among other organizations, circulates its own "clip sheet": a publication containing

[10] Max Ways, "What's Wrong with News? It Isn't New Enough," *Fortune*, October, 1969, p. 111.

stories, editorials, and pictures that in the case of the NAM praise business and preach free enterprise. Some small papers—weeklies, especially—use this material as filler copy, partly because their editors are lazy or harried, partly because their editors share NAM's economic and political viewpoint.

Editors seem especially responsive to the releases issued by government agencies and nonprofit organizations.[11] Thus university news bureaus are able to score with releases that, if they were carefully considered, would not see print: a professor gets included in some obscure *Who's Who*, he makes a routine speech or writes an article for a miniscule audience, the school paper wins a fancy rating in a contest in which every entrant wins. PR men themselves realize that much of this is meaningless, but they turn the stuff out because their fellow practitioners do, and the media continue to use it. The PR man is on a treadmill.

Imagine the appreciation of one editor in early 1968 when an organization sent out a release with this note: "We call . . . [this event] to your attention in the hope that we will get some publicity out of it, and that we will make money from the publicity and that it will cost us nothing." *Editor & Publisher* called it "history's first truthful publicity release."

The PR man ordinarily plays a little game with the editor. How much mention of his client can he get in the story without spoiling its chance of getting into print? At his end, the editor tries to figure out how much of the free advertising he can weed out without hurting the sense of the story. Most editors feel a need to revise the copy, if for no other reason than to make it different from the copy that will appear in a competing paper. PR men have been known to "bury the lead"—put the most important paragraph deep in the story—so the editor will concern himself with moving it back up to the top and not bother to make other changes more damaging to the client.

Client mention in a release is sometimes referred to as "poison." The word typifies what some newspapermen think of the PR man. It goes back to early in the century, to the days of Ivy Lee, the

[11] One editor said he preferred government releases to industry releases because they were more carefully printed with no smears on the reverse sides: he could use them for copy paper.

newspaperman-turned-PR man whose pronouncements were viewed by other newspapermen with some suspicion. Along the way he picked up a nickname: what else but "Poison" Ivy?[12]

It used to be customary for PR men to send a letter with their release saying they were considering an advertising schedule, implying that if the paper didn't run the release, it wouldn't get the advertising. PR men seldom pose such threats to newspapermen these days.

All manner of media

The PR man works with all media.

In the case of radio and TV he takes advantage of a provision of the Federal Communications Commission that directs these media to devote some time to "public service" broadcasting. If the PR man can produce a film, say, that deals with an issue of public concern, and if he confines the advertising content to simple company mention at the end, a station is likely to run it at no charge, though not, of course, at prime time.

In working with magazines, the PR man tries to submit exclusive articles rather than duplicated releases. The PR man probably will not write the article himself; he'll supply information to the free-lancer or staff member who has drawn the assignment. The PR man's chief contribution often is the groundwork which planted the idea with the editor.

Many PR men publish their own magazines—for their employees or for customers and opinion leaders.

PR men get into the book publishing business through the issuing of company histories. Some of these histories are important enough to be published by major book publishers.

PR men also get into film production. They make films primarily for free showing by schools and service clubs. Outside organizations usually handle the distribution of the films.

One of the most important media to the PR man is direct mail. Unlike other print media, direct mail has no frequency schedule. Each piece is a "one shot." When he uses direct mail, the PR man

[12] For Lee's life story see Ray Eldon Hiebert, *Courtier to the Crowd,* Iowa State University Press, Ames, Iowa, 1966.

in effect becomes a publisher. He oversees the writing and design, picks the printer, arranges for the type to be set, decides what kind of paper to use, and takes care of many other production details.

PR men like direct mail because it is so flexible. It can take any shape, any size. They like it, too, because they consider it an intimate medium. When the recipient gets it, he presumably reads it without any accompanying distraction. It doesn't have to fight for attention with other items on a printed page, as, for instance, an advertisement in a newspaper would do. Furthermore, the medium is highly selective. The PR man can rent from one of several brokers a mailing list of exactly the kind of persons he wants to reach.

But the various publics have learned to recognize much of direct mail for what it is: junk. It goes into a waste basket as soon as it's delivered. The various devices PR men use to fool readers into opening the envelope deserve the contempt thoughtful readers feel for them. Mail-order insurance companies are chief offenders with their attempt to hide their identity by printing at the top left of the envelope the address only or the name of the president or by making their envelope look like those used by the government for official business.

Not only does the PR man work with all media; he works with different departments of each medium, helping to supply if not shape editorial as well as news content. A call on the editor of the editorial page may result in an editorial being written siding with the PR man's client. The PR man is especially interested in the letters-to-the-editor column. A newspaper faces a constant problem of weeding out PR-written or -inspired letters from letters submitted by ordinary citizens. This is not to say that the paper doesn't give the PR man a hearing in the column, especially if his company finds itself at the wrong end of a controversy. It's just that it doesn't want professionals taking over a section reserved for readers who are not paid propagandists.

From time to time the PR man finds it necessary to complain about coverage rather than help supply it. A textbook, let us say, makes unfavorable reference to the woods operations of lumber companies. Someone at the American Forest Institute, the PR organization of the lumber, pulp, and paper industry, sees the reference, disagrees with it, and points out to the publisher where the author erred. The author, if he agrees, changes the reference in his next edition.

PR men get in touch with newsmen whenever newsmen unwittingly use language that tarnishes a client's image. Ethnic groups, religious bodies, and various trades and professions are particularly sensitive. The head of a model school some years ago wrote to a London paper protesting what he called "the new and grossly unfair newspaper practice of calling any woman a 'model' who so describes herself. . . ." The "model" in question was Christine Keeler, a call girl linked with a top government official. The head of the model school suggested that because Miss Keeler had just sold her memoirs to a newspaper, it made just as much sense to refer to her as "the well-known journalist."

Euphemism

Just about everybody these days worries about his image. What you call a man is important to him. A name describing his occupation, once perfectly honorable, may strike him as "inappropriate." And so the janitor becomes a "custodian," the garbage man a "sanitary engineer," the hairdresser a "beautician," the undertaker a "mortician" or even a "grief therapist," the journalist a "mass communicator." Printers of high school yearbooks become "publishers."

Words have a way of deteriorating under constant use. What sounds good for a few years changes as people begin reading into a word new and unflattering connotations. Or perhaps the word's real meaning finally catches up with it.

A word or phrase substituted for another because somehow it sounds better than the original is known as a euphemism.

A person uses a euphemism, if not to mislead his audience, then at least to muffle meaning. The late Senator Everett Dirksen once told a story of a man filling out an application for an insurance policy who came upon the question: "How old was your father when he died and of what did he die?" It just so happened the father had been hanged. So the applicant wrote. "My father was 65 when he died. He came to his end while participating in a public function when the platform gave way."

In middle-class society, people don't use toilets, they use "bathrooms" or, in some settings, "powder rooms." In their late years they become not old people but "senior citizens." They don't die, they "pass away."

Some of this is necessary, of course. *Time* in an essay on euphemism quotes what it calls a "familiar saying": "A man who calls a spade a spade is fit only to use one."[13] Bergen Evans, the lexicographer at Northwestern University, suggests that euphemisms are necessary because "lying is an indispensable part of making life tolerable."[14]

Among those who rely heavily on euphemisms are sociologists, teachers, government officials, and even radicals.

To a social worker a slum becomes a "culturally deprived environment." Birth control becomes "planned parenthood." Mentally retarded children are "exceptional children." In California now there is no such thing as divorce: it is, officially, the "dissolution of marriage." To a teacher, students who cheat "depend on others to do their work." A below-average student "works at his own level." A lazy student "can do more when he tries." A library is a "learning resource center."

When the U.S. Information Agency brought out comic books on President John Kennedy for overseas distribution, it called them "illustrated continuities."

The politician who puts his foot in his mouth one day calls a hasty press conference the next to "clarify his position."

When members of the Students for a Democratic Society occupy a building on campus they "liberate" it.

The true disciples of euphemism are PR men and advertising men. A major contribution they make to their clients is putting ordinary or even embarrassing information into attractive terms. The phrasing makes the difference. Store A closes on Sunday; Store B across the street remains open. Store A says: "Closed Sundays so our employees can be with their families." Store B says: "Open all day Sunday as a service to our customers."

In the world of advertising, a TV commercial is "an important word" or "a message"; pimples are "facial blemishes"; false teeth are "dentures"; hair dyes are "tints" or "rinses"; used cars are

---

13 "The Euphemism: Telling It Like It Isn't," *Time*, September 19, 1969, p. 27.
14 *Ibid.*

"pre-owned cars"; houses are "homes"; colors are "decorator colors"; butter is "creamery butter," as if there were any other kind. Jantzen, Inc., makes special swim suits not for fat girls but for girls with "full figures."

When a television network schedules re-runs for summer it calls them "encore performances."

One can understand why the PR man resorts to euphemism in his news releases. He wants to create the best possible climate of opinion for his client. He doesn't want to offend anyone. But why aren't newspaper editors more vigilant in changing the PR man's euphemisms to words that are more direct? As the Eugene, Oreg., *Register-Guard* said in an editorial on "Nice Nellyisms" (another term for euphemisms): "Ah, for a society in which a spade is not an agricultural implement!"

Perhaps the trouble is that the newspaperman himself, in his own writing, has given in to euphemism. The victim in a crime story, for instance, is not raped, she is "criminally assaulted," which can lead to some incongruous phrasing: "The girl, beaten, kicked, and stomped on, lay on the ground bleeding. Her arm and shoulder blade were broken. But she was not criminally assaulted."

Propaganda

The term that best fits the PR man is "propagandist," but that term, especially since World War I days, carries with it unfavorable connotations. People associate "propaganda" with unworthy causes; they think of it as the utilization of dishonest tactics. At one time it was a perfectly respectable word, originating with the Roman Catholic Church and its efforts to propagandize for the faith.

Indeed, one can say that any person who persuades is a propagandist, the clergy included. Certainly the advertising man is a propagandist. Even the editorial writer in a sense propagandizes. But because theoretically he writes as a disinterested observer rather than an idealogue or a paid spokesman for a cause, one would be stretching a point in referring to him as a propagandist.

The propagandist himself regards what he promotes not as propaganda at all but as "information" or even "education." What is the difference between education and propaganda? Again theoretically, education presents both or all sides and permits the listener to make up his own mind. Propaganda presents only one side and tries to make up the listener's mind for him. Another observation about propaganda is that if you approve of what is said, it is, so far as you are concerned, education; if you don't, it's propaganda. The anticigarette campaigns which many Americans consider as educational are considered by some—cigarette manufacturers and tobacco farmers—strictly as propaganda. Some billboards in the South, in North Carolina and Virginia, particularly, where tobacco is the most important single industry, tell the story: "Caution: Anti-Smoking Propaganda May Be Hazardous to Your Economic Health."

Educators like to think that what they do makes the propagandist's job harder. An educated person, it is thought, can see through an appeal, recognizing it for propaganda. But to some extent, education actually helps set the stage for propaganda.

In his book, *Propaganda*, Jacques Ellul calls education "pre-propaganda" because it conditions minds with vast amounts of incoherent information. It remains for the propagandist to come around and make some sense out of the morass for those who are susceptible. Ellul goes so far as to suggest that intellectuals are more vulnerable to propaganda than nonintellectuals because they are used to absorbing information second-hand. Furthermore, they feel a need to form some opinion about almost everything. For this they need help.[15]

But a more universal opinion holds that the less educated person responds more favorably to propaganda than does the intellectual. And that person, propagandists find, responds more surely to emotional than to rational appeals.

The Institute for Propaganda Analysis in the 1930s came up with a list of propaganda "devices" now well known by any school child: name-calling ("Pig"), glittering generalities ("The American Way,"), transfer devices ("U.S. government figures show. . . ."), testimonials ("Recommended by Duncan Hines"), "plain folks" (the political candidate out fishing), card stacking (quoting out of context), bandwagon ("everybody's doing it").

---

[15] Jacques Ellul, *Propaganda*, Alfred A. Knopf, New York, 1965. Malcolm Muggeridge in *Jesus Rediscovered* takes a similar view of education: "For the most part, it only serves to enlarge stupidity, inflate conceit, exchange credulity, and put those subjected to it at the mercy of brainwashers with printing presses, radio, and television at their disposal" (p. 101).

PR men and advertising men still make use of these devices, but they use them subtly. Nor do current propaganda devices—"tactics" might be a better word in this context—fall so conveniently into the basic categories as set up by the Institute. Current tactics include these:

1. *The unstated advantage.* The secret here is to arrange the facts so that the reader will reach a mistaken conclusion—a conclusion that works to the advantage of the client. Example: a correspondence school specializing in training students for work as insurance claim adjusters, runs a picture of a man bent over the prostrate form of a beautiful girl, her dress torn, looking provocative despite the fact she has just been hit by a car. Although the copy doesn't say so, the reader is supposed to get the idea that if he takes the course, he'll spend the rest of his life getting paid for comforting beautiful, suffering women.

2. *The make-believe advantage.* The secret is to get there first with the disclosure of an ingredient that all products in that category have. If you make enough noise about it, people will think you're the only one who has it. A recent example involves the Shell Oil Company with something it calls "Platformate." *Consumer Bulletin* for January, 1968 points out that just about every gasoline has this ingredient, that if you drive a car it's almost impossible to buy gasoline that doesn't have it. *Consumer Bulletin* likened Shell's claim to the claim of a baker: "We bake our cake with flour."

3. *The appearance of modesty.* After a while people turn away from their leader, no matter how much charisma he may have. He becomes too familiar, hence boring.

People like to side with the underdog. So some companies, comfortably settled in first place, would just as soon talk about something else. No sense in rubbing it in. Often when a major company is attacked, it ignores the provocation. To fight back is to dignify the attack.

Sometimes a number-two role can work to the advantage of a company, as Avis Rent-a-Car proved with its "We try harder" campaign. Hertz tried to ignore Avis, and did for a long time; but there comes a time when number one can no longer afford modesty. "For years, Avis has been telling you Hertz is No. 1," read a Hertz ad in 1966. "Now we're going to tell you why."

A PR man shows his worth when he takes a bad break for his client and turns it to an advantage. *The New Yorker* used to advertise it was not edited for the old lady in Dubuque, a reflection on the level of sophistication in that town. The Chamber of Commerce there, seizing the initiative, launched a contest for the ideal "little old lady" and earned some attention for Dubuque.[16]

4. *The long way around.* When a medical clinic decides to charge for phone calls to doctors, it doesn't announce this in the opening paragraph of a form letter to patients. Instead it announces that it is now possible to get advice by phone (it always was) and, oh yes, sort of as an afterthought: "Effective October 1st we will institute a policy of charging for such special services rendered over the telephone."

5. *Pick a reason, any reason.* No store conducts a sale just to conduct a sale. The customer likes markdowns better if he thinks the retailer was forced into it. The manager is away and the assistant manager has gone berserk. Or a new shipment is coming in and there isn't room for it. A dance studio calls you and offers you a free lesson if you can answer a question only a moron could miss.

6. *Phony authority.* People are impressed by footnotes and scholarship. Never mind who the authority is, so long as he looks like an authority. A favorite device of right-wing organizations which like to "document" their cases is the citing of the *Congressional Record.* If something is published there, some people believe, it must be important. But how does an item get into the *Congressional Record?* All that is needed is to get a Congressman to request its inclusion, and it will be published. The *Record* contains not only the texts of what is said in debate in Congress but also all kinds of articles and editorials put there by congressmen to flatter or placate constituents back home.

7. *Leave it out.* A university in the West a few years ago, launching its annual drive for contributors to the Development Fund, published a leaflet listing the names of persons who had given previously. The headline read: "Is Your Name on This List?" It went out to all graduates. A not inconsiderable number kicked in with some money that year, not wishing to be left off a published list the following year.

8. *Buck the trend.* When everybody is writing short letters, you

[16] She turned out to be Mrs. Delbert Hayford, whose favorite magazine was *Reader's Digest.*

write long letters. When the soft sell is in, you use the hard sell. It is a sure way to be noticed.

Bucking a trend often results from an inability to keep up. So the company heads in an opposite direction.

9. *Out of character.* Occasionally a company does the unexpected. In 1966, *Scientific American,* in what was probably the most notable promotion stunt in the history of magazines, ran a paper airplane contest. Eleven thousand entries arrived from all over the world. Eight distinguished judges supervised a "fly off" held in New York's Hall of Science. Winners were duly announced in the press, and Simon & Schuster brought out a book based on the event, showing diagrams of some of the entries.

Stan Freberg in 1967 produced an ad for Pacific Air Lines, a West Coast feeder line, that shocked the industry. "Hey there! You with the sweat in your palms," said the headline. The ad admitted people were frightened about flying. So were Pacific pilots. And this made them more alert.

Freberg drew angry complaints from other airlines because the ad, they said, would frighten all airline passengers. But Freberg argued that by facing up to fears, timorous prospective passengers would take heart—and take a plane next time. He even wanted to hand passengers "survival kits," including copies of Norman Vincent Peale's *The Power of Positive Thinking.* And he planned to substitute porters for stewardesses, pipe in the sound of clacking railroad wheels over the loud speaker system, and pull the shades and project pictures of telephone poles going by. During the uproar over the campaign, the line merged with another, and the campaign was quietly dropped.

The ethics of persuasion

Persuasion can be a perfectly honorable activity. Our society is based on the premise that people have a right to make their ideas known and influence others to accept them. A man can do this for himself—or as a hired hand for someone else or for some organization. To most of us, persuasion is far preferable to coercion.

But questions do arise over the *means* used by the persuader and the *cause* he advocates. Perhaps the cause is more crucial than the means. When a person criticizes public relations or advertising his motive often is that he doesn't identify with the cause. He may approve a blatant appeal to the emotions, for instance, if the purpose is to alleviate hunger among underprivileged children but he may not approve such an appeal if the purpose is to elect to office a politician with unshakable middle-class values.

Regardless of the cause, most PR and advertising men agree that certain means should be avoided. While these rules are not spelled out by law or even through formalized codes of ethics, they are acknowledged as desirable by almost all persuaders whether or not persuaders at all times live up to them:

1. The persuader should not resort to lies or distortions of the truth. This does not mean he will tell *both* sides of the story. Just as a lawyer does for his client, the PR man and the ad man tell only as much of the story as will benefit the client.

2. The persuader should not resort to appeals to bigotry, hatred, fear, anxiety, or ignorance. He should not encourage people to make decisions that are obviously against their best interests.

3. The persuader should not resort to an emotional appeal if he knows that reason, were he to use it, would lead his audience to an opposite opinion. But the persuader insists that an appeal to the emotions, rightly used, is entirely legitimate. Man does not— can not—make many of his decisions rationally; it would be unrealistic to appeal to him purely in rational terms.

In their *Persuasion: A Means of Social Control*[17] Winston L. Brembeck and William S. Howell criticize the "cult of reason" which puts emotion off limits for the persuader. "Since at least a great many decisions made by people are more nonlogical than logical, the voluntary self-limitation of the persuader to the tools of facts and reason may purify his ethics to some degree but do little for his effectiveness (which is also a matter of ethics, since he may not have the moral right to be ineffective in a crisis). Quite possibly he may misrepresent the facts of his case through attempting to reason logically about matters of nonlogical motivation."[18]

4. The persuader should not hide the name of the sponsor or the real purpose of the public relations or advertising he produces.

These standards seem modest enough, but the PR man and adman

[17] Prentice-Hall, Englewood Cliffs, N.J., 1952.

[18] See the book edited by Richard L. Johannesen, *Ethics and Persuasion: Selected Readings*, Random House, New York, 1967, pp. 10, 11.

on the job experience difficulties living up to them. The nature of the cause adds further to the persuader's dilemma.

Some PR and admen work for causes or products or companies they are enthusiastic about. Others are not so fortunate. If the persuader works for an agency serving a *variety* of clients, he may be able to avoid that client—or those clients—of which he doesn't approve. For instance, a confirmed nonsmoker would not be expected to work on a cigarette account. In some cases, the agency itself may refuse to accept such a client.

But there is a prevailing spirit among PR men and admen that holds that every client deserves a hearing in the court of public opinion provided no law prohibits the distribution of his product or service. Under this concept, the persuader owes some consideration to his publics, but, unfortunately, his first loyalty is to his client.[19]

[19] For more on public relations see William L. Safire, *The Relations Explosion*, The Macmillan Company, New York, 1963.

CHAPTER SIXTEEN

When rights conflict

As has been noted earlier, the press operates behind the secure shield of a special constitutional guarantee against government interference. That safeguard is justified—in fact, necessitated—by the importance of the press to the system of representative democracy under which we live.

Yet the right of the press to publish is not an absolute one. It sometimes happens that the media of information, in carrying out their essential function of informing the public, infringe upon other guarantees that are also vital to our system; some of them, indeed, have just as impressive constitutional underpinning as does the concept of press freedom.

When such conflicts of rights occur, it is often difficult to sort out the values involved and determine which has priority.

Guidelines exist for resolving these conflicts, sometimes in the form of statutes, sometimes in common law, and sometimes only through an evolving consensus. But in all cases the guidelines are imprecise. Substantial expanses of gray areas are left, stretches of no man's-land across which opposing forces shift back and forth and the issue remains in doubt.

One of these gray areas involves the law of libel and its limiting effect on the freedom of the press to publish without hindrance.

The 50 laws of libel

Freedom to publish is spelled out in the First Amendment's provision that "Congress shall make no law . . . abridging the freedom of speech, or of the press. . . ." and in the extension of that prohibition to the states by means of the Fourteenth Amendment.

As the courts have interpreted it, the First Amendment affords assurance to anyone who publishes that the government will not impose prior restraint on his publishing activity; that is, there can be no censor who must approve the content of a publication before it comes out, and no agency of government can prevent the appearance of a publication by a court injunction, a sheriff's order, or other attempt to restrain a potential publisher *before* he commits his work to the presses.

But the courts have also held that the First Amendment does not render the publisher immune from responsibility *after the fact* of publication, if what he has published injures other well-established and safeguarded rights.

Among these rights is that of any citizen to his own good name and reputation.

The way a man is thought of by others in his community usually depends on the things that he has said and done through the years, on his pattern of conduct. He has gradually built up his standing and character by this accumulative record. And, the courts have held, this reputation belongs to him. It has value. If that reputation is damaged by something that appears in the newspaper or something that is broadcast over radio or television, the injured man is entitled to take legal steps to re-establish his good name and to recover monetary losses that he may have suffered. The laws of libel provide the means by which he can take these steps.

There is no federal law of libel, but each of the 50 states has its own set of statutes. These differ in some respects, and anyone who wants to gain a full understanding of libel codes as they affect him must take the trouble to examine in detail the laws of his state. It is possible, however, to consider the subject in general terms, since there are more similarities than differences among the various statutes.

All of the state laws are in approximate agreement in defining what libel means: a publication of some kind that in some manner damages the reputation of an individual or group of individuals. (A particularly useful definition is that devised by Harold Cross, a former counsel for the New York *Herald Tribune*. It well reflects the ambiguity and uncertainty that are so much a part of the laws of libel. According to Cross: "A newspaper publication is libelous of any person if its natural effect is to make those who read it think worse of that person.")

In the several definitions of libel, the term "publication" has broad meaning. It embraces not only the obvious ways of publishing, such as in a newspaper, magazine, or book. Publication, so far as libel law is concerned, also includes the dissemination of a statement over radio or television (even though verbal or visual, it has been "published" to hundreds or thousands of listeners and viewers, with the same effect as if it had appeared in print).

In some cases, the courts have held that damaging material that was reproduced on a copying machine for only a few readers represented "publication" so far as the law of libel is concerned; even handwritten letters that were passed around to several persons have been held to be "published" libel. In other words, the damaging or defamatory material need not have been distributed to many persons in order for it to be considered libel.

Moreover, the definition includes material in any form—not only the substance of a newspaper story, but also the headline, an accompanying picture, an advertisement, or a cartoon sketch. Whatever is published and causes injury to a person's good name is by definition libel.

If the statutes stopped there, they would constitute a sweeping limitation on the freedom of the press. A cursory skimming of any newspaper would yield numerous examples of published material that would be damaging to the reputations of the persons mentioned in the stories. An account of an arrest of a man on a charge of burglary certainly is likely to dim his good name among those who read it; the report of a debate in Congress wherein the President's motives and policies are bitterly attacked could well damage his standing; a photograph of a dignified citizen caught in an amusing but embarrassing mishap may expose him to ridicule and diminish his reputation. All of these instances are, under the law, libelous. Why, then, isn't every publication constantly under legal siege by aggrieved citizens demanding satisfaction for injuries done them through the news report? Chiefly because the laws of libel, after defining the term, go on to spell out various specific ways by which a publisher can defend himself against libel suits and escape the damages that might be sought by a reader who felt himself injured by something that had been published about him. The defenses thus provided to the publisher enable him to sidestep some of the hazard represented by the law of libel.

Through the loopholes

If you consider the concept of libel law as a kind of limitation on the freedom to publish, then the defenses specified in the statutes must be considered as loopholes or exemptions to that limitation. It should be noted, however, that each such specified exemption rests upon a determination that in this specific instance the public's right to be informed takes precedence over the individual's right to safeguard his good name against unwarranted injury by the media of information.

One of these defenses is that of *privilege*. A newsman invoking this defense claims the right to publish material from official and public records (such as the testimony given in a trial) even if that material is defamatory and damaging to the reputation of some citizen or group of citizens. And if the newsman's report taken from such records is a fair and accurate one, this defense of privilege will protect him even if he is sued for libel damages by someone mentioned unfavorably in the report.

The rationale for this exemption to the general concept of libel responsibility is persuasive. It goes back once again to the First Amendment. The purpose of the guarantee of press freedom contained in that amendment is to ensure that the public will be well and fully informed. It is particularly necessary that the public be kept informed about the way in which its elected and appointed representatives are carrying out their responsibilities as public servants.

It follows, then, that the press should be free to report for the public the ways in which the public's business is being conducted by the legislators, the judges, the administrators, and others who have been given a public charge. And the news of how the public's business is being conducted is found in large part in the proceedings of legislative, judicial, and administrative agencies.

So in reporting material from the records of those proceedings, the press is considered to be the public's agent; it is also considered to have immunity from liability if some of the material it reports from the records happens to be defamatory. It has a privilege, in short, to report public and official records without fear that it might later have to run the post-publication gauntlet of the libel laws.

The defense of privilege is invoked by newsmen to shield their reports of Congressional or legislative debates, proceedings in the various state and federal courts, and official actions by administrators or administrative agencies.

As a practical matter, this means that if something bad is said about you by a state senator during a debate on the floor of the senate, and a newspaper publishes a story quoting the senator's unpleasant comment, you will very likely be unable to win a libel suit against the newspaper. The senator, of course, has absolute immunity conferred on him by the state constitution, so you can't reach him, either.

But if that same senator were to make exactly the same statement about you in the course of a talk at the local Rotary Club, he *would* be open to suit. And if the newspaper quoted his comment in its news story of the club meeting, the newspaper would be vulnerable to libel action as well. The Rotary speech is not an official occasion, and no privilege attaches to what is said or written about it. The defense of privilege applies *only* to public and official proceedings about which the public has a special need to be informed.

If the press were not given the right to invoke the defense of privilege, it would be inhibited from reporting many kinds of news about the public's business that in one way or another involved defamatory material. And as a result the public would not be fully informed about the activities of its governmental representatives.

Some are fair game

A second defense that newsmen can use against a libel suit also has constitutional roots. It is the defense of *fair comment and criti-*

cism. The reasoning behind this defense runs thus: A person who runs for public office, or accepts appointment to a public office, thereby solicits the public's trust and confidence. He also lays himself open to criticism of his performance as a public representative; sometimes that criticism may be painful to bear, but he has asked for it. He has, in effect, yielded up some of his rights as a private citizen and made himself subject to scrutiny and comment in his role as a representative of the public; and he cannot expect to be protected by the laws of libel to the same extent as when he was a private citizen.

So if a news report quotes a constituent who has some unflattering things to say about his congressman, the congressman will be frustrated by the defense of fair comment and criticism if he attempts to sue either the disgruntled voter or the newspaper.

Supreme Court decisions during the 1960s considerably broadened and strengthened what had been up to then a somewhat limited fair comment and criticism defense. Under these interpretations, a public official may be the subject of very harsh treatment by critics in or out of the press, and even be the victim of false statements made about the way in which he is fulfilling his public responsibilities, without being able to rehabilitate his reputation by means of a libel action.

The landmark case is *New York Times* v. *Sullivan,* 1964, in which the Supreme Court held that a libelous statement about a public official could be defended as fair comment even if parts of it were shown to be false—provided that the publisher had not printed it with malicious intent or foreknowledge that it was false.

The broad sweep of the Sullivan-*Times* doctrine is perhaps best conveyed by an interpretation made by former U.S. Attorney General William P. Rogers (who later became Secretary of State in the Nixon cabinet): "A newspaper is not liable for anything said about a public official, true or false, if what is said concerns public conduct and is said without malice."

In a subsequent case dealing with an extension of the Sullivan-*Times* doctrine, Supreme Court Justice Hugo L. Black observed that "unconditional freedom to criticize the way such public functions are performed . . . is necessarily included in the guarantees of the First Amendment. . . . And unconditional right to say what one pleases about public affairs is . . . the minimum guarantee of the First Amendment."[1]

Not all of the justices then on the bench agreed with this interpretation, however. One of them, Justice Abe Fortas, voiced a concern that was shared also by some editors and observers of the news media: "The First Amendment is not a shelter for the character assassinator, whether his action is heedless or reckless or deliberate. The First Amendment does not require that we license shotgun attacks on public officials in virtually unlimited open season. The occupation of public officeholder does not forfeit one's membership in the human race."[2]

But it does, so far as majority decisions of the Court have held, constitute a forfeiture of many of the protections that a nonofficeholder has under the laws of libel. The fair-comment-and-criticism defense has developed into a broad shield for the press in its treatment of public officials, both great and small.[3]

The concept of the fair-comment defense also extends to other kinds of persons who may not be public officeholders but who in one way or another put their efforts before the public and solicit

---

[1] *Rosenblatt* v. *Baer*, 1966. In the view of one academic observer, the *Times* decision could be explained more in terms of the context of the era than on the basis of the single case:

The most pertinent reality behind the ruling, however, was that in the decade preceding *Times* the Supreme Court had made a sweeping commitment to the cause of Negro equality. . . . The direct antecedents of *Times* resulted from Negroes' adoption of direct action techniques of dramatizing their grievances. This produced the sit-in and demonstration cases in which the First Amendment guarantees of free speech, assembly, and the right to petition for a redress of grievances were the bases of Negroes' legal arguments. Though not all the justices were persuaded in each case that First Amendment rights should prevail over the rights of states to secure order and property, after 1954 the court held for the Negro petitioners in every single case it accepted prior to *Times*. . . . It is clear that the racial undertones of the *Times* case were well within the Court's attention. (Daniel Pfaff, "Race, Libel, and the Supreme Court," *Columbia Journalism Review*, Summer, 1969, pp. 23–26.)

[2] *St. Amant* v. *Thompson*, 1968.

[3] Subsequent cases have extended the Sullivan-*Times* doctrine to apply not only to elected public officials but also to persons who had formerly been public officials and to persons who had made themselves "public figures" by engaging in controversial political debate. In some cases in lower courts, the attempt has been made to apply the doctrine to such minor public officials as a candidate for mayor, or a police patrolman.

public approval and support, such as actors, authors, and enter-tainers.

These persons also are assumed to have laid themselves open to criticism of their creative efforts and must not wince and rush to court if that criticism wounds. The courts have been fairly strict, however, in ruling that the freedom to criticize extends only to the artist's creative effort—not to his private life or to his personality. A reviewer can criticize an author's new novel in acid terms and be protected by the defense of fair comment, but he cannot, under the same shield, attack the author as a bad father or as a despicable human being.

The truth, the whole truth, and . . .

There is a third major defense that a publisher can use to defeat a libel action brought against him—that of *truth*.

In most state jurisdictions, if a publisher can prove to the satis-faction of a jury that the defamatory material he published about the plaintiff was true in all respects, *and* was published without any malicious intent but only as a part of the news report, he will be able to escape damages.

That second provision is very important to the success of the defense of truth. If, in the course of reporting legitimate, *bona fide* news, an editor publishes material that is damaging but true, he is doing no more than performing the role contemplated in the First Amendment. If the defamatory story is true, the editor is not re-sponsible for the injury it causes, and the wounded party has no recourse.

But note that this line of reasoning rests on the assumption that the defamatory material is *legitimately* part of the news report. If it is included frivolously by the editor, or if it is dragged into a news story when it really isn't a part of the news, then the court is likely to assume that spiteful or malicious intent was involved. In that case, even if the material happens to be true, the editor will be held accountable for the damage the report has caused. He was act-ing *not* in his role as unbiased disseminator of the news, but as one who had a special purpose to injure the person mentioned unfa-vorably in the published account.

But where it is possible for the publisher to demonstrate the defense of truth, without any malice being shown, this defense is sound and solid and will defeat most libel actions.

It can be a solid defense without being based upon its literal truth. So long as it can be demonstrated to the jury and court that the *gist* of the report was indeed true, it is not necessary to establish that every word or syllable of the account was factual.

(In one case, a newspaper published a story claiming that an alderman had a terrace constructed in his back yard by city workers, who used city-owned bricks for the job. In fact, such a terrace had been built, but of dismantled paving stone, not bricks. The alderman brought suit against the paper, and his attorney argued that the paper could not offer a defense of truth because the story contained an error, the reference to bricks rather than paving stone. The court ruled that this error was a "triviality," and that the gist of the story was indeed correct and the paper's defense of truth a good one.)

But if truth as a defense need not rest on literal accuracy, it must embrace the whole impact of the defamatory publication. That is, the defense must be as broad as the charge, and if the effect of the defamatory material is in part created by innuendo and suggestion, then the defense of truth must extend to the innuendo and suggestion as well as the flat statement. In such cases the use of crutch phrases such as "it was reported," or "it is claimed" does not reduce the liability of the publishing agent. Attribution of the defamatory material to someone else does not relieve the publisher of responsibility for whatever damage the material may cause (unless, of course, the attribution is to a privileged official record, such as a warrant or a grand jury indictment).

"Oops, sorry . . ."

These three—privilege, fair comment, and truth—are the principal defenses that newsmen can employ to defend themselves and their publications against a libel action. There is one other device, however, that an editor or broadcaster can use in some states to enable him to escape at least some of the damages he might have to pay if he lost a libel action. In those states (in the late 1960s there were 29) the publication of a retraction—an acknowledgment that an error was made and an apology for having made it—frees the publisher from some damage liability even if he has no defense to offer against the suit.

In most states that have retraction laws, the provision is intended to free the publisher only from responsibility for inadvertent libel —the kind that stems from an accident in the news handling process, such as a typographical error, or the transposition of names. Usually a retraction will not ease the liability of a publisher for a libel published with malice.

Assuming that the publisher of a libel has no good defense to offer, he can be brought to account in court for the damage that his publication has done.

In theory, anyone who has had a significant role in the publication of the defamatory material is vulnerable to suit—the reporter who wrote the story, the copyreader who edited it and put a headline on it, the editor who assigned the reporter to the story, and of course, the publisher who bears ultimate responsibility for anything the paper publishes. As a practical matter, however, the chief target of a libel action is usually the ownership—the moneybags that have the means to pay the damage awards, if the jury decides that damages are due.

Often the damages sought by a plaintiff in a libel action sound astronomical. Suits for $5,000,000 and even $12,000,000 have been filed, and rarely does the injured person seek less than $100,000.

To a considerable extent these vast claims are window-dressing. The plaintiff really doesn't expect that a jury will agree with him that his reputation has been injured a million dollars' worth. But even the act of filing a suit for such a staggering amount may accomplish at least part of the plaintiff's purpose—persons reading of the action will think to themselves: "He *really* must have the goods on that paper if he's going after *that* much," and to an extent the plaintiff's reputation will already have been rehabilitated in that the reader has by implication accepted the guilt of the publisher.

There are occasions, of course, when the jury takes seriously the formidable damage claims of a plaintiff. Georgia athletic director Wally Butts sued *The Saturday Evening Post* for libel on the basis of an article in the magazine that accused Butts of conspiracy to fix a football game between his team and that of the University of Alabama. In that case the jury awarded Butts $3,000,000 in damages. This award was, however, reduced to $460,000 by an appeals court.

Usually a successful plaintiff receives a much more modest sum. The award may be in several parts: "special" damages that are to repay actual monetary loss the plaintiff suffered as a result of the libel (such as in the case of a shopkeeper who lost business because it was said that he had a dirty store); "compensatory" or "general" damages that are intended to recompense the injured person for loss of good name and reputation; and "punitive" damages that may be added to the award by the court if the offending publication was particularly outrageous.

Some plaintiffs may win the case so far as the court record is concerned but gain little else. This happens if nominal damages—such as $1, or $100—are awarded when the suit had asked for $500,000. What the court is in effect saying in such cases is that the plaintiff's reputation has indeed been damaged by the publication, but not much—or else that he didn't have much reputation to damage in the first place. In either instance, the outcome represents a rather sour triumph for the plaintiff and really constitutes a moral victory for the defendant.

A substantial damage award in a libel action can be a crippling blow to a publication or broadcasting station (the *Butts* case crucially weakened an already staggering *Saturday Evening Post* and contributed to its eventual demise). Moreover, the court costs of defending against a rash of libel suits can themselves be a serious burden, even if every case is won by the publication at the trial or appellate level.

So the libel statutes do represent one type of limitation on the freedom of the press to publish whatever it pleases, and a significant safeguard of the rights of the individual who finds himself in conflict with one of the media of mass communication.

Privacy: a new doctrine

There is another area somewhat akin to libel wherein the right of the press to publish the news conflicts with an individual right—that of privacy.

Here there are few statutes to serve as guidelines. In fact, the concept of a "right of privacy" is relatively novel in the law; it was first enunciated in an 1890 *Harvard Law Review* article by Samuel D. Warren and Louis D. Brandeis, later to become a distinguished justice of the Supreme Court, and its evolution since has been chiefly through court decisions.

The underlying reasoning is similar to that having to do with libel. An individual is presumed to have a right to keep his private life free from intrusion, just as he is also presumed to have a right to his good name and reputation. If his privacy is unwarrantedly invaded by a reporter or photographer bent on getting the news, the citizen ought to have some means of recourse.

Many of the early court cases involving violation of the right of privacy had to do with advertising in which an individual's picture or name had been used for commercial purposes without his consent. The findings in favor of the plaintiff in most such cases were clear-cut and uncontroversial.

The privacy issue takes on more complexity, however, when the offending publication involves news rather than advertising, and when the plaintiff who is complaining that his rights have been invaded is someone who has in some fashion become a part of the news. How, then, to distinguish between invasion of privacy and legitimate reportage of a newsworthy person?

The decisions have been made on a case-by-case basis, and in the process the concept of invasion of privacy has taken on some outlines, though not precise ones.

One illustrative case involved a man who in his youth had been a boy genius in mathematics. He had attracted wide attention, and news stories recounted his brilliant and precocious grasp of the field. Then he dropped out of sight for a number of years, until much later a reporter discovered him working in a humdrum job as a minor statistician, his initial promise faded. When the reporter wrote a "where are they now?" kind of story, the man sued the newspaper that published it; the basis for his suit was invasion of privacy.

In that case the court held that he could not recover damages. Having once been so much in the news he had lost his claim to privacy and could not reinstate it now, even though circumstances had changed.

In other, somewhat related cases, the courts have held that privacy cannot continue to exist where there is a legitimate public interest in the news. Public officials, for example, have little claim to privacy. Yet other cases have suggested where the boundaries may lie. In one of these, decided in the mid-1960s, a woman sued a newspaper after it had published a picture of her with her skirts flying in the updraft of a carnival fun house. She was awarded damages, and the judge observed that "to hold that one who is involuntarily enmeshed in an embarrassing pose forfeits her right to privacy . . . would be illogical, wrong, and unjust."

A recent illustrative decision with respect to the right of privacy was *Time, Inc.* v. *Hill*[4] which came down from the U.S. Supreme Court in 1967.

This case involved a family named Hill, the members of which had been held hostage in their home for several days in the early 1950s by three escaped convicts. Their ordeal was widely reported in the news of the time.

Several years later a book, *The Desperate Hours*, appeared on the market, presenting in fictional form an episode that in some respects resembled the Hill family story. *Life* magazine published an article about the book and about a forthcoming play made from the book, and in the article clearly identified the fictional works as being based upon the *Hill* case. The members of the Hill family sued *Life* for invasion of privacy, claiming that the book and play described a situation quite different from the one they had gone through and contending that the representation in *Life* was "false and untrue."

A jury found for the Hill family and awarded damages, but the Supreme Court reversed the verdict on the ground that the right of privacy doctrine cannot supersede the First Amendment guarantee where legitimately newsworthy matter is concerned, even if some incidental error may have been present in the published version of the newsworthy material.

Some courts have held that a person who is shown in a news picture as part of a crowd gathered at a public place is not entitled to claim that his privacy was invaded, but that if a cameraman singles him out for no particular news-connected reason, then he may have a case.

The rules of the game with respect to invasion of privacy are still in the process of evolving, but it is clear that they already constitute at least a moderate form of restraint on the freedom of the press to seek the news wherever it is to be found.

[4] 385 U.S. 374, 17 L. Ed. 2nd 456, 87 S. Ct. 534 (1967).

Keeping trials fair

There is a third point at which the right of the press to publish news clashes with an equally respected constitutional right. This conflict has received a good deal of attention in recent years under the shorthand label of "Fair Trial *vs.* Free Press."

At seeming odds in this issue are two articles of the Bill of Rights, the First Amendment with its provision for freedom of the press, and the Sixth, which states that "In all criminal prosecutions, the accused shall enjoy the right to a speedy and public trial, by an impartial jury of the state and district wherein the crime shall have been committed. . . ."

The operative phrase here is "impartial jury." And the argument arises over whether it is in fact possible to empanel a truly impartial jury to try a man if the community's newspapers and newscasts have been filled with accounts of his arrest and the preliminaries to his trial.

To the lay observer, the argument is a difficult one to follow, since the two sides often seem to be espousing very similar positions. But there are crucial points of disagreement, and they are not likely to be resolved soon or easily.

Consider first the viewpoint held by most lawyers and judges. They contend that only the barest minimum of information should be published about an accused person prior to the time he is actually placed on trial. Legal purists would allow publication only of such items as the fact that someone had been arrested, the nature of the charges filed against him, and the legal sequence that will be followed in handling his case.

They argue that if additional information is given out—such as a report that the accused has confessed, or a prediction by a prosecutor that a guilty verdict will be returned, or details of the accused person's prior criminal record—the minds of potential jurors in the community will be prejudiced. It will then become difficult to select 12 persons who can honestly say that they have not formed an impression about the accused's guilt or innocence, and the accused person will be deprived of his right to a trial by unbiased jurors who are prepared to hear the case with open minds.

In support of their position, spokesmen for the legal profession can cite and document a succession of celebrated cases in which "trial by newspaper" did indeed take place. They can point to headlines in which the guilt of an accused person was assumed ("Police Name Seaman as Slayer of Eight Nurses") and to even more blatant instances in which the press appeared to be trying to direct a verdict ("Why Isn't Sam Sheppard in Jail?" and "Quit Stalling—Bring Him In"). They can also enumerate various cases in which pictures, such as a staged reenactment of a crime, had implanted in the public's mind an impression of an accused person's guilt long before he was brought into the courtroom to be tried on the charge brought against him.

(A spectacular, but hardly typical, instance took place during the trial of Charles Manson in 1970. Manson had been charged with master-minding the killings of actress Sharon Tate and seven other persons. Shortly after Manson's trial had gotten underway in California, President Nixon held a press conference in Denver and commented on a number of topics, including the press coverage of the Manson case. In the course of his comments he inadvertently convicted Manson: "Here is a man who was guilty, directly or indirectly, of eight murders without reason." Although the President's press secretary later issued "clarifications" that emphasized that the President had not intended to imply that the defendant was guilty, large headlines resulted, and Manson's attorney immediately moved for a mistrial—a motion denied by the presiding judge after a poll of the jurors convinced him that they had not been affected by the Nixon comment.)

As remedy for what it considers to be an impediment to justice, the legal profession has brought forward a program of restrictions on the release of pretrial information. These restrictions were developed first in the form of a report by an American Bar Association committee, and later were adopted formally as part of the canons that guide the behavior of lawyers and officers of the court.[5] Such canons—once they have been adopted by the individual state and local bar associations and courts as well as by the ABA—become a part of the ground rules of the courts, and a judge has the

---

[5] The so-called Reardon Report, presented in December, 1966, by the ABA's Advisory Committee on Fair Trial and Free Press, headed by Justice Paul Reardon of the Massachusetts Supreme Judicial Court, and formally adopted by the ABA House of Delegates in February, 1968.

power to enforce them by contempt of court citation or by instituting disciplinary procedures through a bar association.

In some respects, the position taken by the newsmen in the Free Press-Fair Trial debate does not seem markedly different from that of the jurists. Most editors will concede that there have been some spectacular abuses of news coverage of criminal cases; they will not attempt to defend such excesses. Most editors will also acknowledge that the ABA formula for limitation of the release of pretrial information would allow for the reporting of *most* of the facts that the public needs to know in *most* criminal cases.

But the editors balk at the rigidity of the ABA approach. They insist that the public has a need to know how the machinery of justice is working at all of its stages, and that in some instances this requires a close and detailed account of the course of a case from the time that a crime has been committed until a verdict has been reached.

In support they can cite numerous instances in which the rights of an accused person were violated in secrecy by corrupt law enforcement agencies that were able to avoid press scrutiny (black persons in small Southern communities have frequently been the victims of such tactics). And they can point out cases in which bargains were struck behind the scenes by prosecutors and defense attorneys at the expense of the public interest.

The press must have discretion, the editors argue, to consider each case by itself, and to push for full coverage when the public interest would be served by such an approach. The ABA formula, were it to be widely adopted by individual courts and bar associations, would throw a universal blanket over the handling of court cases and in the process would raise the specter of judicial contempt power as a club to keep the press from getting at facts that in some instances should be aired.

The concern of newsmen about the threat of use of the contempt power is a genuine one, based on some unhappy experiences in earlier eras.

The power to cite and punish for contempt is available to all judges. It is a power usually not based on statute but on a common law assumption that a judge must be able to maintain order in his court so that justice can be administered. When anyone or anything threatens to interfere with the orderly processes by which justice is dealt out, the judge is assumed to have the authority to put an end to that interference and to punish those responsible for it.

Under this doctrine, judges have punished not only outbursts of violence in the courtroom itself, but also statements made or publications disseminated at a distance from the court which the judge concluded were likely to affect the attitude of a jury or apply pressure to a judge and thus obstruct the administration of justice.

As it was exercised in early English courts (and American practice derives from the English model) the power was swift and harsh. A judge could cite an offender at the moment his actions began to constitute interference with the decorum of the court or with the administration of justice. Having cited the contemptuous behavior (or, in effect, stated the charge) the judge could proceed on the spot to find the offender guilty, pronounce his sentence, and order a bailiff to haul him off to a cell (or to the scaffold in very early times)—all in the space of a few moments, and with no provision for trial by jury or right of appeal.

While the common law basis for the contempt power is still recognized in the courts of this country, there have been some limits placed on the exercise of the power. In some cases the limits have been statutory. (For example, the law provides that if a contempt penalty of imprisonment for more than six months is to be assigned, the offender must be given a jury trial. Appeals are also provided for in most cases involving contempt citations.) In other respects the contempt power has been limited by judicial decisions, and these limitations are of particular interest to the press.

In *Bridges* v. *California*[6] in 1941 and later in *Pennekamp* v. *Florida*[7] in 1946 the United States Supreme Court held that for a newspaper publication to constitute contempt it must represent a "clear and present danger" that it would have the effect of obstructing justice in the pending case. In these two decisions, the court held that the publication of news articles or editorials could not be held to represent such a clear and present danger, and reversed contempt penalties that had been imposed on newsmen by trial judges and upheld in the lower appellate courts.

To many editors, the American Bar Association recommendations that the contempt power be invoked to assure adherence to the pro-

[6] 314 U.S. 252, 86 L. Ed. 192, 62 S. Ct. 190 (1941).
[7] 328 U.S. 331, 90 L. Ed. 1295, 66 S. Ct. 1029 (1946).

posed limitations on pretrial publicity raised the prospect of a revival of earlier, pre-*Bridges* interpretations. They feared that individual judges, encouraged by the ABA recommendations, might begin utilizing the contempt power to prevent publication of information about the working of the court system that the public should be entitled to have.

Which right is paramount?

And thus we work our way down to the heart of the matter: two basic rights in conflict. The press wants to keep its hand free to report the news the public needs to know; the legal fraternity wants a firm rule assuring every accused person who comes into court that he will confront a jury which has not been prejudiced against him by reading or hearing news accounts that suggest his guilt.

One difficulty in the way of a resolution of the clash is the lack of hard evidence about certain aspects of the question. We know little, for example, about how a juror's attitude toward a case is affected by what he has read prior to coming to the courtroom. Very little research has been done on the matter, and most of it has been fragmentary and inconclusive. As Alfred Friendly, managing editor of the Washington *Post*, observed:

The question is: how big a house are we proposing to burn down for the sake of how big a pig we wish to roast? I think we are in considerable doubt about the dimensions of both. As to the pig, we do not really know how serious is the danger to a fair trial from prejudicial pre-trial or pending-trial publication. Nobody has ever made much of a quantitative measurement. How many cases involving unfair trials are there? The President of the American Bar Association has said that they have become a commonplace, but I would challenge him to find ten cases in the last ten years within his own particular state where a serious charge has been made that justice miscarried because of prejudicial publicity in the press.[8]

Another editor, Raymond Spangler of the Redwood City, Calif., *Tribune*, sought to boil the whole controversy down to its essentials:

When a crime is committed by someone else, the average citizen

[8] In a pamphlet, *Fair Trial vs. A Free Press*, published in 1965 by the Center for the Study of Democratic Institutions.

wants to know all about it; he calls that Free Press. But when he is himself involved in a crime, the average citizen wants it kept out of the papers; he calls that Fair Trial. Question: Can we in this country honor the principles of both Free Press and Fair Trial?[9]

Mr. Spangler's assessment somewhat oversimplifies the matter, but his question is the central one—can we honor both?

One attempt at an affirmative answer has been the development in several states of joint bar-press codes, drawn up by newspapermen, lawyers, judges, and broadcasters. These codes set out standards of behavior for both the press and the officers of the court, and they usually include many of the same kinds of provisions that were embodied in the ABA's recommendations.[10]

An attempt was begun in 1969 by the American Society of Newspaper Editors and the ABA, working with other press and legal organizations, to encourage the spread of the bar-press code concept. Officers of both groups expressed hope that the widespread use of such codes would reduce the need for imposing the restrictive ABA canons.

It should be noted, however, that the joint codes are entirely voluntary in character, with no provision for effective enforcement. Their success depends on the good faith of the signatories, and most of them have yet to undergo a test under crisis conditions.

Another proposed solution was put forward by magazine author Irwin Ross, but it has not as yet been given much hearing by either side in the debate. Ross proposed that restrictions be imposed on defense attorneys, police officers, and the prosecution to prevent them from releasing pretrial information, much as the ABA formula provides. But, to safeguard against instances where a defendant was being railroaded, and where only publicity on the proceedings could give him relief, Ross proposed that all the restrictions on information release should include a provision allowing the defendant to waive them at his option. Thus, if he felt his rights were in jeopardy, he could authorize his attorney to speak out through the press, in which case the canonical restrictions on the prosecution would also be lifted.

[9] Quoted in *The Nation*, April 11, 1966.

[10] One of the earliest, in Oregon, was put into effect in 1962, six years before the Reardon Report was adopted.

Ross concluded: "This may not be a perfect solution, but it is one which is likely to prevent the excesses of trial by newspaper without relinquishing the safeguards of a crusading press."[11]

An editor might argue that a defendant would not always be aware when his rights were jeopardized, and that the press ought to be free to monitor the processes of justice in all cases, not just when called upon.

Neither the Ross proposal nor any other currently under con sideration seems to represent a solution acceptable to all the parties involved. The prospect is that this particular stretch of no man's-land will continue to be contested for some time to come.

According to ——?

There is still another sector where the issue is similarly unre-solved. Here a less momentous problem than the Free Press—Fair Trial question is involved—whether under certain circumstances a reporter should be allowed to keep his news sources secret, even when ordered by a court to reveal them.

On the face of it, this seems a paradoxical matter. The mission of the press usually is to tell what it knows, not to suppress it. And that includes the source of news; in many instances knowing where a given item of information originated is essential to an understand-ing of that item. So why would a reporter want to conceal his sources?

It doesn't very often happen, but there are times when newsmen feel that the claim to secrecy must be made. And when they make it they often find themselves on a collision course with the courts.

These infrequent situations almost always involve an investigative story, often an exposé of wrongdoing on the part of some agency of government. The initial tip for such a story typically comes from an informant willing to blow the whistle on his superiors so long as he can be assured that his own name won't be brought into the case. The tipster may fear for his job, or even his life, if it becomes known how the newspaper got on the trail of the story.

So the reporter gives his word, gets the leads he needs, and pro-

11 Irwin Ross, "Trial by Newspaper," *The Atlantic*, September, 1965.

ceeds to develop the story. If it involves laying bare extralegal activities, the chances are pretty good that sometime later on the reporter may be called before a judge or a grand jury and asked to provide what evidence he can on the matter under investigation— including the names of the persons who fed him the original tips.

In making such a request, the authorities are only doing their job, of course. Most of us, as citizens, subscribe to the doctrine that law enforcement officials are entitled to the cooperation of the public, and that they ought to be able to seek out and obtain information that they need to carry out their responsibilities. When a citizen is summoned to court to give evidence, he is expected to give what help he can, so long as his rights are not violated.

The newsman's contention, however, is that he should in certain cases be exempted from this obligation;[12] he should be permitted to remain silent about the identity of his news sources because to expose them would jeopardize future access to the kind of information that he obtained in this instance. The reporter argues that the public interest is better served by keeping such channels open than it would be if he were compelled to expose his informants and thus dry up the only avenues through which certain kinds of news can find their way to the attention of the press and the public.[13]

So the issue is drawn. The court and the prosecutor contend that the reporter as citizen must give evidence that is needed to further the ends of justice; the reporter as representative of the press responds that he must withhold the evidence in order to be faithful to his obligation to inform the public. Each side claims that righteousness and the public interest are in its corner.

In sixteen states, resolution of the matter has been attempted by statute. By law in those jurisdictions, reporters may refuse to reveal news sources under certain specified circumstances. In the rest of the states, newsmen take their chances individually. In some cases they have clung to their professional code even in the face of judicial

[12] Most states, for quite different reasons, provide exemptions from the obligation to testify for certain categories of citizens such as doctors and lawyers, who receive information in confidence and must be allowed to preserve that confidence if they are to continue to be useful to their clients or patients.

[13] One such tip from a secret informant led in recent years to a newspaper exposé that resulted in the trial and conviction of the State Treasurer of Illinois for malfeasance in office.

order and have paid fines or gone to jail as a result.[14] In other instances the authorities have backed down from a final confrontation and tacitly conceded the newsman's claim, even though it had no statutory support.

The situation here is akin to that in the other gray areas in which the right of the press to find and print the news is in some fashion at odds with other rights that are also vital to our way of life. The drawing of simple boundary lines is very difficult and the continuation of a see-saw shifting of forces seems likely to be the pattern for the foreseeable future.[15]

[14] Marie Torre, columnist for the New York *Herald Tribune*, went to jail in the 1950s rather than reveal the source of a story she wrote about actress Judy Garland. A decade later, an editor of the University of Oregon student newspaper, Annette Buchanan, finally paid a $300 fine for contempt of court rather than reveal the names of persons interviewed in a story about use of marijuana on campus. The case had been carried to the Oregon Supreme Court and had been supported by *amicus curia* briefs on behalf of the Oregon Newspaper Publishers Association, the American Society of Newspaper Editors, and Sigma Delta Chi, professional journalism society. The issue was raised in a somewhat different form late in 1969 and early 1970, when several newspaper and magazine reporters and some broadcast newsmen were requested to testify before a grand jury probing into the activities of the Black Panthers. The newsmen were directed to bring with them unedited files, films, photos, and notebooks containing information gathered on a confidential basis.

One of the reporters, Earl Caldwell of the New York *Times*, was backed by the newspaper in a court test of the matter. He requested a federal court to quash the subpoena or else to direct that his questioning before the grand jury be strictly limited so that he would not be forced to jeopardize his relationship with the Panthers as news sources.

Federal District Court Judge Alfonso J. Zirpoli held that Caldwell would have to respond to the subpoena and appear before the grand jury. But then he also held that in the absence of an "overriding national interest" Caldwell should not be compelled to reveal information developed out of confidential relationships. This was interpreted by some press spokesmen as the first holding by a federal court that newsmen have a First Amendment privilege not to reveal the identity of news sources.

[15] For additional reading on the subject matter of this chapter see Zechariah Chafee, Jr., *Government and Mass Communications: A Report from the Commission on Freedom of the Press*, J. B. Lippincott Co., Philadelphia, 1956; Alfred Friendly and Ronald L. Goldfarb, *Crime and Publicity*, Twentieth Century Fund, New York, 1967; William A. Hachten, *The Supreme Court on Freedom of the Press*, Iowa State University Press, Ames, Iowa, 1968; Donald M. Gillmor and Jerome A. Barron, *Mass Communication Law: Cases and Comment*, West Publishing Co., St. Paul, Minn., 1969; and Harold L. Nelson and Dwight L. Teeter, Jr., *Law of Mass Communications: Freedom and Control of Print and Broadcast Media*, The Foundation Press, Mineola, N.Y. 1969.

CHAPTER SEVENTEEN

Who watches the watchdog?

The first chapter of this book suggested that the only meaningful quality control being brought to bear on the mass media today lies within the consciences of the men who own and operate those media.

Various other forces exert intermittent pressure for improved performance, to be sure. But the response to those pressures varies directly with the degree to which the public-service responsibility of the press is honored at the decision-making levels of a given newspaper, magazine, or broadcasting station. Except for the fitfully exercised powers of the Federal Communications Commission with respect to radio and television, there is no agency—public or private—that stands guard over media performance on behalf of the public in anything other than a pro-forma fashion.

Yet the chapters preceding this one have spelled out in detail how crucially important it is that the media of information *do* function in the public interest. These chapters have also catalogued the internal and external factors that militate against the achievement of this ideal.

The question inevitably works its way to the fore: is internal conscience enough protection? Does society's watchdog itself need watching? If so, what kind of mastiff would be appropriate to the assignment?

"There ought to be a law . . ."

The handiest answer is the one that has been applied to so many other sectors of life in recent decades: government regulation. But that could be a ruinous answer.

If an agency of government were to be established to ensure quality performance by the mass media, it would presumably have to be empowered to license quality practitioners and to punish substandard ones in some fashion. Once such power had been acquired by an arm of government, the long struggle for freedom of expression would have been nullified, for the power to license can be—and usually is—the power to destroy insofar as the media of information are concerned.

And there is no need to turn back to the Alien and Sedition laws, or to any other distant period of press repression, to sense the force of that truism.

Consider for a moment the severe temptation that the existence of a government licensing power would have posed for President Lyndon Johnson during his final year in office. Day by day he saw the press reflecting in its headlines the mounting chorus of dissatisfaction with his policies. Day by day he saw his hopes of another term in office shriveling. Day by day he read the pollsters' findings that showed his standing with the public sinking further and further.

Had there been ready at hand an instrumentality by which he could have cut off that crippling, fatal flow of criticism in the press (as being "inimical to the public interest") would Johnson—or would anyone in his situation—have been able to resist the impulse to apply the clamps so that he could win the breathing space he felt he needed in order to make his Vietnam policy succeed?

Perhaps most persons rarely, if ever, have occasion to concern themselves about the hazard implicit in governmental power over the press. And it is true that those who are involved with the press as practitioners or observers (including the authors) are particularly sensitive about the issue. But most libertarians in every age have been aware of its menace. Even the critics of the press have backed away from this kind of corrective; the 1947 report of the Hutchins Commission, *A Free and Responsible Press*, observed:

> If modern society requires great agencies of mass communication, if these concentrations become so powerful that they are a threat to democracy, if democracy cannot solve the problem simply by breaking them up—then those agencies must control themselves or be controlled by government. If they are controlled by government, we lose the chief safeguard against totalitarianism—and at the same time take a long step toward it.

We cannot afford such a stride toward totalitarianism; on that all of us would be able to agree. But, some analysts of the press contend, this country has found ways of utilizing the power of government to provide varying degrees of regulation over other aspects of our society and our economy without pushing on all the way to totalitarianism. They point to the pure food and drug laws, the regulations of advertising and marketing practices, the use of statutes and court actions to prevent the spread of corporate trusts. Isn't there, then, some middle way also with respect to the press? Couldn't the agencies of government somehow be employed in the public interest to ensure responsible performance by the press without in the process destroying the freedom of expression that is the breath of life to our democratic system?

As was noted in the preceding chapter, there are some laws (libel, invasion of privacy) and some court powers (the contempt citation) that do constitute government controls on the press. Yet press freedom has not perished because these controls exist. Is this a pattern that might be further developed?

One who thinks so is Jerome A. Barron, a professor of law at George Washington University.[1] In two articles, one published in the *Harvard Law Review* in 1967 and the other in the *George Washington Law Review* in 1969, Barron developed what he called "A New First Amendment Right—Access to the Press."

Mr. Barron's thesis is that freedom of the press is not synonymous with freedom of expression for the average citizen, since he has little chance to avail himself of the channels of communication in

---

[1] And coauthor, with journalism professor Donald M. Gillmor, of the excellent text on law of the press, *Mass Communication Law*, mentioned in Chapter Sixteen.

order to disseminate his own ideas. ". . . A right to expression is somewhat thin if it can be exercised only at the sufferance of the managers of mass communications."

He urges that the interpretation of the First Amendment be broadened to embrace a doctrine of free access to the channels of communication so that it would "require opportunity for expression as well as protection for expression once secured."

The practical result of such an interpretation might be to apply to the newspaper press a version of the equal-time doctrine imposed by the FCC on broadcasters. A citizen who had been mentioned unfavorably in the press would be ensured a right to reply in the next day's paper. An unpopular or minority opinion would be guaranteed a chance to be aired through a letter-to-the-editor or an advertisement. Either the courts or statutes might be resorted to as means of obliging the managers of the mass communications media to provide such access.

Mr. Barron's *Harvard Law Review* article concludes:

The changing nature of the communications process has made it imperative that the law show concern for the public interest in effective utilization of media for the expression of diverse points of view. Confrontation of ideas . . . demands some recognition of a right to be heard as a constitutional principle. It is the writer's position that it is open to the courts to fashion a remedy for a right of access, at least in the most arbitrary cases, independently of legislation. If such an innovation is judicially resisted, I suggest that our constitutional law authorizes a carefully framed right of access statute which would forbid an arbitrary denial of space, hence securing an effective forum for the expression of divergent opinions. With the development of private restraints on free expression, the idea of a free marketplace where ideas can compete on their merits has become just as unrealistic in the twentieth century as the economic theory of perfect competition. The world in which an essentially rationalist philosophy of the first amendment was born has vanished and what was rationalism is now romance.[2]

As might have been expected, the Barron proposal had a mixed reception. The American Civil Liberties Union saw promise in it,

---

[2] "Access to the Press—A New First Amendment Right," 80 *Harvard Law Review* 1641, June, 1967. Copyright 1967 by the Harvard Law Review Association.

and its biennial conference in 1968 voted to support law suits challenging denial by publishers of the right of reply. But many editors and observers of the press were dubious.

They saw the prospect of publishers being forced to publish selected items as a clear threat to press freedom ("When any group —even government seeking to remedy certain ills which it believes it detects—tells a publisher what he must print, it is taking upon itself an omnipotence and paternalism which is not far removed from authoritarianism").[3]

Another critical reaction focused on the practical difficulties that a right-of-reply and right-of-access concept would create for the press. Walter Wilcox, professor of journalism at UCLA, pointed out that newspapers might be flooded with demands for space: "The possibilities are staggering: the society matron who is miffed at the coverage given her latest bash, the pseudo-scholar who wishes to set the record straight, the crank, the crackpot—not to mention the special pleaders who haunt the city room."[4]

Even professional press critic Ben H. Bagdikian, who has frequently raised his voice to complain about journalistic sins and omissions, was skeptical of the Barron approach.

> The . . . likely extension of Professor Barron's idea is that news organizations would tend to become common carriers of other people's views with no control over content, like telephone and telegraph companies. This is already true for most advertising. The courts have made plain that they will not permit arbitrary denial of advertising space in a monopoly or near-monopoly medium. Is this a reasonable doctrine for news? It is not. One function of news is the professional judgment of what is more and what is less important at any given hour. . . . Despite all the flaws in these decisions, someone has to do it, and judges and legislators are not able to do it better.[5]

Whether the Barron proposal for a broadened First Amendment as a guarantee of a right of access for individuals will take root perhaps depends less on the reaction of academic observers than

[3] John C. Merrill, University of Missouri, and Dennis Brown, San Jose State College, in an essay, "Regulatory Pluralism in the Press?" in *Freedom of Information Center Report No. 005*, October, 1967, published by the Freedom of Information Center of the University of Missouri.

[4] *California Publisher*, February, 1968.

[5] Ben H. Bagdikian, "Right of Access: A Modest Proposal," *Columbia Journalism Review*, Spring, 1969, pp. 10–13.

on the way in which the courts view the doctrine. And some years may pass before the deciding cases find their way through the judicial system.

From the viewpoint of the journalist, the proposal appears to be more hazardous than helpful. As one journalism educator put it, the Barron concept "will take root only when our society has proceeded much farther along the road toward Orwell's 1984, wherein a paternalistic and omnipotent power structure makes our individual decisions for us."[6]

But if there hasn't yet been found a safe way to bring government into the picture as a guarantor of press quality, what alternatives are there?

The editor's conscience has thus far served us fairly well, but not in every instance. And its leverage may be growing less in an age of increasing monopolization of the channels of communication, of increasing chain control of newspapers and broadcast outlets, and of consequent dilution of the role of the individual in the large, corporate structures that many of the communication channels have become. So where else can we turn for help in maintaining and improving the level of performance of the mass media of information?

Various answers, or partial answers, have been put forward. Some of them have been tested; others have never progressed beyond the drawing-board stage.

Codes and committees

One that has gotten at least some testing represents, in effect, an extension of the concept of quality control through individual conscience. It has involved the establishment of various professional societies and associations of editors and others engaged in the gathering and disseminating of information. Such groups—among them the American Society of Newspaper Editors, the National Conference of Editorial Writers, the Radio Television News Directors Association, the American Newspaper Publishers Association, the National Association of Broadcasters—have devised codes of professional conduct that have an impressive and reassuring ring.

[6] John C. Merrill, *Freedom of Information Center Report No. 005, op. cit.*

It is likely that these codes have had some influence on the professionals who by their membership in the associations indicated a willingness to adhere to their standards. But where that happened, it was once again by virtue of the integrity and sense of responsibility of the individual editor or broadcaster. The associations have no effective enforcement apparatus, nothing comparable, for example, to the threat of disbarment that a bar association ethics committee can wield.

In the few recorded instances in which any of these associations attempted to exert any disciplinary pressure on an erring brother, the effort was ineffectual.[7]

A proposal was made in 1969 that one of the groups, the American Society of Newspaper Editors, attempt to invest its code of ethics with new significance by establishing a standing grievance committee. Norman Isaacs, president of ASNE and executive editor of the Louisville newspapers, described the proposed committee as an agency that would stand ready to "consider complaints of substance as they relate to the Society's Code of Ethics." Such complaints might come from members of the public, or they might be lodged by one editor or newsman against another. The ASNE leaders estimated that such a grievance committee might receive "from one or two such complaints a year to perhaps six or seven at the outside." That would appear to be either: (a) a strikingly conservative assessment of the number of unheard grievances floating about, or (b) an acknowledgment in advance of the limited scope of the agency. In commenting on the idea, the magazine *Editor & Pub-*

---

[7] Carl Lindstrom, a former newspaper editor, describes one such episode in his book, *The Fading American Newspaper:*

Ethics gave the newly organized American Society of Newspaper Editors birth pangs that nearly proved fatal. The records of the Society do not tell the whole story because more of the initial agonies occurred in the Board of Directors. . . . The story was that a member of the Society had misused his newspaper in a way that seemed a clear violation of the newly adopted code. The Board of Directors voted his expulsion, but he was to have a hearing. At this hearing the accused was represented by counsel and made it clear that, if expelled, he would sue individually and personally all members of the Board. The directors also consulted counsel, who found that under their loosely written constitution they had no right to expel anybody and were, indeed, sitting ducks for a lawsuit. Hence, no expulsion. The issue was resolved by the resignation of the accused member. . . .

lisher observed that "the committee will have no teeth or punitive powers except the power of public opinion,"[8] and that brings us back to the point at which the discussion began.

This is by no means to suggest that the associations and their codes—or their grievance committees—are meaningless. But their leverage for good is, in the last analysis, a moral rather than a tangible force, and those who are likely to respond to that leverage are the ones who were behaving responsibly in the first place and didn't really need a disciplinary curb.

The yardstick concept

Another approach was suggested back in 1930 by that same Robert M. Hutchins who 16 years later served as chairman of the commission to investigate press freedom. In a speech to the annual meeting of newspaper editors in 1930, Dr. Hutchins proposed that there be established one or more model newspapers that would be published by endowed foundations. With no commercial influence to modify their purpose, such journals would be free to develop to the fullest the potentialities of the newspaper for public service. They would constitute yardsticks of ideal performance, by which all other papers could be measured.

The very existence of such yardstick newspapers would, Dr. Hutchins reasoned, be a spur to all other publishers to improve their product. Their existence would also remind the reader of the kind of superior product he *could* be getting, if he would only demand it of the local newspaper proprietors.

This idea never got a trial on Mr. Hutchins's terms, and in another speech to the same society of editors in 1955 he acknowledged that "I take this proposal less seriously than I did twenty-five years ago." He pointed out that there did exist one journal that somewhat approximated his ideal, but that it had not been particularly effective. "*The Christian Science Monitor* undoubtedly has a good influence on the press of this country, but the conditions under which it operates, with its foundations in heaven rather than on earth, are so different from the ordinary that any publisher has an adequate

[8] *Editor & Publisher*, October 11, 1969, p. 6.

excuse for not following the *Monitor's* example. So I fear it would be with an endowed newspaper."[9]

How about a press council?

The other proposal for improvement of the quality of press performance that is associated with Hutchins's name also went for many years without any field test. That was the proposal by the commission on press freedom that there be set up a national press council that would monitor the performance of the media on behalf of the public. As the commission's 1947 report envisioned it, "such an agency would . . . educate the people as to the aspirations which they ought to have for the press." It would be independent of government as well as of the media of information. Its support would come from gifts, perhaps from foundations. It would report annually to the public and might also establish machinery for investigating specific complaints about inadequate or unsatisfactory press performance.

While the press council idea has as yet had no full-dress trial on a national scale (most publishers promptly rejected the concept as an invasion of press freedom) its possibilities have at least been investigated at the local level.

Through the years a very few individual publishers experimented on their own (Houston Waring of the Littleton, Colo., *Independent* was one of them), but it was not until two decades after the release of the Hutchins commission report that the idea was given a systematic tryout.

This came about through the sponsorship of the Mellett Fund for a Free and Responsible Press, a nonprofit foundation established by the American Newspaper Guild. The fund provided a series of grants to several journalism educators who undertook to set up experimental local press councils in several parts of the country during the 1967–68 academic year and report on the results they achieved.

[9] In the field of broadcasting the existence of the National Educational Television network and the Public Broadcast Laboratory has provided the viewing public with some basis, at least, for judging what the medium is capable of providing in the way of public service. Whether the example of these yardstick projects has had an uplifting effect on the quality of commercial television programming is debatable.

One of the educators, William B. Blankenburg of Stanford University, described some preliminary conclusions about his part of the experiment in an article in *Columbia Journalism Review*.[10] Blankenburg had been an assistant to Professor William L. Rivers of Stanford when Rivers established and monitored the activities of two Mellett-sponsored local press councils at Bend, Oreg., and Redwood City, Calif.[11] In each case, the local council consisted of a cross-section of citizens who agreed to meet once a month with the publisher of the local daily to advise him of the information needs of the community and to criticize the newspaper's performance.

How did it all work out? Blankenburg reported that there were very few fireworks, and that the publishers—at first wary as tom-cats—found that they didn't get the raking-over they had expected and that no attempt was made to infringe their editorial freedom. For the council members it proved an educational experience.

"In retrospect," reported Blankenburg, "it seems clear that a press council can have effect because of its sheer presence. A hidden value in press councils is their ability to require busy journalists to reflect on their work. Likewise, council members acquire an appreciation of the journalistic craft, its opportunities and limitations."

The Stanford educator did not claim for the councils he monitored any dramatic results in terms of improved newspaper performance, but he pointed out that the time span had been a brief one, and that many of the benefits from the experiment may have been subsurface.

"Will this country have more press councils?" he asked. "I think so, but not a great number." The Mellett Fund experiment "may have planted some good seeds in the weedy field of press responsibility."

In these and all other trials of the concept thus far undertaken in this country, the cooperation of the local publisher has been obtained. Since the councils had no leverage of their own, their effectiveness depended upon the willingness of the publisher to accept their suggestions and criticisms.

[10] "Local press councils: an informal accounting," Spring, 1969 issue, pp. 14–17.

[11] The others were organized at Seattle, St. Louis, and two small Illinois communities, Sparta and Cairo. An account of the experience with the Illinois councils can be found in Kenneth Starck, "Community Press Councils in Southern Illinois," *Grassroots Editor*, November-December, 1968, pp. 3–7.

In Great Britain, where the press council concept has had a more extensive trial than in this country, the approach has been made on a national rather than a local basis. After several Royal Commissions had taken extensive looks into the press and its practices, a national Press Council was established in 1953. This body, made up of laymen and newspapermen, accepts complaints about the press, conducts extensive investigations through a complaints committee, and issues findings which may criticize a given newspaper or editor, or hold the original complaint to be unfounded. But, as has been the case with the experiments in this country, there is no provision for enforcement of the council's rulings. As John M. Harrison, a journalism educator who made a study of the British experience, explained it:

As a voluntary organization, the Press Council has no power to impose sanctions against the newspapers it censures. The impact of its findings is dependent on their publication in the press, based on general releases summarizing each adjudication. It is assumed that a newspaper against which a complaint has been brought will publish the Council's finding, and this has been done in all but a very few instances, though sometimes a reader must make a considerable effort to locate it. Other newspapers may publish these releases or not, and only a few of the larger ones generally do. . . . The degree to which the Council has effected an improvement in the performance of the press is a matter for speculation. To the casual reader, accustomed to American newspapers, much of Britain's popular national press still seems to be unbelievably trashy and sensational—certainly no model of responsible and ethical conduct.[12]

Yet many British observers, Harrison reported, feel that the situation today is much better than it was before the Press Council came into existence. There has been, they contend, an increasing emphasis on solid news and a greater acceptance of responsibility.[13]

---

[12] "A Look at the British Press Council," *Nieman Reports*, September, 1969, pp. 10–14.

[13] The British Council has built up the equivalent of "case law" by its handling of complaints. In the year ending June 30, 1968, the council dealt with 384 complaints, of which 88 received full adjudication, with hearings, testimony taken, and decisions rendered. As the record of case decisions has accumulated, it has provided guidelines for British press performance. (From a report by Charles L. Bennett, "The British Press Council," *Bulletin of the American Society of Newspaper Editors*, November, 1969, pp. 14–15.)

Whether a similar body could have like impact on the press of this country is not clear. A national press council makes sense in Great Britain because many of the British newspapers are national journals—they circulate throughout that compact nation. We have no counterparts in this country. As Harrison observed, "If the Press Council concept were imported, it must almost certainly be on some kind of regional basis. This imposes the limitations of a multiplicity of operating groups, each with its own inevitable variations in standards and unlikely to achieve the prestige a single national council might have."

However, some journalism educators and foundation heads have not abandoned the idea of a national press council in the United States, and a trial may yet be made of the proposal put forward by the 1947 report of the Hutchins Commission.[14]

From the sidelines

In addition to the specific proposals for quality controls that have been advanced, there are some diffuse and continuing influences that act upon the press and to some extent, at least, help to raise its standards of performance. Among them are a very few regular journals and an occasional article or book that offer critical appraisal of the various media of communication.

The books, however, do not often become best sellers, and the journals typically have only modest circulations. *Columbia Journalism Review*, published by Columbia University, and *Nieman Reports*, published by the Nieman Foundation of Harvard University, are among the best of the critical journals, but together they

[14] Another kind of organization to monitor press performance was set up in 1969 by Frank L. Kluckhohn, former correspondent for the New York *Times*. Kluckhohn and other conservatives planned to use their "Press Ethics Committee" to fight "one-sided reporting." Kluckhohn had complained that the news media "glorify rioters, demonstrators, hippies and yippies. . . . We see pleas for surrender in Vietnam, while draft card burners are publicized nation-wide. . . . We see declarations that the U.S. has no right to defend itself against nuclear bombs. . . . We see heroes made out of Black Power advocates who openly cry for revolution and incite riots. . . . We see yells [*sic*] of 'police brutality'—our policemen as vicious bullies, while lawless mobs receive sympathetic treatment. . . ." Kluckhohn said the public deserved objective reporting, and he promised to publicize instances where the public did not get it. (See "Ethics Group Would Serve as Watchdog for All Media," *Publishers' Auxiliary*, May 17, 1969, pp. 1 ff.)

reach only a few thousand readers four times a year.[15] *Chicago Journalism Review*, a publication launched by critical Chicago newspapermen who were disappointed by the local press coverage given to the 1968 Democratic National Convention and attendant riots, reaches an even smaller circle.

The Press section in *Time*, the Media section in *Newsweek*, and the monthly Communications section in *Saturday Review* have a wider audience, as do the occasional analytical articles on the press published by such magazines as *Harper's*, *The Atlantic*, *Esquire*, and *The New Yorker*. Yet this is sporadic and uneven scrutiny at best, and hardly represents the kind of searching, ongoing appraisal that would keep the press on its toes and alive to its obligations of public service.

There are a great many trade publications dealing with the various media of communication, but their appeal is to the practitioners and their concern is largely with the "how-to" approach and with promotion of the media they serve. Publications such as *Advertising Age*, *Editor & Publisher*, *Marketing/Communications*, *Publishers' Auxiliary*, or *Broadcasting* do not often deal in hard-nosed appraisal or criticism.

A logical source from which to expect regular and perceptive evaluation of press performance is the Academy—the schools and departments of journalism in the nation's colleges and universities. They are staffed—in part, at least—by former professionals who would be likely to know what soft spots to probe and what reforms to advocate. And they are sufficiently detached from the workaday journalistic scenes so that they should be able to play the critic's role constructively.

And to some extent they do. Leading journalism educators contribute their insights and suggestions through *Columbia Journalism Review* and similar journals, and sometimes break into the publications of more general circulation as well. And the findings of researchers at the universities, reported in the academic quarterlies,

15 Another publication of regional significance is *Montana Journalism Review*, published by the University of Montana School of Journalism at Missoula. An outstanding student-edited publication dealing with the media is *News Workshop*, published by New York University's Department of Journalism.

sometimes throw light on problems of the mass media and the ways in which those problems might be resolved.[16]

Some of the educator-critics, however, are reluctant to indulge very often or very forcefully in appraisal of media performance. They don't want to alienate the people who are the prospective employers of their students, and they know well that the typical editor or publisher is fiercely resentful of criticism.

As Louis M. Lyons, former curator of the Nieman Foundation at Harvard once put it, "Some publishers' reaction to criticism is at times practically paranoiac. It has restrained all but the hardiest souls from criticism. . . ."[17]

A meeting of the national organization of journalism teachers, the Association for Education in Journalism, received a report from one of its standing committees that had undertaken to investigate how well the educators' group was fulfilling its responsibility to evaluate the performance of the various news media. The committee found that "journalism educators are not doing all that they properly should to provide critical appraisal of the performance of our newspapers, magazines, and broadcast outlets." The report quoted the response of one journalism department head who had been queried about the activities of his staff in the role of critics:

> Except for classroom discussion we're not doing a darn thing here in the area of press criticism or appraisal. We have a faculty of 11 content to teach their subject matter and remain inconspicuous except to bend an occasional elbow with representatives of the press. There are so many pressures and deterrents to our engaging in a truly professional relationship with the press. And meantime we're letting an important responsibility go by default. . . .[18]

But even if they do not provide as much day-by-day evaluation of press performance as they might, the journalism educators do have the opportunity to exert a significant influence on the quality

[16] A handy summarization of such research findings is published annually by the American Newspaper Publishers Association Foundation under the title *News Research for Better Newspapers*. Copies are available from the Foundation offices at 750 Third Avenue, New York, N.Y.

[17] Quoted in *Newsweek*, November 29, 1965, p. 56.

[18] Report of the Committee on Professional Freedom and Responsibility, presented to the annual meeting of the Association for Education in Journalism at the University of Nebraska, August 28, 1963.

of the news and information media through the students that they train. There is a steady flow of journalism graduates into the newspapers, wire services, magazines, and broadcast channels. Some of them are equipped with no larger ambition than to fit in comfortably with things as they are; but a good many others have learned not only how things are but how they *could be*, and they are hoping for the chance to do what they can to improve the quality of the mass media.

The leavening influence of the schools is sometimes effective through old hands as well as first-year cubs. A number of programs have been established at the universities to provide some updating for working newsmen who have been on the job for some years and now see the value in returning to the campus for a time to soak up new insights. In 1938 the Nieman Foundation was set up at Harvard to provide an opportunity each year for ten or a dozen newsmen to spend the academic year at the university studying some subject area (such as economics, law, or government) that would help them to become more knowledgeable reporters or editors.

A few years later Columbia University founded the American Press Institute, which annually sponsors a series of short courses (typically three weeks) for newsmen interested in brushing up their writing or editing skills and in talking over with their colleagues the problems confronting the media. Programs like the Nieman fellowships at Harvard have been established at other universities, among them Stanford and Northwestern. And the short-course approach has been adapted in various ways by a number of institutions. The cumulative effect of these various efforts at upgrading the quality of journalism has presumably been significant, even though relatively small numbers of individual newsmen have been directly affected.

Still to be heard from

One influence that could be more effective than any other in bringing about improvement in the mass media—consumer reaction —has rarely been brought to bear.

Not many readers or viewers are familiar enough with the potentialities of the press so that they can recognize when they are being poorly served. And even when they do sense that something is wrong, they are more likely to respond with a "what's the use?" shrug than to register a complaint and demand improvement.

Their attitude is doubly wrong. Every consumer of the mass media ought to make the relatively modest effort required to inform himself about the workings of these channels of news and information on which he is so crucially dependent (that, of course, is the underlying thesis of this book). And every consumer ought to avail himself of any opportunities at hand—a local press council, a letter to the editor, a demand for correction of a factual error, a note of praise for fine reporting—to let the managers of the media know what kind of service he wants.

None of this effort would be wasted. Editors and broadcast station managers are sensitive to criticism, as has been noted; by the same token they *do* pay attention to the expressed reactions of readers and viewers. Many of the men who make the decisions for the media scan their mail as carefully as a congressman testing the wind in his district. A clear expression of consumer preference would not fall on deaf ears; some editors and broadcasters, in fact, are straining to hear such an expression and are ready to respond to it.

J. Edward Murray, editor of the *Arizona Republic*, Phoenix, told a group of his colleagues at an Associated Press Managing Editors meeting that "the newspaper audience is growing in intellectual capacity and appetite more rapidly than we are upgrading newspaper content." And another newsman, Executive Editor Norman Isaacs of the Louisville *Courier-Journal*, declared: "Imagination, inventiveness, and a sense of adventure are needed, and the newspaper people of my generation seem to have lost it. I can get you a raft of American papers and clip off the mastheads and defy you to tell where they are printed. Editors take refuge in a lot of shibboleths and half-baked adages. All my life I've heard: 'It can't be done that way.' What I want to know is why not?"[19]

Yet in the absence of any informed reaction from the consumer, some media managers will see no reason to institute costly, wave-making changes. If the readers and viewers are content with the present mix, why alter comfortable, if archaic patterns? If sensa-

[19] *Newsweek, op. cit.,* p. 57.

tionalism sells, why replace it with in-depth reporting of complex news developments? If shallow trivia on the networks racks up the top ratings, why take a chance on something more solid?[20]

It may indeed be the case that the American consumers of the various products turned out by the mass media have been fortunate in that so many of the individual editors and decision-makers through the years have been responsive to an inner conscience and sense of public service, even without prodding. But it is equally the case that the level of quality has been uneven; and in no single medium have the potentialities been fully realized.

It is likely that they never will be realized until the voice of the knowledgeable and discriminating consumer has been raised— and heard.

[20] Some internal pressure for improved performance may eventually develop as the result of an effort recently begun by reporters on some newspaper staffs to assert their right to share with editors in the decision-making process. They want to help make the policies that govern the newspaper's day-by-day operations and thus determine its quality. (See Edwin Diamond and Jean Schwoebel, "The Coming Newsroom Revolution: 1. The Miracle *Le Monde* Wrought; 2. 'Reporter Power' Takes Root," *Columbia Journalism Review*, Summer, 1970, pp. 8–18.)